Empirical Law and Economics

Maki provides an empirical analysis of law and economics by reevaluating Myrdal's value premises and Weber's separation of analysis and policy.

In modern civil society, individuals and businesses conduct economic activities through markets. The mainstream economic theory is the general equilibrium theory, which assumes a perfectly competitive market. The upshot is that transactions through competitive markets maximize the economic welfare of society, with policies such as deregulation and privatization being implemented with the backing of the law. However, in the real economy, legal transactions do not always take place, and this book analyzes price-fixing and bid-rigging cases. These cases show that there is a gap between competition philosophy and legislation. Using the real economy as data, this book conducts an empirical analysis of law and economics and illustrates issues related to the ideals of economics and the proper application of law. Accumulating empirical results will provide the means to form a healthy civil society.

A useful reference for graduate students and researchers in economics and legal research, and an interesting read for those who consider economics to be an empirical science.

Atsushi Maki is Professor Emeritus at Keio University. His research focuses on the empirical analysis of consumer behavior. He published books such as *Introduction to Estimating Economic Models* and *Poverty, Inequality and Growth in Developing Countries*, and articles in several journals such as *Review of Economics and Statistics*, *Economics Letters*, and *Economic Record*.

Empirical Law and Economics

Price-Fixing and Bid-Rigging Cases in Japan

Atsushi Maki

Routledge
Taylor & Francis Group
LONDON AND NEW YORK

First published 2025
by Routledge
4 Park Square, Milton Park, Abingdon, Oxon, OX14 4RN

and by Routledge
605 Third Avenue, New York, NY 10158

Routledge is an imprint of the Taylor & Francis Group, an informa business

British Library Cataloguing-in-Publication Data
A catalogue record for this book is available from the British Library

Library of Congress Cataloging-in-Publication Data
Names: Maki, Atsushi, author.
Title: Empirical law and economics: price-fixing and bid-rigging cases in Japan/ Atsushi Maki.
Description: Abingdon, Oxon [UK]; New York, NY: Routledge, 2024. |
Includes bibliographical references and index. |
Contents: Where the problem lies: freedom and justice – Empirical analysis of law and economics: on the philosophical foundation and analytical procedure – Case of petroleum product price-fixing and cases related to damages – Case on price-fixing of bearings and the particular field of trade and market – Case of water meter bid-rigging: scattering of winning bids given changes in contract methods and claiming for damages – Government bid-rigging: cases of the central procurement office of the defense agency and the Hokkaido development agency – Case of stalker furnace bid-rigging: scattered target prices of the properties and high winning bid rate – Tama District in Tokyo bid-rigging case: a bid-rigging case in which the winning bid was polarized – Tama District bid-rigging case: compensation of damages by local residents – Sewerage facility bid-rigging case in Tokyo: changes in the behavior brought about introducing the announcement in advance for target prices – Policy theory based on empirical analysis of law and economics.
Identifiers: LCCN 2024004390 (print) | LCCN 2024004391 (ebook) |
ISBN 9781032440996 (hardback) | ISBN 9781032441009 (paperback) |
ISBN 9781003370444 (ebook)
Subjects: LCSH: Price fixing–Law and legislation–Japan. | Letting of contracts–Japan. | Government purchasing–Law and legislation–Japan. | Law–Economic aspects–Japan. | Antitrust law–Japan.
Classification: LCC KNX3276 .M35 2024 (print) | LCC KNX3276 (ebook) |
DDC 343.5207/25--dc23/eng/20240205
LC record available at https://lccn.loc.gov/2024004390
LC ebook record available at https://lccn.loc.gov/2024004391

ISBN: 9781032440996 (hbk)
ISBN: 9781032441009 (pbk)
ISBN: 9781003370444 (ebk)

DOI: 10.4324/9781003370444

Typeset in Galliard
by Deanta Global Publishing Services, Chennai, India

To my mentor late Hendrik S. Houthakker and my family—Michie, Chiori, and Hisashi

Contents

Figures

Tables

Preface

Queen Elizabeth II's question to a London School of Economics professor about the 2008 financial crisis caused by Lehman Brothers's bankruptcy is well-known: *Why did nobody notice it?* Economists said they initially judged the risk to be small and could not have predicted the escalation of the crisis and the imbalances in financial markets.

If economists had recognized that the financial crisis transcended the framework of existing economic theories, the crisis could have most likely been mitigated. However, economics is less predictive than classical mechanics in the natural sciences. The conditions assumed as premises in the economic model are insufficient to predict actual economic phenomena. In science, when a theory is wrong or the premises of the theory are not sufficient to explain reality, the result will be wrong.

This book emphasizes Gunnar Myrdal's value premises of *respect for life* and the *egalitarian principle*. Economic models based on standard economic theory have insufficient explanatory power for predicting actual economic activities. The book stresses the need for a new analytical framework that includes jurisprudence in addition to the existing economic models. Thus, it utilizes the knowledge obtained from judicial precedents and research on legal philosophy since the modern era.

The insufficient predictive power of economic models means they might not produce clear solutions to economic conflicts in the real world.[1] Max Weber argued that policy is not an extension of analysis and that analysis and policy should be separated. There are sometimes discrepancies between reality and the reasoning of economic policies based on economic theory.

In economic models, Myrdal's value premises are not expressed explicitly. This situation leads to the separation of analysis and policy described by Weber. Policy should incorporate the value premises, based on conclusions from empirical economic analyses. This book examines the concept of law, which idealizes the realization of justice in society. In social science, social

1 Although the conclusions obtained from economic models are simple and clear, their policy effects are often questionable.

justice exists as a major premise in the search for truth. Deviating from this premise, economic analysis as a branch of social science might be meaningless.

Empirical science tests the validity of theories using data. If the theory is solid, scientific truth is established. Classical mechanics is an important physical theory in natural science. Social science, however, explores the truth in a society that is a collection of individuals.

This study conducts empirical economic analysis on the premise that civil society is the basis of society. Japan, like many democracies, has a highly developed civil society. Under constitutionalism, Japanese society is characterized by the sovereignty of the people, separation of the three powers, respect for basic human rights, and pacifism. The development of civil society has as ideals the realization of social justice and the establishment of economic freedom. Under the premise of justice, there is economic freedom, which is indispensable for the pursuit of efficiency for improving the standard of living of the people.

The study empirically analyzes economic behavior in society through economics and law. It stresses the need for empirical science-based law and economics. Economic models are important as a basis.[2] However, economic models alone cannot explain the causes of economic conflicts in society, as humans do not conduct economic activities solely based on economic rationality. A diversity of human values shapes economic activities. Concretely, as per the history of philosophy, *sympathy* by Adam Smith, *tolerance* by Jean-Marie Arouet Voltaire and John Locke, and *passion* by René Descartes supplement economic rationality in guiding human activities in the real world. The individual assumed in the standard economic model only maximizes a certain criterion (utility or profit); the model does not adequately consider human diversity. An economic model for explaining economic behavior is not sufficient for developing economic policy that satisfies people in the real world. Any shortfall of economic analysis will be left to the debate of the legislative bodies (the Diet in Japan) representing the people. This is the meaning of Weber's *separation of analysis and policy* in social science.

Economics is an academic field that values efficiency, but the concept of justice is lacking in economics. Though justice is challenging to define, this study employs the concept of legal justice in its empirical analysis using judicial precedents. Another premise lacking in economics is the *principle of liability for negligence* that exists in jurisprudence. This principle states that a person is liable for damages to another person only when there is intent or negligence. Economic activities are not always legal transactions. Illegal trade exists. When one excludes such realities, the usefulness of theory for describing reality can be questionable. Simply put, there are problems that economics cannot bridge in explaining the gap between theory and reality. This book attempts to find a solution to this problem through empirical analysis of law and economics.

2 In empirical economics, after setting up a theoretical model, researchers test the validity of various hypotheses using data.

There are several things to note when conducting empirical analysis of law and economics. Adam Smith, the founder of economics and the author of the *Wealth of Nations*, was a professor of moral philosophy at the University of Glasgow. He was also the author of *Theory of Moral Sentiments*, a book on legal philosophy. His work suggests that economics emerged from law.

Today, however, economics and law are each specialized, with a deep chasm between the two. Mutual understanding between economics and law has become challenging for various reasons. For instance, while economics is strongly analysis-oriented, law is focused on hermeneutics. Economists who conduct economic analysis on economic problems understand facts through theoretical models and make decisions based on them. However, legal scholars and practitioners see the facts through the texts of the law and make judgments based on them. How the texts are interpreted greatly influences their judgments. Thus, economics and law have different standards for addressing economic problems.

The standards for recognition and evaluation of facts are not the same in economics and law. For example, economics emphasizes the results of economic activities, while law emphasizes the intentions that encourage economic activities. Therefore, judgments on the same economic problem may not necessarily be the same.

In the economic analysis, this study creates mathematical models based on economic theory and obtains qualitative features such as theorems.[3] It conducts a quantitative analysis using data to test the validity of the model. In policy evaluation, a perfectly competitive market is used as the basis of such economic analysis. The fundamental theorems of welfare economics mathematically prove that equilibrium in a perfectly competitive market meets the Pareto efficiency criterion and maximizes economic welfare. The assumptions of perfectly competitive markets and the fundamental theorems of welfare economics express an economic ideal. Accordingly, the study evaluates how far the real economy is from perfectly competitive markets.

This book conducts empirical analysis using judicial precedents as basic data. Case law, of course, includes the notion of justice. Evaluating this data solely in terms of economic theory obliterates the notion of justice. However, it is possible to maintain the concept of justice inherent in the data by devising appropriate analytical procedures and experimental designs.

3 There are general cautions when performing analysis. Considering the facts through the filter of theory, researchers sometimes ignore some of the information contained in the facts given the inherent nature of theory. One example is the issue of economic inequality, examined in the Chapter 11 of the book. An economic theory based on efficiency yields the fundamental theorems of welfare economics and posits that a competitive market is the optimal market. However, no unique optimal solution for the distribution problem is found. To solve this problem, it might be necessary to establish the definition of equality, such as equality of opportunity or equality of outcome. This is an issue related to justice in legal philosophy. Moreover, it is essentially determined by the consensus of the people.

This book focuses on cases with trouble in the process of economic transactions that were adjudicated in the trial or other courts: the petroleum product cartel price-fixing during the first Oil Crisis in the 1970s and the related damage claims from consumers, bid-rigging cases related to public works that occurred since the 1990s, and claims for damages by residents and local governments. Many of the primary victims in these cases were consumers as taxpayers. Bid-rigging cases involving public works resulted in a waste of tax money. Measures to curb the wasteful spending of taxpayers' money—which is one of the causes of Japan's chronic deficit—involved fiscal consolidation policies in macroeconomics. Proposals to legally prevent bid-rigging cases and curb wasteful spending of taxpayers' money are important issues today in Japan. This book examines this issue by going back to Keynes' thinking. Moreover, in treating economic disparities that cannot be resolved by economic theory, it examines policy from the perspective of justice, which is the theme of legal philosophy.

In approaching economic problems, economics (law) emphasizes analysis (interpretation). Even with such differences, there is a lot of room for each to effectively utilize information from the other. This book incorporates the aspect of fairness to efficiency. Hence, economics and law can cooperate to realize justice in society.[4]

Finally, I would like to thank Yukihiko Kiyokawa, Lam Yong Ling, Kendrick Loo, Chisugi Mukai, Akira Rokusha, and Tom Wells for their comments and suggestions.

4 The field of "Law and Economics," generally understood, is a research area that examines legal systems and legal phenomena normatively (Sollen) but not empirically (Sein) through microeconomics to contribute to policy and legislation.

1 Where the problem lies

Freedom and justice

1.1 Purpose and background

This book explores efficiency (regarding freedom) and fairness (regarding justice) in economics through empirical analysis using economic statistics and legal data, such as decisions of the Japan Fair Trade Commission (JFTC) and judgments by the courts.[1] It focuses on consumer behavior using both materials and concentrates on consumers, households, individual investors, and taxpayers.[2] By using legal data, it considers where frauds and torts in economic activities took place and how they can be eliminated. When examining the materials necessary for empirical economic analysis, it sometimes found cases of economic disputes outside economic statistics.

Below is an explanation of the circumstances of the Japanese economy in which the cases of price-fixing and bid-rigging occurred. Japan experienced a high economic growth era called the "economic miracle" from the latter half of the 1950s to the early 1970s. The growth rate of real GDP averaged 10% *per annum*. The postwar economic growth in developed countries changed the supply-demand balance of crude oil, which was an important source of energy for households and industries. In oil-producing countries, supply restriction policies on crude oil were implemented to maintain resources for the future;

1 The concept of justice in this book is legal justice. Economic freedom and legal restraint are contradictory from the legal philosophy perspective but not contradictory from the societal viewpoint. Economic freedom involves the principle of freedom to make contracts between individuals. However, to maintain social stability, society will not accept illegal contracts, irrespective of how much individuals want them. Moreover, the standard of judgment is the law. Historically, the idea of civil liberty arose as a way of freeing citizens from the shackles of feudal lords and royal decrees. If this idea is generalized, freedom becomes unlimited; however, this notion is unreasonable. In a civil society, individual freedom does not infringe on the freedoms and rights of others. Individuals who can make decisions independently and freely as presented in economics are free to the extent that they do not infringe on the dignity and rights of others. It is challenging to specify such a concept of freedom mathematically. Furthermore, as a premise of economics, there is room for empathy and tolerance. The introduction of these abstract concepts beyond the concept of justice is one of the ways in which analysis and policy can be separated, as advocated by Weber and emphasized in this book.

2 Economics usually considers three economic units: household, firm, and government.

DOI: 10.4324/9781003370444-1

therefore, crude oil prices soared. Though the price of crude oil was $3 per barrel in the early 1970s, it had quadrupled by 1973. In 1974, the consumer price index (CPI) in Japan rose given soaring crude oil prices, and the GDP growth rate was negative. The Japanese economy experienced stagflation, indicating a decrease in GDP under inflation. During the first Oil Crisis in the early 1970s, Japanese oil distributors made a cartel price agreement to prepare for uncertain earnings fluctuations given unstable crude oil prices.

In 1979, the price of crude oil at $36 per barrel further tripled, and the world economy was jolted by the second Oil Crisis. After the first Oil Crisis, the Japanese economy succeeded in transforming its production structure through energy-saving investments. Thus, the international competitiveness of Japan increased in the world economy, and Japan's trade surplus also increased. During the stable economic growth era in the 1980s, Japan's economy was on quite a roll. In those days, the trade imbalance between Japan and the United States widened, and the Japan-US Structural Talks were built up to resolve economic frictions between the two countries. The United States claimed Japan's retail prices were high given the closure of Japanese markets and that collusion plagued bidding on public works. In the history of the Japanese economy, bid-rigging on public works was not uncommon. Such economic conduct violates the principle of equal opportunity in market competition. It hinders competition and breeds economic inefficiency. Bid-rigging also leads to wasting taxes.

This book uses judicial precedent to analyze several bid-rigging cases that occurred since 1990. It considers the factors that enable such collusion, estimates the amount of damage claims of consumers, and proposes some measures to prevent collusion.[3] Eliminating the wasteful use of taxes caused by this collusion is key to implementing fiscal consolidation policy, which is one of the most important issues of the Japanese economy in the 2020s.

1.2 Cases and laws regarding economic disputes

The occurrence of an economic dispute suggests that the transactions through the market were not necessarily fair transactions per legal rules. The study examines the unfair transactions of the markets through the JFTC's decisions and judgments by the courts.[4]

3 The author became interested in collusion because I attended a seminar at Australian National University titled "Dango" (collusion) held by John McMillan in the early 1990s (cf. McMillan, 1990, 1992). At the seminar, he reported that the cost of public works in Japan was 15% to 30% higher given collusion.

4 Some argue that cases brought to the courts are not representative of the general problem of unfair transactions because each case has different circumstances. However, that is not valid. One of the roles of the Supreme Court is to unify the conflicting judgments made in the lower courts. When the Supreme Court makes a judgment, it is binding on all future-related cases. That is, similar court requests are unlikely to re-occur.

Economic statistics record economic transactions on the premise that they were conducted under the condition of freedom in making contracts. However, the law is enforceable. Violations of the rules will result in penalties through legal force. Victims can claim damages from the perpetrator for infringement of their rights. Fair competition in the market will be enhanced by enforcing legal rules in economic activity.

Consider an in-depth look at *fairness*. The purpose of law is to realize justice in society. What is justice is an important issue in the philosophy of law, but the definition of justice is diverse given the diversity of individual values. However, it is a common understanding in the philosophy of law that *justice*, *equity*, and *fairness* are synonyms (see *Black's Law Dictionary*). Fairness is a concept that belongs to *legal justice*, and it is justice when the law is obeyed. In this way, legal justice is just like fairness, and JFTC's decisions and judgments by the courts are made to realize justice per the law.

The rules are clearly written in JFTC's decisions and judgments. It is possible to understand the decision-making process by examining the testimony and evidence of both parties. Empirical analysis using such legal data makes it possible to bridge law and economics.

1.3 Basic factors that cause economic conflict

Three major factors cause economic disputes: (1) problems with the nature of the market and the process of achieving market equilibrium, (2) problems with laws and institutions, and (3) problems with legal decisions and judgments. The following is an explanation of these three issues as they pertain to the cartel price agreement by Japanese oil distributors and bid-rigging on public works discussed in this book. First, consider the conditions where there is a problem in the market. Factors that determine the market price of a product are (a) the shape of the market demand curve, especially when demand is inelastic; (b) the characteristics of the market, such as whether it is a monopoly, oligopoly, or competitive market; and (c) the shape of the production function and the cost function of the firms in the market. When demand for a good is inelastic, price-fixing and bid-rigging can be easily accomplished.

Consider the cartel price agreement on kerosene (obtained from oil), as discussed in-depth in Chapter 3. Regarding the distribution channels, the main suppliers of kerosene are less than a dozen oil-refining companies. The retailers of kerosene considered are Tsuruoka Co-op and general retailers. Consumers are residents of Tsuruoka City. An important property of kerosene is that it is homogeneous. Consumers must not necessarily buy kerosene from a particular retailer linked to a particular oil company. If another oil company wholesales kerosene to retailers on favorable terms and the retailer offers consumers a favorable price, consumers will buy it. For consumers, kerosene is a necessary energy source for cooking and heating. Necessary goods are classified as price-inelastic goods in terms of the elasticity of demand. Kerosene is a good that can be available in stock in the distribution channels; thus, supply adjustment of kerosene is possible in the short term. Given these characteristics of the supply of and demand for kerosene, it is easy for oil-refining companies to agree on price.

Regarding bid-rigging in public works projects ordered by the central and local governments, the contractor was often decided by bidding, where the party ordering the project must calculate the target price ruled by the law. The winning bidder will be the one who offers the lowest bid price below the target price. In some cases, the lower limit of the winning bid (called the minimum limit price) may be specified together with the target price. Hence, the condition for the winning bid is that the upper (lower) limit is the target (minimum limit) price. The winning bidder offers the lowest bid in the range between those two prices.

The essence of bid-rigging is to keep the winning bid high and distribute the resulting profits among the companies in the industry. To achieve the former, the bidders decide the winning bidder through negotiations, and they collude such that the winning bidder can win the bid at the desired price. The bid-rigging is a kind of redistribution system of unfair profits among the companies in the industry.

The second factor in economic disputes is problems with the law or legal system. One of the reasons for the collusion involved in oil price-fixing is that the amount of the surcharge imposed on the price-fixing is cheap. That is, it is profitable to collude despite the surcharge. There have been three changes to the surcharge thus far. The surcharge system was established by the JFTC in 1977. At the time, the rate was 1.5% of sales. The ratio increased to 6% in 1991 and has since increased to 10% given the revision in 2005. Moreover, a premium rate is applied to those who have repeatedly engaged in price-fixing or are judged to have played a leading role. When the JFTC determines that the present rate is not effective enough, it will raise the surcharge rate as stipulated in the Anti-Monopoly Act (AMA), which essentially plays the same role as antitrust legislation in the United States.[5]

To prevent collusion in bidding, a comprehensive evaluation method for bidding has been implemented (e.g., Enforcement Order Article 167-10-2 of the Local Autonomy Act). This method focuses on the price when bidding, evaluates the technical aspects of the bidding process, and adds other types of evaluations, such as consideration for environmental protection.

5 In 2013, the AMA was amended. The hearing process of the JFTC was abolished. Before the revision, when a cease-and-desist order or a surcharge payment order was issued by the JFTC, and the parties were dissatisfied, they had three opportunities to appeal. The first trial was held at the trial court of the JFTC, the second trial was held at the High Court in Tokyo, and the third trial was held at the Supreme Court. Today, after the revision, when either of the noted orders is issued by the JFTC, and the parties are dissatisfied, the first trial is held at the District Court in Tokyo, the second trial is held at the High Court in Tokyo, and the third trial is held at the Supreme Court.

The third issue that causes economic disputes is problems with court decisions and judgments. Given the libertarianism (the principle of independent evaluation of evidence) of the judges, judgments of three trials may occur in the same case, which are then unified by the final judgment, as a precedent, in the Supreme Court.

1.4 Fundamental theorems of welfare economics and the Coase Theorem

The study here introduces the fundamental theorems of welfare economics and the Coase Theorem, which are the theoretical products of microeconomics. A central purpose of economics is the pursuit of economic efficiency, and there are two basic theorems of welfare economics:

1. The equilibrium of a perfectly competitive market always achieves a Pareto-efficient resource allocation (Pareto efficiency is a state in which one's utility cannot be increased unless the utility of another person is reduced).[6]
2. Assuming lump-sum taxes and subsidies, any Pareto-efficient resource allocation can be achieved with proper income redistribution through a perfectly competitive market.

The fundamental theorems of welfare economics prove that if the utility function of the consumer and the production function of the producer satisfy certain conditions, a Pareto-efficient equilibrium can be obtained through a perfectly competitive market.

The Coase Theorem posits that, under the following five conditions, resource allocation in equilibrium based on everyone's consensus is always Pareto efficient: (1) The legal rights of each individual are guaranteed, (2) Individuals act rationally to maximize their self-interest, (3) No transaction costs are incurred, (4) Each individual is free to negotiate in economic society, and (5) Society has a mechanism to effectively enforce contracts.

Of course, the actual economy is not a perfectly competitive market. There are frauds and torts, and transaction costs are not zero. The actual economic society deviates from the ideal type (*idealtypus*) assumed in the basic theorems of welfare economics and the Coase Theorem. However, it is possible to

6 A competitive market meets the standard of Pareto efficiency. In the actual economy, what is known as *market failure* cannot be left to the market mechanism. Specifically, examples of market failure include underprovided public goods, increasing product returns in industries, and harmful externalities. Notably, in the actual economy, the economic field related to market failure is not negligible. Further, the basic theorem of welfare economics is not a theorem to determine the optimal solution to the problem of economic disparity.

approach the ideal type that achieves efficiency and fairness by amending laws and promoting competition through policy.

This book describes the relationship between the Coase Theorem and claims for damages through the cases of price-fixing and bid-rigging. In the case of the increase in the price of kerosene given the cartel price agreement, direct negotiation between each consumer and the oil-refining companies is almost impossible. The transaction cost related to the negotiation would be enormous. Therefore, claims for damages at a court are the most reasonable solution. There may also be settlements before the judgment is finalized. Chapter 5 discusses a settlement that was made between consumers and water meter companies in the case of water meter collusion.

1.5 Method of empirical economic analysis

This section explains the empirical economic analysis and its significance. Empirical analysis tests the validity of economic theory using observed economic data. From the empirical science view, the conditions required for empirical economic analysis are logical consistency and reproducibility. In empirical economic analysis, researchers aim for logical consistency when setting economic models based on a theory. As long as logical consistency is maintained, the economic models are valid. Indeed, logical consistency is a prerequisite for setting a model.

The economic model that can withstand empirical economic analysis must be theoretically consistent and empirically valid. The study employs observational data for the verification. The relationship between the variables in the model is restricted by the theory. Therefore, empirical economic analysis is performed to verify the empirical validity of the functional relationships inevitably derived from the theory via observations.

The empirical economic analysis specifies the experimental design in addition to the theory. The contents of the experimental design are the (1) determination of the economic unit, (2) determination of the unit period of observations, and (3) correspondence between theoretical variables and observational variables. By specifying these factors, the same result can be obtained irrespective of who retests the theory, and the reproducibility of the empirical analysis can be ensured. Moreover, by specifying such an experimental design, it is possible to compare the empirical results with prior results. Accumulation of such results leads to the development of economics as an empirical science.

Now, using consumer behavior as an example, the study denotes the correspondence between theoretical and observational variables, which constitutes a part of the experimental design. According to the theory of consumer behavior, a consumer has a utility function that expresses the ordering of preferences, and income y and prices p_i (n = 1, ..., N) are given exogenously where the number of goods and services are classified into N. The amount of demand q_i (i = 1, ..., N) is determined by a mathematical operation where the utility is maximized under the budget constraint and exogenously given prices p_i ($i = 1, ..., N$). In the empirical analysis, the demand function of each good is obtained using the observed income and prices. The demand function is formulated as

$$q_i = f(y, p_1, ..., p_N)$$

where $i = 1, ..., N$. The demand function f is constrained by the specification of the utility function.

It is necessary to pay attention to the price p_i when conducting empirical analysis of consumer behavior. In the empirical analysis of consumer behavior, whether the observed prices the consumer pays are equilibrium prices in competitive markets is inconsequential. The prices observed are often the market prices determined not in competitive markets but in imperfect markets, such as oligopoly markets (e.g., the markets of automobiles and electric appliances). In the modern market economy, the percentage of perfectly competitive markets is low. There are also government-determined official prices such as utilities prices. Consumers may also be subject to retail prices that are products of illegal pricing given cartel price agreements.[7] However, empirical analysis of consumer behavior does not consider whether the observed retail prices are those in competitive markets or by a cartel price agreement. One simply assumes prices are given in the markets and that individual consumers optimize their decisions given the prices and their income.

Consider empirical analysis regarding the Coase Theorem. In conducting empirical economic analysis, it is challenging to measure the theoretical variable of transaction costs. Theoretically, it is defined as expenses regarding all possible transactions or as a burden of elements such as time, labor, and money required for transactions of goods and services.[8] However, in empirical economic analysis, such conceptual theoretical variables must correspond with the observational variables when estimating the model.

1.6 Structure of the book

The cases in this book involve the claims of damages by consumers given price-fixing of kerosene or ball bearings or by bid-rigging in public works projects and defense procurement that wasted taxes. The price-fixing and bid-rigging cases entailed collusion.

7 If a retail price given illegal pricing is presented to the consumer, it can be the basis of a claim for damages from the consumer. By applying appropriate laws, oil-refining wholesalers who have agreed with the cartel price and committed illegal acts of bid-rigging will be punished. Judiciary decisions on frauds and torts have the effect of making resource allocation more efficient.

8 Beyond transaction costs, there is a theoretical variable called *basic needs*, defined as the general needs of goods and services required for people's livelihoods. Though basic needs are often used in theoretical analysis, the concept is also challenging to operationalize through observational variables.

Chapter 2 examines the philosophical basis of empirical analysis of law and economics. It begins with the ideas of British empiricism and Continental rationalism on scientific methodologies since the early modern period. It then considers Kant's epistemology that integrated the two and Weber's ideas in the context of Neo-Kantianism. It discusses Myrdal's value premises. Further, it explains the procedure required for empirical analysis while introducing the concept of experimental design. This chapter furnishes the ideas to understand the empirical analysis of law and economics.

Chapter 3 examines the cases of consumers claiming damages from petroleum wholesalers given price-fixing during the first Oil Crisis in the 1970s. The Supreme Court did not award damages since the causal relationship between the rise in the wholesale price of kerosene and the rise in the retail price was not proven and the basis for calculating the amount of compensation for damages was unclear. This chapter verifies the causal relationship between the two prices by performing the Granger causality test based on time-series data. It calculates the amount of the claims for damages as the difference between the observed price, which includes the effect of price-fixing, and the theoretical price that excludes the effect of price-fixing.

Chapter 4 examines the cases of the price-fixing of bearings. The three criminally charged companies proceeded differently. The case of the first (second) company closed at the District (High) Court, and that of the third company was appealed to the Supreme Court. The differences in the companies' price-fixing perceptions were evident in their actions.

Chapters 5 to 10 consider five bid-rigging cases. Several prices will appear in bid-rigging cases as follows. The target price is the upper limit for the property calculated by the party ordering the bids based on the law. Bidders who bid above the target price are disqualified. The minimum limit price is 80% of the target price, and any bidder who submits a lower bid is also disqualified. The bid price is the price offered by the bidder for the property. The winning bid price is the successful bid price. The competitive price is a conceptual price, which is the price that would have been established if there was a competitive market. A fair price, defined in the Criminal Code for collusion, is also a conceptual price: it is the price established when there is competition among bidders. In bid-rigging, there is a high possibility of cooperation among firms in bidding near the target price, and decisions by the courts are inclined to recognize the existence of this collusion, while competitiveness is recognized to take place near the minimum limit price. In the latter case, the trial decisions and judgments are more likely to perceive no bid-rigging.

Chapter 5 analyzes the water meter bid-rigging case. The bidding companies were accused of bid-rigging three times from 1989 to 2001. The bidding method changed from making a discretionary contract through designated competitive bidding to general competitive bidding. In the process, the unit price of the standard water meter dropped significantly. Given this decline, the profitability of the industry declined. However, the change in the bidding method increased competitiveness in the industry. This chapter employs the statistical significance test of difference to determine whether the winning bid price was the same under the different bidding methods and contract regimes.

Chapter 6 analyzes two cases of government collusion in bid-rigging involving the Central Procurement Office (CPO) of the Defense Agency and the Hokkaido Development Agency. The empirical analysis reveals that neither institution followed the established procedures and that both thwarted efforts to promote competitive bidding.

Chapter 7 analyzes the case of stoker furnace bid-rigging. Stoker furnaces are a type of waste incinerator. Stoker furnace bid-rigging demonstrated the horizontal connection between major firms in the industry and the vertical connection between major, second-tier, and outsider contractors. Second-tier contractors and outsiders sometimes colluded with major contractors. This bid-rigging stifled competition and distorted market forces.

Chapters 8 and 9 examine a case of bid-rigging in public works in the Tama district in Tokyo. Local residents filed lawsuits claiming compensation for illegal acts given the bid-rigging.

Chapter 10 analyzes bid-rigging cases in the installation of sewage pump facilities in Tokyo. In some properties, the party ordering the bidding announced the target price in advance; in others, it did not. The advance announcement of the target price changed the bidding behavior of manufacturers. Announcing the target price in advance seems to eliminate bid-rigging. This situation is empirically verified using qualitative response models in econometrics such as probit and logit models.

Chapter 11 considers policy theory. It assesses whether deregulation and privatization regulated by the law were effective policies to ensure competitiveness. It also examines how bid-rigging and inflated construction costs contribute to government budget deficits. Finally, it shows that economic policy theory for the benefit of the people cannot come only from economics and that it must embrace diversity to be based on empirical knowledge obtained from economics. Chapter 12 describes conclusion of the book.

2 Empirical analysis of law and economics

On the philosophical foundation and analytical procedure

2.1 Introduction

The market economy is a system adopted in many countries. Its theoretical background is indicated by the general equilibrium theory based on microeconomics. The theory yields two fundamental theorems of welfare economics.[1]

According to the first fundamental theorem of welfare economics, the competitive market maximizes economic welfare, and the appropriate economic policy for that is deregulation and privatization. As the fundamental theorems of welfare economics are obtained by a mathematical operation specified by a mathematical model with some assumptions, there is no mathematical inconsistency in the solutions derived. In recent years, though economic policies of deregulation and privatization by the government have been implemented, there is a question as to whether these policies benefit the people. The practical validity of some of the assumptions in the economic model has not been empirically verified. Moreover, while appropriate income redistribution through lump-sum tax and subsidy can achieve economic efficiency per the second fundamental theorem of welfare economics, it is debatable who specifically decides the appropriate redistribution among the people.[2]

Furthermore, economic theory is based on the principle of maximizing economic welfare, but there is also a debate as to whether the basis of policy evaluation should be only maximizing economic welfare. For example, societies aim to accomplish goals such as economic welfare goals; Sustainable Development Goals; and Environment, Social, and Governance goals. Given the differences between views of the ideal type of economic model and the actual world, there is a theory-policy disparity. Empirical economic analysis needs economic

1 See section 1.2 in Chapter 1 for the fundamental theorems of welfare economics.

2 Consider one example: people will accept *equal wages for equal workers* from the standpoint of fairness. There exists a wage gap between regular and non-regular workers in the actual world. According to the second fundamental theorem of welfare economics, when appropriate lump-sum tax and transfers of wealth are arranged, it will yield a Pareto optimal outcome through competitive markets. The problem is: Who decides the Pareto optimal point concretely? People and politicians decide it. However, economists do not decide it from the economic model.

DOI: 10.4324/9781003370444-2

statistics that capture the facts, economic theory as the basis of the analysis, and the econometric method for hypothesis testing and estimating the parameters of the model. After verifying that the test results of a working hypothesis are statistically significant, the study analyzes how the actual economy deviates from a competitive market as an ideal type.

The following four issues in this book will help readers understand the significance of its objectives: (1) the relationship between economics and law and the aspects of the field of law and economics that connect economics and law, (2) the relationship between normative analysis and empirical analysis in economics, (3) the history of empirical research in economics, and (4) the features that distinguish the methodologies of the social science from those of the natural science.

Section 2.2.1 of this chapter examines the history of empirical economic analysis (issue 3). It mainly focuses on the economic statistics that are essential for empirical economic analysis rather than the economic models. The history of empirical economic analysis shows that the accumulation of observations began recently relative to that of the astronomical observations that made important contributions to the completion of classical mechanics. This relates to the discussion of whether the methodology of the social science differs from that of the natural science (issue 4).[3]

Section 2.2.2 discusses the essence of ordinal utility, which is one of the most important tools in microeconomics when conducting empirical analysis of consumer behavior. It describes the relationship between normative and empirical analysis in economics (issue 2), particularly as it relates to the consumer. Section 2.2.3 examines the philosophical foundation of the methodology of social science based on the philosophical history of British empiricism and Continental rationalism since the early modern period. It focuses on works by Francis Bacon, René Descartes, and Immanuel Kant, who synthesized British empiricism and Continental rationalism. It then addresses a 1904 paper by Max Weber that examined the relationship between analysis and policy. Finally, it discusses Gunnar Myrdal's value premises, which are closely related to Weber's way of thinking on the roles of analysis and policy. Section 2.2.4 explains the procedures of empirical economic analysis and its flow chart.

Section 2.3 introduces two empirical economic analyses related to consumer behavior based on microeconomic theory. Section 2.3.1 explains Japanese consumer demand regarding the price differences between domestic and foreign markets. This research empirically verifies that Japanese consumers had to purchase goods and services at higher prices in the domestic market. The reason for the higher prices in the domestic market was that it was closed by business practices and regulations implemented by the government; therefore,

3 Astronomical observations were made on the determination of planetary orbits and constellations. These were observations conducted by Hipparchus circa 150 BC, by Ptolemy circa 120 BC, and by Tycho Brahe circa 1550, whose observations derived the Kepler's three laws of planetary motion. The accumulation of astronomical observations had a history of 1800 years by the time of Newton, who was born in 1642 and perfected classical mechanics.

there is a need for deregulation. Section 2.3.2 empirically verifies the favorable effect of deregulation on New Zealand consumers. Deregulation improved the standard of living of these consumers, but the changes in the magnitude of the standard of living were different among low-income, middle-income, and high-income earners.

After confirming from the two empirical analyses the necessity of deregulation to ensure competitiveness, Section 2.4 considers the policy implications based on the fundamental theorems of welfare economics. It examines the difference between deregulation to ensure competitiveness proposed by the fundamental theorems of welfare economics and the actual deregulation policy of the government. It also discusses the differences between deregulation, privatization, and marketization.

Section 2.5 explains in some depth the empirical analysis of law and economics, which is, of course, the main theme of this book. Sections 2.5.1 and 2.5.2 present the basic preconditions of the theoretical model of law and economics and a flow chart of empirical analysis of law and economics. Based on the concept of legal justice, the sections explicitly argue that victims of illegal economic transactions have the right to claim damages. Section 2.5.3 introduces examples of concrete empirical analysis of law and economics. Section 2.6 concludes the chapter.

2.2 Empirical economic analysis

Section 2.5 of this chapter argues that the empirical analysis of law and economics is based on empirical economic analysis and is an extension of it. Before that, this section gives an example of empirical economic analysis and shows that it constitutes the empirical analysis of law and economics.

2.2.1 Economic statistics used for empirical economic analysis

Empirical economic analysis requires economic statistics that capture facts. Typical economic statistics include those in household surveys, censuses, market statistics, and System of National Accounts (SNAs). Originally, the population census aimed to tally the number of soldiers, and the household surveys aimed to know the nutritional status of the people. It was not until the 20th century that economic statistics were systematically and comprehensively compiled and used for empirical economic analysis.

The following is an overview of the history of economic statistics from the perspective of empirical economic analysis. As an example of empirical economic analysis, the study mainly focuses on an analysis involving consumption-related statistics. It also introduces production statistics and national income statistics. Important data in empirical consumption analysis includes data from household surveys, market statistics, and macroeconomic statistics. As specific examples of empirical analysis, the study introduces (1) consumption analysis using household surveys (cross-sectional data), (2) demand analysis using market statistics (time-series data), and (3) data debated during the consumption controversy in the United States mainly in the 1950s. During the controversy, various hypotheses were proposed that aimed at a unified explanation of consumer behavior; three different tendencies were indicated in the economic statistics of household surveys, short-run macro time-series data, and long-term macro time-series data.[4]

Let us start with a cross-sectional analysis using household surveys. Before Ernst Engel analyzed the living expenses of Belgian workers' families, David Davies, a clergyman in England, conducted a household survey focusing on poor households in 1789–1793 (see Stigler, 1965). He surveyed 127 poor households to appeal for poverty alleviation. However, the beginning of household survey analysis covering a wide range of income groups was the analysis by Engel (1895), which is famous for the discovery of Engel's law. His Belgian household survey, conducted in 1853, established the empirically based law that the ratio between food expenditure and income (usually called Engel's coefficient) decreases as income increases. Allen and Bowley (1935) estimated Engel's curve from cross-sectional data as the income-consumption line of the indifference map based on ordinary utility theory (see Hicks, 1939). After confirming that Engel's law was validated by a 1904 British household survey, they estimated the linear Engel curve using household survey data in the 1910s, 1920s, and 1930s in England, the United States, Finland, Norway, Denmark, Germany, and Belgium. Moreover, Prais and Houthakker (1955) conducted a large-scale consumption analysis in England.

Gregory King's Law is well-known as the empirically based demand law on the relationship between the price of corn and demand for it. It states that the price of corn increases as its quantity decreases. According to an observation by Charles Davenant in 1699, a 10% decrease in the quantity of corn increases the corn price by 30% (the price elasticity is –0.33), and, when the quantity is reduced by 20%, the price rises by 80% (the price elasticity is –0.25). Engel also confirmed the downward-sloping curve using the demand for rye in Prussia from 1846 to 1861.

An empirical analysis of consumer demand was conducted in the early 20th century. In the United States, Moore (1914) derived the demand function for potatoes using market statistics from 1870 to 1918. Schultz (1938) estimated the demand function for sugar from 1875 to 1925 and for beef and pork from 1922 to 1930. In Europe, Wold (1953) conducted an analysis using household surveys and market statistics from 1921 to 1939 in Sweden. Moreover, an empirical analysis by Stone (1954) used pooled cross-sectional and time-series data from 1920 to 1930. These researchers estimated demand functions to calculate the price effect, such as the price elasticity of demand for commodities.

4 This session focuses on the explanation of economic statistics used in empirical economic analysis but not on the explanation of the theory and hypotheses for consumer behavior.

During the *Consumption Controversy* in the United States in the 1950s, three data sets on consumption and savings had different characteristics. The first set was the long-term macroeconomic time series created by Kuznets (1942), indicating that the savings rate (i.e., 1 minus the consumption rate), with 10 years serving as one unit, was constant during the period from 1879 to 1938. The second data set was the short-run macroeconomic time series compiled by the US Department of Commerce. It indicated that though consumption increased as income increased, the consumption rate (i.e., the ratio of consumption to income) tended to decrease as income increased. Therefore, the savings rate was not constant and rose as income increased. Smithies (1945) and Duesenberry (1949) used short-run macroeconomic time-series data from 1923 to 1940 in their analysis (this time-series data is still published as part of the *National Income and Product Accounts in the United States*). The third data set is the 1935–1936 and 1941–1942 household surveys compiled by the Bureau of Labor Statistics. The household surveys found that there was a difference in consumer behavior between urban and rural households and between white and black households, even at the same income level.

Using these three types of data sets with different tendencies, several working hypotheses were proposed. They included the absolute income (originally in Keynes, 1936), relative income (Duesenberry, 1949), liquid asset (Tobin, 1951), permanent income (Friedman, 1957), and the life cycle (Ando and Modigliani, 1963) hypotheses.

Switching focus to economic statistics other than consumption data, Douglas (1934) contributed greatly to the field of empirical analysis of production. He is famous for estimating the Cobb-Douglas production function using the production, capital, and employment index from 1899 to 1926. Leontief (1941) prepared what is known as the input-output table for 1919 and 1929. Richard Stone proposed creating the SNA for each country through the United Nations. The SNAs have five accounts: national income statistics, the input-output table, the flow of fund table, the balance of payments table, and national wealth statistics. The data of the macroeconomic model of the United States by Klein (1950) was compiled by the Department of Commerce from 1920 to 1941. Thus, excluding market statistics, economic statistics used for empirical economic analysis were created in the 20th century, especially after 1930. Nowadays, it is possible to obtain consistent economic statistics and perform highly accurate empirical economic analysis.

Microeconomics is the theoretical basis of the field of law and economics. Areas such as general equilibrium theory, ordinal utility theory, and the indifference curve are basic analytical tools in microeconomics. The 20th century witnessed the development of economic theory that enabled empirical economic analysis in response to the enrichment of economic statistics. The beginning of general equilibrium theory occurred with Walras (1874, published in French). Pareto (1906, published in Italian) and Hicks (1939) contributed greatly to the introduction of ordinal utility theory and the indifference curve in microeconomics.

2.2.2 *Economic theory on which empirical analysis is based: The ordinal utility theory*

Ordinal utility theory is a basic concept in the theory of consumer behavior; it is also used in Edgeworth's box diagram to help explain the fundamental theorems of welfare economics. The ordinal utility theory states that an individual can judge the following three opportunities regarding commodity sets A and B: (1) commodity set A is preferred to that of B, (2) commodity set B is preferred to that of A, or (3) commodity sets A and B are equally preferred (the consumer is indifferent about them). According to the theory, the individual can compare the commodity sets such that their utility for the individual can be determined relative to each other but not by their absolute value. The individual selects the commodity set such that the utility index for it is the highest feasible as restricted by income.

Importantly, it is not possible to compare the utility of a commodity between different individuals when they have different shapes of indifference curves of consumer choice between two commodities. When the commodity sets A and B are presented to individuals a and b, one (the other) may prefer commodity set A (B) according to the shape of the indifference curves. Thus, a utility comparison between them is not possible in ordinal utility theory.[5]

Many different research results have been obtained in empirical economic analysis of consumer behavior based on ordinal utility theory. In the empirical analysis of consumer behavior, the economic agent is not the individual per se but the *representative* individual (representative household). The behavior of the representative individual corresponds to the observed value of economic statistics. In the ordinal utility theory, it is possible to compare the relative magnitude of satisfaction of consumer choice only if the indifference map is the same during the observation period in a time series or among individuals in a cross-section. If the shape of the indifference map is different at different times in a time series, it is not possible to compare the utility between different periods. Similarly, when the shape of the indifference map differs for each income class in the cross-section, it is not possible to compare the utility between individuals.

5 Individuals a and b appear in the Edgeworth box diagram. There, the utility comparison between a and b is not performed, but the route to reach the higher level of the indifference curve is searched for each of the individuals. Modern economics textbooks use the ordinary utility theory. However, sometimes, they use cardinal utility to explain a topic. For example, the theory different from the ordinal utility theory is the Gini coefficient, which indicates the degree of inequality in income distribution among the individuals in the society. When deriving the Gini coefficient, the sum of utilities among the different individuals is taken. Another exception is game theory, which deals with negotiations between different individuals. It only allows linear transformation of the utility function. In welfare economics, the measures of compensation standards—Kaldor's, Hicks', and Scitovsky's standards—implicitly include a comparison of utility between different individuals.

2.2.3 Philosophical foundation of the methodology of social science

Next is an examination of the history of philosophical thinking related to the methodology of social science since the early modern period. In the methodologies of natural and social science, as debated in modern philosophy after the 16th century, there were two major trends. One is British empiricism influenced by thinkers such as Francis Bacon, Thomas Hobbs, and John Locke, and the other is Continental rationalism represented by thinkers such as René Descartes, Benedict de (Bauch) Spinosa, and Gottfried Wilhelm von Leibniz in exploring the truth about the natural and social sciences. Empiricism and rationalism sought to establish research methods that excluded theology (scholasticism) or the authority of the church. The essence of empiricism is the inductive approach, and that of rationalism is the deductive approach. Induction derives a general proposition or empirical law from individual facts. Deduction draws inevitable conclusions from presupposed propositions according to the rules of logic regardless of experience. Before the modern ages, truth was God, and theology (Scola philosophy) was the search for the existence of God. However, after the modern ages, truth was confined to laws that exist in nature (natural laws) and society (social laws), and people seek such truth. Broadly, the academic purpose is the search for truth.

Immanuel Kant fused rationalism and empiricism from the rationalism standpoint. He argued that a perception of truth must be a judgment that combines universality and necessity. Moreover, although logical judgment reveals the content of a concept, it is not recognition. For a judgment to be recognized, there must be a substance that corresponds to the concept. This shows that true cognition must be conceptually true and have objective substance to support the concept. Knowledge is achieved through the synthesis of concept (*a priori*) and experience (*a posteriori*) (see Scruton, 2002).[6]

Neo-Kantian philosophy emerged from the late 19th century through the early 20th century. It started with the dualism of existence (Sein) and purpose (Sollen). Among the Neo-Kantian schools, the Neo-Kantian Southwestern German School argued that there was a world of *culture* between existence and purpose. This concept of culture had a great influence on the sociologist, Max Weber. The impact of Weber (1904) on empirical analysis begins with constructing a model, which accords with empirical economic analysis. In

6 Though Bacon was one of the pioneers of British empiricism, and Descartes was one of the pioneers of Continental rationalism, neither Bacon nor Descartes unilaterally stated the superiority of their theories of empiricism and rationalism. Bacon (1620) stated that it is necessary to ascertain a general law after gathering individual-specific experiences. However, Descartes (1637) also stated that, by making experiments, it is necessary to confirm the validity of the proposition to be deduced. He recognized that it takes much time and money to conduct the experiments. Accordingly, both had a flexible way of thinking about the method of seeking the truth. There is a difference in the starting point of philosophical thinking and the methodology for obtaining results.

Weber's methodology, for social science, he made an important observation on the relationship between analysis and policy.

When Weber's paper on the methodology of social science was published in 1904, empirical analysis was the method of natural science; there were no cases of empirical analysis in social science (especially in economics). The Econometric Society was established in 1930, centering on Irving Fisher, Ragnar Frisch, Joseph Schumpeter, and Jan Tinbergen. Since then, empirical economic analysis has been conducted widely, economic statistics have accumulated, and econometric estimation methods have been developed. Thus, economics has made incomparable progress relative to the early 20th century when Weber's treatise was published. Although Weber recognized the importance of empirical economic analysis, he died in 1920 and could not witness the subsequent development of economics.[7] Weber's *ideal type* is a mental image that is not historical reality and certainly not "true" reality; less so, it is meant to serve as a schema into which it would be possible to fit reality as a specimen. It has the status of a purely ideal concept against which reality is measured and compared to extract significant parts of the empirical substance of reality.

Policy is not an extension of analysis. It is simply naive when even professionals occasionally still assert that what is important above all is to set up "a principle" for practical social science and to corroborate its validity by scientific

7 At that time, Weber was a sociologist with a unique view on the controversy among the younger German Historical School, such as Gustav von Schmoller, the Austrian School, such as Karl Menger, and the Marxian School. The main arguments according to Weber (1904) are as follows. (1) About the model: [The ideal type] is a mental image that is not historical reality and certainly not "true" reality; less so, it is meant to serve as a schema into which it would be possible to fit reality as a specimen. It has the status of a purely ideal limiting concept against which reality is measured—with which it is compared—to bring out certain significant components of the empirical substance of [that reality]. (Weber, 1904, Page 127). (2) Analysis and policy are not on a continuous basis: It is simply naive when even professionals occasionally believe that what is important is above all to set up "a principle" for the practical social science and to corroborate its validity [by scientific means] such that norms for the solution of individual practical problems can be unambiguously deduced from it. There is a definite need within the social science for "fundamental" discussions of practical problems; that is, for uncovering the ideas underlying the value judgments that unreflectingly push themselves forward; and this journal, in particular, has the firm intention of devoting itself to precisely those kinds of discussion. However, it certainly cannot be the task of the journal or any science of empirical experience to establish a practical common denominator for the problems in the shape of generally valid ultimate ideas (Weber, 1904, Page 104). (3) Regarding the distinction between analysis and policy: The goal is to strengthen once more the ability to distinguish between knowing [something] and judging [it] and to fulfill the scientific obligation to see the truth of facts and the practical duty of standing up for one's ideals (Weber, 1904, Page 105). The term "ideal type" is indifferent to evaluative judgments; it has nothing to do with any other "perfection" than a purely logical one (Weber, 1904, Page 130). (4) Economic factors alone cannot address social phenomena: The reduction solely to economic causes is never in any sense exhaustive within any sphere of cultural phenomena, not even in the sphere of "economic" processes (Weber, 1904, Page 113).

means such that the solution of practical problems can be unambiguously deduced from it. There is a definite need for fundamental discussions of practical problems within social science; that is, for uncovering the ideas underlying the value judgments that are unreflectingly pushed forward. However, it certainly cannot be the task of empirical analysis to establish solutions to our problems.

Regarding the distinction between analysis and policy, the goal is to strengthen the ability to distinguish between knowing something and judging it and to fulfill the scientific obligation to seek the truth and the practical duty to stand up for one's ideals. An "ideal type" is indifferent to evaluative judgments; it has nothing to do with any "perfection" but is purely logical. Economic factors alone cannot be utilized to solve social issues. The reduction of social problems solely to economic causes is never in any sense exhaustive, not even within the sphere of economic processes.

Weber argued that analysis (recognition) and policy (practice) are different things. Policy does not flow from analysis and the two must be separated. Weber emphasized separating economic analysis and economic policy. He argued that researchers in economic science perform economic analysis, while economic policy is done through politics based on empirical economic analysis (see Weber, 1919a, b). Weber also stated that it is not necessary to equate the methodology of social science with that of natural science. There are two possible reasons. First, social science has relatively little accumulation of empirical analysis and data that verifies theory. Therefore, the correspondence of theory with reality is weaker in social science than in natural science. Second, the activities of human beings are more complicated than the movement of objects. In natural science, it is relatively easy to conduct experiments in an isolated system; in social science, it is challenging to analyze the activities of human society in that way.[8]

Regarding the methodology of social science, Gunnar Myrdal (1969) proposed the value premises as universal values of human society. They are respect for life and the egalitarian principle. Myrdal's premises of equality and

8 According to Weber, from the perspective of astronomy, only the ***quantitative*** relationships of the celestial bodies, which can be measured with precision, engage our interest; [but] what matters in social science is the ***qualitative*** aspect of events. Moreover, social science is concerned with the influence of processes in the ***human minds***, and the reexperiencing "***understanding***" of such processes is of course a task that is different from that which the formulas building on the exact knowledge of the natural world are at all able or designed to solve (Weber, 1904, Page 115).

Social science studies human behavior in society. Economics focuses on economic society (especially markets) and human economic behavior. Humans act as consumers in the field of consumption and as a factor of production (labor) in the field of production. In policy theory, individuals appear as creators and beneficiaries of policies. Notably, in policy discussions, there is the possibility of a conflict of interest for certain individuals, which overlaps with Weber's separation of analysis and policy.

respect for life are a problem of economics and the philosophy of law.[9] Various declarations of human rights emphasize respect for life along with freedom. However, modern economics does not specifically address life (or the fact that an individual lives). Consumption and labor are conducted on the premise that people are alive, but the conditions for human survival and human rights are left out. In modern economics, influenced by natural science, humans exist as a factor of production. Modern economics recognizes that individuals have diverse abilities and theoretically argues that any individual with any ability contributes to the improvement of productivity. This notion is expressed in the *theory of comparative advantage*. However, it applies only when individuals are self-employed or employed in the labor market; it does not apply to the unemployed. Even so, employment and unemployment are directly related to human life and human rights.

2.2.4 Procedure of empirical economic analysis and its flow chart

The study employs econometric methodologies in empirical economic analysis. First researchers collect the data necessary for the analysis. The data include various economic statistics compiled by the government and data from international organizations such as the United Nations and the Organisation for Economic Co-operation and Development (OECD). Data collected as reference materials include papers and commentary of other researchers, newspaper articles, and industry reports. The analytical methods are based on British

9 In the history of legal philosophy and political history, the concepts of freedom and independence are incorporated into various declarations of human rights as components of civil society. *The Declaration of Human Rights* of the French Revolution of 1789, which reflects the ideas of Rousseau (1762) and others, is famous, but the basis for this declaration is the *United States Declaration of Independence* and the *Virginia Declaration of Rights* in 1776. The Virginia Bill of Rights, approved in June 1776, states the following about individuals:

That all men are by nature equally free and independent and have certain inherent rights, of which, when they enter a state of society, they cannot, by any compact, deprive or divest their posterity; namely, the enjoyment of life and liberty, with the means of acquiring and possessing property and pursuing and obtaining happiness and safety. The *United States Declaration of Independence* of July 4, 1776, holds these truths to be self-evident, that all men are created equal, that they are endowed by their Creator with certain unalienable Rights, that among these are Life, Liberty, and the pursuit of Happiness. Article 1 of the *French Declaration of Human Rights* of 1789 notes that people are born and live free and equal in rights. Social discrimination can only be made in the common interest. Article 4 states that freedom comprises being able to do everything that does not harm others. Consequently, the exercise of each person's natural rights has no limits other than to ensure the enjoyment of these same kinds of rights by other members of society. These limits can only be defined by law. In Article 6, law is an expression of consensus. All citizens, either personally or through their representatives, may contribute to its creation. The law must be the same for all, whether it protects or imposes punishment. All citizens, being equal in the eyes of the law, are entitled to all public ranks and offices according to their abilities and are equally subject to discrimination other than their virtue and talent.

empiricism. *Empirical law* is law based on systematic observations and data accumulation.

The researchers conducting empirical economic analysis create a theoretical model to generalize from the empirical facts. The models take mathematical forms. For example, the study utilizes the mathematical operation of maximizing utility when examining theories of consumer behavior and that of maximizing profit when studying theories of producer behavior. This stage is influenced by Continental rationalism. The procedures for the collection of facts and the creation of theoretical models are influenced by Kant's philosophy.

The next step is to set up the experimental design. This procedure is unique to empirical analysis; the methodology of empirical economic analysis comes from natural science. The experimental design includes (1) the determination of economic agents, (2) the determination of the unit period of observation, and (3) ensuring correspondence between theoretical variables and observational variables. The objectivity of the empirical results is maintained by the experimental design. That is, if anyone analyzes the data according to the experimental design, they should obtain the same results. The theoretical concept alone is not sufficient to conduct the empirical analysis; the substance is in the observation.[10]

When the model and data are ready, the study estimates the parameters included in the model and tests its validity. There are two principles in the estimation: the least squares and maximum likelihood principles. The former was invented by a mathematician, Karl Friedrich Gauss, and the latter, by a statistician, Ronald Fisher. The study employs statistical methodologies in estimation and testing. When the model is finalized, forecasting and extrapolation techniques are used to test the robustness of the model.

After confirming the validity of the model, the conducts various policy simulations. Per Weber (1904), confirming the robustness of the model is the responsibility of economists, and making amendments to the law and taking new legislative measures are the role of politicians. Figure 2.1 shows the flow chart of empirical economic analysis.

10 The task of setting the experimental design is not done in the normative analysis of economics. In the normative analysis, when a theoretical model is set, the variables included in the model may not always correspond to the observed variables. Examples include the concept of transaction costs, basic needs in welfare economics, and costs and benefits in cost-benefit analysis. In the normative analysis, these concepts do not necessarily correspond exactly to the substance. In the wealth maximization hypothesis used in law and economics, social wealth is defined as the sum of the market value of goods and services (obtained from the National Income statistics), and the consumer and producer surpluses. In the empirical analysis, how to measure consumer and producer surpluses is a significant problem. The concept of fairness used in the normative analysis of law and economics includes corrective justice, the principle of keeping promises, and the principle of proportionality in criminal punishment. How to contrast these concepts with the observed data would be a much more difficult problem.

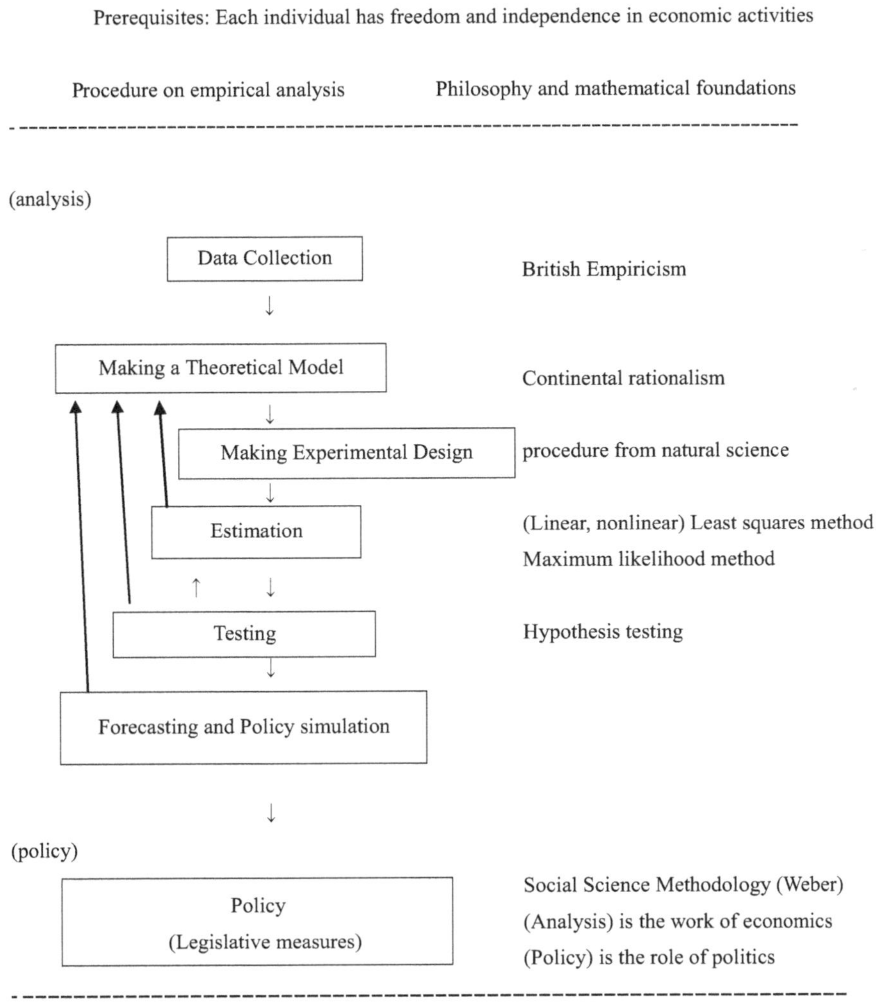

Figure 2.1 Flow chart of empirical economic analysis

2.3 Two examples of empirical economic analysis

The study introduces two analyses. One is the analysis of domestic and foreign price differences given various regulations introduced in the Japanese economy in the 1980s. In those days, Japanese consumers purchased goods at high prices in the domestic markets relative to international markets. The other is the analysis of changes in living standards among three income groups of consumers given deregulation in New Zealand since the 1980s. The study employs prior empirical analyses (Maki, 1998, 2002) on these two issues.

2.3.1 *Problems of price differences between domestic and foreign markets and deregulation policy*

Since the 1980s, the Japanese economy has had a trade surplus and been known as a major asset-holding nation. Thus, the trade imbalance between Japan and the United States widened, and Japan-US Structural Talks were held to consider solutions. The US side noted inappropriate business practices in Japanese distribution industries in wholesale and retail sectors and noted that collusion in bid-rigging occurred in the construction industry. They noted that given the closed nature of Japanese markets, consumer prices in Japan are higher than in the United States and Europe.

For the econometric model constructed when conducting an empirical analysis of the price differences between domestic and foreign markets (Maki, 1998), the study utilized two cross-sectional data sets for international comparisons with the same classification as the SNA. These data sets are the *Price Report* compiled by the Economic Planning Agency (EPA), currently in the Cabinet Office of the Japanese government, and the *Purchasing Power Parities and Real Expenditures* prepared by the OECD. The EPA provided data on consumption expenditures and the corresponding prices in Tokyo, New York City, London, Paris, and Berlin. The OECD provided data on consumption expenditures and the corresponding prices in Japan, the United States, the United Kingdom, France, and Germany.

The study considered a situation where an individual living in Japan had an indifference map of consumer preferences specified by the utility function. It sought to answer the following question: When the Japanese live in a specific foreign city or a country with prices that are different from those in Japan, how much does the Japanese pay for the minimum amount of total consumption under the condition that the Japanese obtain the same level of satisfaction (i.e., the utility level is the same) as in Japan? The study calculated the minimum total consumption expenditure using the minimum expenditure or cost function of consumer behavior by applying the estimated econometric model.[11]

Figure 2.2 explains the present simulation. It illustrates three indifference curves (u_1, u^*, u_2) and two income lines (y^J and y^A) that are tangent to the indifference curve of u^*. y^J is the total amount spent by the individual to maintain the utility level of u^* in Tokyo or Japan with the relative prices P^J. Further, y^A is the total amount spent by the same individual with the relative prices P^A in a particular foreign city (e.g., New York City) or a foreign country generally (e.g., the United Kingdom). The relative prices are shown by the gradient of the income line, and they are not the same in Japan and other

11 When converting the local currency to Japanese yen, this study employs the exchange rate. Maki (1998) explains the econometric model and how to calculate the minimum total consumption expenditure in detail. Maki (2011) explains the dual approach of consumer behavior regarding the cost function in consumer demand theory.

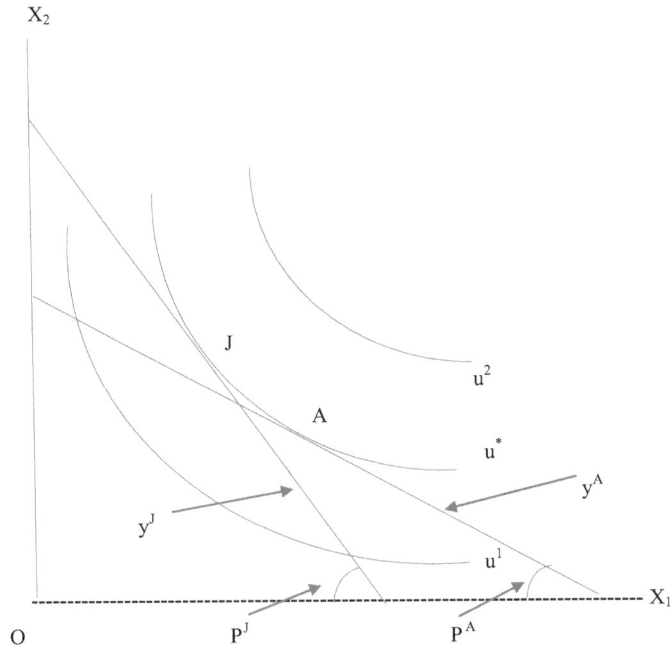

Figure 2.2 Consumption expenditure at the same utility level when Japanese live in overseas cities and countries

countries. If the ratio of the total expenditure consumed in Japan (y^J) to the total expenditure consumed outside of Japan (yA) is greater than unity, the prices, on average, in Japan are higher than those in foreign cities or foreign countries.

Table 7 in Maki (1998) shows the results of the empirical analysis, some of which are reproduced here in Table 2.1.

Table 2.1(a) indicates the statistical price index reported by the *Price Report* compiled by the EPA as an approximation to the constant-utility price index. Table 2.1(b) indicates the statistical price index, called purchasing power parity, reported in *Purchasing Power Parities and Real Expenditures 1993* compiled by the OECD. These two statistical price indices stem from the Fisher price index formula, which is the geometric mean of the Paasche and Laspeyres price indices. Although a statistical price index is based on a completely different concept than the constant-utility price index, it can be used as an approximation of it.[12]

12 See Maki (2005) for the magnitude of the divergence between the constant-utility price index and the statistical price index. Maki (2005) confirmed that the statistical price index has a high degree of approximation to the constant-utility price index.

Table 2.1 Constant-utility price index and two statistical price indices

(A) Constant-utility price index with a certain utility level and the livelihood cost index (statistical price index) prepared by the Economic Planning Agency (currently the Cabinet Office)

	Tokyo	*New York City*	*London*	*Paris*	*Berlin*
Constant-utility price index reference:	1.00	0.757	0.694	0.709	0.704
Statistical price index	1.00	0.709	0.685	0.735	0.724

(Note) The Economic Planning Agency Livelihood Index is based on the *Price Report*.

(B) Constant-utility price index with a certain utility level and purchasing power parity prepared by the OECD (statistical price index)

	Japan	*US*	*UK*	*France*	*Germany*
Constant-utility price index reference:	1.00	0.568	0.561	0.685	0.727
Purchasing power parity	1.00	0.552	0.557	0.674	0.712

(Note) OECD Purchasing Power Parities are based on the *Purchasing Power Parities and Real Expenditures 1993*.

According to the empirical results of the analysis, the price level in Japan was higher than in other developed countries. Indeed, on average, prices in Japan were higher than those in foreign cities and countries by 20% to 40%. The Japan-US Structural Talks concluded that there were inefficiencies in the distribution sectors of the Japanese economy, particularly in retail industries. The United States requested deregulation in the Japanese retail markets as a means of removing these inefficiencies.

Specific deregulation policies were accompanied by amendments to the law. As part of the policies to improve efficiency in the distribution industries, the Department Store Law enacted in 1973 was abolished in June 2000. Chapter 11 discusses the results of the policies.

2.3.2 Changes in living standards among income groups of consumers given deregulation in New Zealand

There was a global trend of deregulation in the 1980s and 1990s. In those days, deregulation policies in New Zealand worked well. The improvement of the New Zealand economy was called a "miracle" worldwide. To examine the impact of deregulation on New Zealand households, the study analyzed the change in living standards of households by income group using household surveys conducted between 1984 and 1996 (Maki, 2002).[13]

It reports an overview of this empirical analysis, where the representative household has an indifference map derived from the utility function that is common to all income classes in the observation period (If each income class has its utility function and, therefore, its indifference map, one cannot make utility comparisons among income classes using the indifference map.). Figure 2.3 shows this relationship.

The study compared changes in living standards over time by income class as follows: For any income class, the study calculated the minimum expenditure required to maintain the utility level of the previous year under the prices in the present year and compared the minimum expenditure calculated by the model with the observed expenditure that year. If the minimum expenditure was greater than the observed expenditure that year, the standard of living that year declined, and vice versa. When the minimum expenditure is greater than the observed expenditure that year, the household does not maintain the standard of living of the previous year given the lack of income. However, when the minimum expenditure is less than the observed expenditure that year, the household

13 The *NZ Household Income and Expenditure Survey* classifies the decile income class. The econometric model was estimated using pooled data of time series (1984 to 1996) and cross-section (ten income classes). However, to examine the effects of deregulation, the ten income classes were reorganized into three income groups: low-income, middle-income, and high-income groups. Of the 10 quantile income classes classified in the household survey, the low-income group in the analysis is the 1st to 3rd quantile income class, and the high-income group is the 10th quantile income class. Therefore, the middle-income group is in the 4th to 9th quartiles.

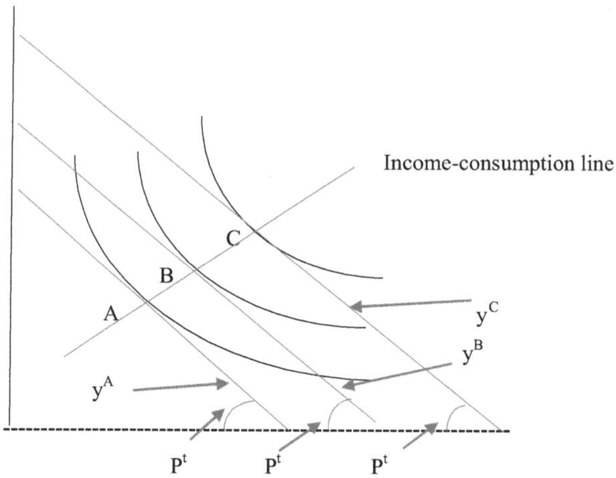

Figure 2.3 Indifference map and three budget lines by income class

consumes more using the extra amount of income. Therefore, additional consumption yields a higher indifference curve and a higher utility level. In this case, the standard of living improved relative to the previous year. Figure 2.4 illustrates the criteria for determining whether the standard of living improved.

Table 2.2 shows the results of changes in living standards by income class. It shows the number of years the total spending was greater than the upper bound of the confidence interval of the estimated minimum expenditure derived by the model. The greater the number of years, the greater the improvement in living standards in the income class.[14]

The effect of deregulation on New Zealand households should be a remarkable improvement in the living standards of the high-income group (10th quantile), followed by the level of improvement of the middle-income group (4th to 9th quantiles). The low-income group (1st to 3rd quartiles) would show the least improvement. However, the results of the empirical analysis contradicted intuition. As expected, the improvement in living standards of the high-income group was the highest among the three income groups. However, the second-highest improvement in living standards was in the low-income group, not the middle-income group. The empirical results accord with the feelings of New Zealand people. Even in the period of deregulation, the philosophy of the welfare state since the beginning of the 20th century has been to focus on maintaining the New Zealand social security system. The high-income group was strongly affected by the deregulation, and the low-income group benefited from the traditional social security system. However, the middle-income

14 To obtain the confidence interval of the minimum expenditure for each income class, the study employed the bootstrap method. Refer to Maki (2002) for the details of the analysis.

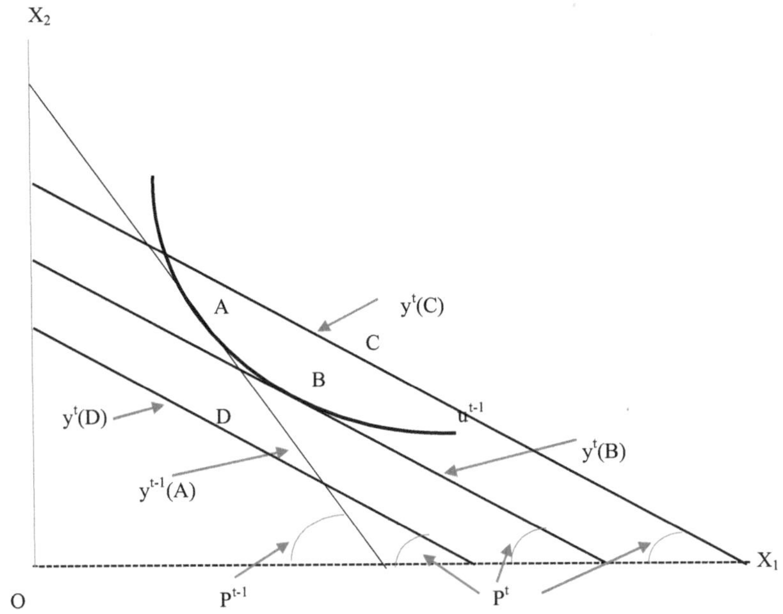

Figure 2.4 Judgment of improvement of living standards

Table 2.2 Number of years where living standards improved by income group during the 1985–1996 period

Income class									
1st	2nd	3rd	4th	5th	6th	7th	8th	9th	10th
4	4	6	3	5	3	5	3	4	7
33 (%)	33 (%)	50 (%)	25 (%)	42 (%)	25 (%)	42 (%)	25 (%)	33 (%)	58 (%)

group enjoyed relatively little benefit from either. The study verified the results of the analysis using data compiled by Statistics New Zealand. It calculated the time-series changes in the real-term consumption expenditure of households by adjusting the nominal-term consumption expenditure divided by the CPI. Table 2.3 shows the results.

The yearly changes in the number of income classes with improved living standards and consumption based on the official data shown in this table show that the higher the number of income classes with improved living standards relative to the previous year, the greater the change in consumption from the previous year, except for two (1986 and 1994) out of 12 years. Household consumption in New Zealand has steadily increased given deregulation. However, inequality of income distribution has also increased because the growth rate of

Table 2.3 Yearly changes in real consumption

Year											
1985	*1986*	*1987*	*1988*	*1989*	*1990*	*1991*	*1992*	*1993*	*1994*	*1995*	*1996*
1	4	1	3	4	6	2	1	5	5	6	6
–	–	–	+	+	+	–	–	+	–	+	+

real consumption was not the same among income groups.[15] The reduction of the middle-income class can induce a crisis of democracy because it suggests a tendency for society to become polarized.

2.4 Gap between the results of empirical economic analysis and the desired policy from the normative analysis perspective

In normative analysis, the first fundamental theorem of welfare economics states that the competitive market maximizes economic welfare in society. However, the results of the empirical analysis revealed that economic policy did not necessarily produce results consistent with the purpose of deregulation and privatization. An economic policy for deregulation is based on the enforcement of the law, but it is not necessarily for the realization of competitive markets defined by microeconomics. Figure 2.5 shows the principles of deregulation, privatization, and the realization of competitive markets (marketization).

The conditions of a competitive market shown in Figure 2.5 are (1) a large number of small-scale market participants, (2) homogeneous goods, (3) perfect information, and (4) free entry and exit. The idea of creating a competitive market under these conditions is to create fair markets (i.e., markets regulated by fair rules) such that each consumer and producer participating in the market can be equally competitive.

However, given the deregulation in the markets, the strong won and the uncompetitive weak lost and exited from the market. There was a decrease in competitiveness among the participants in the market, contrary to the purpose of deregulation. Deregulation means loosening the restrictions imposed by the current laws. It will, thus, weaken beneficial restrictions protected

15 Deregulation improved the standard of living of the people. Meanwhile, income inequality had widened. The Gini coefficient is an index that indicates the degree of income inequality among households. According to the OECD statistics, the Gini coefficient in 1985 was 0.271. However, it increased yearly from 0.318 (in 1990), to 0.335 (in 1995), to 0.339 (in 2000). Hence, income inequality widened in the process of deregulation. However, the Gini coefficient was 0.335 in 2003 and 0.330 in 2008, indicating that the income disparity has been shrinking. It seems the government's redistribution policy functioned.

Facts: There are inhibition factors for competition such as inefficient business customs

↓

Policy Goals: Creating a competitive market that maximizes the economic welfare of the society

↓

Means: deregulation ruled by law and economic policies aimed at privatization

↓

Ideal Result: Realization of fair competitive markets (Ensuring equal competitiveness of the market participants, and securing the law to prevent torts and illegal activities)

Figure 2.5 Difference between the principle of deregulation and privatization and that of marketization

by regulations. For example, in the labor market in Japan, deregulation has resulted in an increase in non-regular workers and a growing economic disparity between regular and non-regular workers.

Based on the fundamental theorems of welfare economics, the final objective of economic analysis and policy is to create competitive markets. However, policies must embrace various values, such as a law-abiding spirit, human rights, equality, peace, and environmental protection, not just efficiency. Although economics scholars are experts in economics, they are not experts in these diverse values. When policies are made based solely on economic knowledge, they may not promote social justice. Policymaking and enforcement are the job of politicians, not economists.

2.5 Empirical analysis of law and economics based on judicial precedent

Economics advocates the principles of *freedom of contract* and the *absolute right of private property* and presupposes that an individual can make transactions independently and freely of his own will. The basic principles of property law are *freedom of personality rights*, *freedom of ownership*, *freedom of contract*, and *liability for negligence*. Liability for negligence means a person is liable for damages to another person only when the act is intentional or entails negligence. The premises of economics and the basic principles of property law contain common elements, except the principle of liability for negligence. By excluding the principle of liability for negligence from the premise of economics, it is not feasible to express economic theory in a simpler model. However, it can result in a lack of relevance of economics to reality. In particular, it affects judgments when evaluating the appropriateness of economic policies.

There is a difference in the approaches of economics and law to actual economic problems. Economics explores ways to solve problems based on economic models as ideal types, while law seeks to solve problems based on legal provisions. Consider the jurists' approach to social problems. Legal scholars or lawyers try to solve problems based on legal texts. Law forms an enormous system, and legal scholars and lawyers search for ways to solve problems while keeping an eye on the whole system. As a precondition for finding ways to solve problems, they consider elements such as the realization of justice, protecting the weak, and valuing human beings.

Despite the difference between economics as a model and law as a text, the economic model and the legal system are based on rationality or logical consistency. Conducting empirical analysis in the area of law and economics warrants considering the relationship between *free* transactions in economics and *justice*, which is the purpose of law. According to the philosophy of law, the demand for legal justice is backed by coercion. However, coercion contradicts the free and unrestricted activity of the individual assumed by economics. That is, justice does not enter the realm where the full autonomy of individual action is allowed. Hence, the economic behavior of the individual based on freedom and efficiency is rational but neither justice nor injustice.

In society, freedom and coercion can coexist. The following is an examination of this from the standpoint of Kant's philosophy of law. There are two categorical imperatives. The first is the a priori moral law that people *act so that the maxim of the subjective will become a universal law*. The second categorical imperative is that *human beings should always be treated as an end in themselves, not as a means*. It is difficult for us to uniquely judge the good or evil of individual actions by the abstract concept of an autonomous ethical personality. Thus, the law is necessary to judge good and evil in society. The law must uphold the freedom of the individual as an autonomous personality. If the behavior of one individual is compatible with the freedom of all others, then the behavior is just. However, if the action of one individual interferes with the freedom of another, it is unjust. Individuals whose freedom is infringed upon have the right to address the infringement by law with coercion.

The law is the substantive basis for judging people's actions, whether it is correct or incorrect. Going back to economics, Pareto efficiency corresponds to the right thing to do. When there is an infringement, economics simply says that it is not Pareto efficient. However, law says that when there is an infringement of rights, legal remedies are possible and necessary.

Consider disparity, discrimination, and bullying in this context. Kant's philosophy of law states that if another person feels bullied (discriminated against) by an individual's actions, it is bullying (and discrimination). However, it is impossible to uniquely define bullying and discrimination given the diversity of individual emotions and values. Therefore, the concept of right and wrong, as it pertains to individuals, is unified by social rules called law. That is, the reason for legal justice. The influence of Kant's philosophy of law is seen in Myrdal's value premises of respect for life and the egalitarian principle.

2.5.1 Basic prerequisites for empirical analysis of law and economics

In setting up a theoretical model of law and economics, start with the Coase Theorem. It includes the following five assumptions:[16]

> (1) The legal rights of each individual are guaranteed, (2) Individuals have rationality to maximize their self-interest, (3) No transaction costs are incurred, (4) Each individual is free to negotiate in economic society, and (5) Society has a mechanism to effectively enforce the performance of contracts.
>
> (C.f. Tsuneki, 2015)

Table 2.4 classifies these five assumptions into those to be maintained and those to be relaxed in the empirical analysis of law and economics. It also summarizes the relationship between these assumptions and the empirical economic analysis explained in Section 2.2.4 of this chapter.

Removing Assumptions (1) and (5) would deviate from the democratic rule of law principle. Therefore, the two assumptions may be held in empirical economic analysis. Of course, they are maintained in empirical analysis of law and economics. Illegal acts occur in economic transactions. In such cases, legal actions are taken per Assumptions (1) and (5): a claim for damages from the victim and punishment for the perpetrator. When the empirical analysis of law and economics is an extension of empirical economic analysis, the transaction cost in Assumption (3) becomes the focus.[17]

In conducting empirical analysis of law and economics, it is important to consider how to include conditions such as freedom in economic transactions, legal coercion given torts and illegal acts, and Myrdal's value premises. Though it is necessary to incorporate these conditions into the analytical framework as explicit mathematical formulas or implicit statements as null hypotheses, the egalitarian principle is a policy issue that goes beyond the framework of the fundamental theorems of welfare economics. Therefore, the egalitarian principle cannot be solved by economics.

Table 2.4 Correspondence between the assumptions of the Coase Theorem and the empirical economic analysis

Assumptions	*(1)*	*(2)*	*(3)*	*(4)*	*(5)*
Empirical economic analysis	Potentially maintain	Maintain	Potentially maintain	Maintain	Potentially maintain
Empirical analysis of law and economics	Maintain	Maintain	Loosen	Maintain	Maintain

(Note) The correspondence may be loosened in the empirical analysis of law and economics.

16 See Section 1.2 in Chapter 1 for the contents of the Coase Theorem.

17 The transaction costs in this book include the specific costs payable if the consumer's claim for damages is successful and the expenses related to court.

The study now presents the analytical procedure of the empirical analysis of law and economics with freedom and coercion as the basic components. It divides the whole system into three blocks—the economic transaction block (freedom), the damage compensation block (coercion), and the policy block (regarding the egalitarian principle)—following the second of the four simple doctrines by Descartes (1637).[18] At the first stage as preconditions, the study sets Myrdal's respect for life and the egalitarian principle as the value premises and sets legal justice. The second stage is similar to empirical economic analysis premised on freedom in economic transactions. In this stage, it sets *economic agents can freely and independently trade* as a null hypothesis. The null hypothesis is that there is no illegal act in the behavior of the economic agents. The study conducts an empirical analysis to test the null hypothesis.

To determine if torts and illegal acts were found by the JFTC to have occurred (i.e., the null hypothesis would be dismissed), this study scrutinized its decisions and judgments by using the logic of economics and that of law. It tested the validity of its decisions and the judgments and estimated the amounts of damages claimed utilizing methods of empirical economic analysis. The study created a damage compensation block corresponding to the coercion of the law when illegal acts occurred. In the block, it examined the causal relationship required for claiming damages for infringement of rights and the estimation of the amounts of claims for damages. Figure 2.6 shows the conceptual correspondence between economic and legal acts in the damage compensation block.

Most of the economic transactions are normal transactions and legal acts for contracts. There were, however, a small number of torts and illegal acts. Here, there is a significant difference in the focuses of economics and law. Economics focuses on normal transactions and is uninterested in illegal transactions. Law is relatively uninterested in legal acts; law pays attention to torts and illegal acts.

Considering the case of public works collusion in the construction industry, consider the difference between the information in the analysis based on economics and that obtained from JFTC's decisions and the judgments. Based on economics, the bid-rigging mechanism becomes a matter of coordination or competition between general contractors, which is a theme for game theory. However, when utilizing game theory, it is important to specify the pay-off matrix of each player and the risk of being caught bid-rigging. It is important to determine how to make the pay-off matrix based on the observed data and how to obtain the probability that bid-rigging will be detected. However, searching for observational data may be a big problem in itself. Nonetheless, there are data of empirical facts and evidence related to the collusion in the JFTC's judgments and decisions.

18 Researchers will divide the problem to be solved into smaller parts. Then, they will solve the problem by giving the solutions to the individual parts.

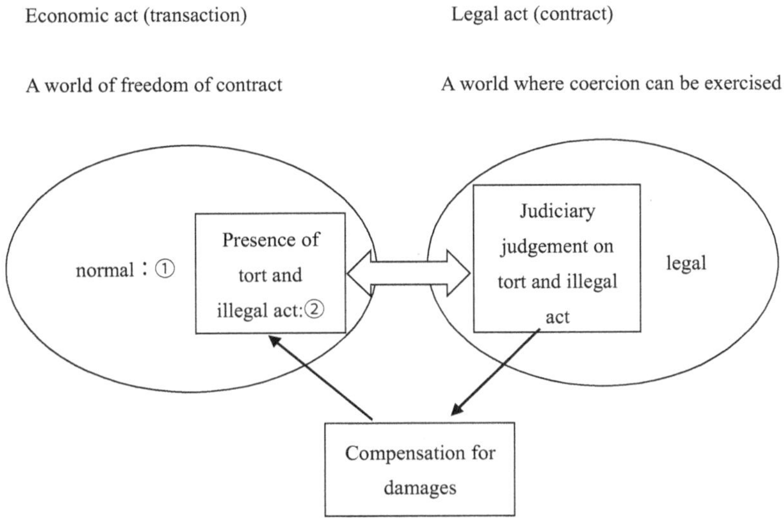

(Note) ① and ② correspond to ① and ② in Figures 7 and 8.

Figure 2.6 Normal transactions and torts and illegal acts as the target of damage blocks

As a critique of British empiricism, this study considers the issue of distinctiveness and generality. It may be difficult to determine the general factors involved in the rigging from a single case. However, as with Bacon (1620), one can extract general factors by collecting several similar cases. It is possible to confirm those factors via statistical tests. After going through the damage compensation block, the study shifted to the policy block. With normal economic transactions, the economic transaction block does not fall within the damages claim block. Economic transactions are conducted based on the free will of the parties. If the transaction violates the law, the judicial system is used to achieve justice. According to law, the judiciary determines whether the act is illegal. Ultimately, if deficiencies in existing laws become apparent, the consensus of the society will lead to amendments to existing laws and new legislative measures.

Next, the study explains the flow of empirical economic analysis and empirical analysis of law and economics using as examples the empirical economic analysis of the Japanese and foreign price differentials and the deregulation in New Zealand and the empirical analysis of law and economics of the cartel price agreements and bid-rigging in Japan. Figure 2.7 shows the basic analytical procedure for empirical analysis of law and economics.

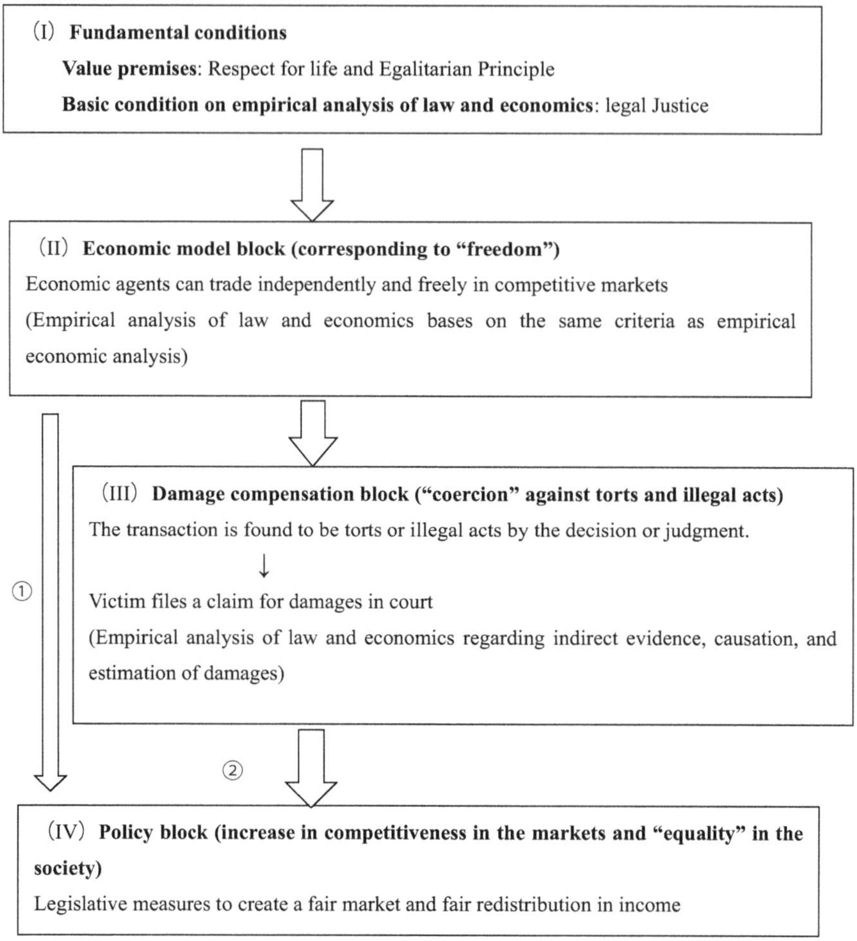

Figure 2.7 Basic analytical procedure for empirical analysis of law and economics

In the empirical economic analysis of the price differentials and the deregulation, the damage compensation block is not necessary. In the analysis of the domestic and foreign price differences, the retail prices were higher than those of other countries given the closed state of the Japanese market. The study also discussed the necessity of deregulation. However, economists do not care about cases where consumers claim damages from infringement. In the empirical analysis of deregulation in New Zealand, the deregulation policy improved the living standards of consumers overall. The deregulation widened the income disparity among them, and the size of the middle-income classes declined. The empirical results simply show that deregulation has improved living standards and widened economic disparities. Politicians must reduce the disparities by conducting suitable economic policies.

In an empirical analysis of law and economics of the cartel price agreements and bid-rigging in Japan, it is possible to enter into the damages claim block from the economic model block and consider the victim's damages claim. The study examined the validity of the claim for damages in the case where the infringed individual claimed damages on the premise of legal justice. A lawsuit for damages was filed by local residents, and there was a dispute between the plaintiffs and the defendants over whether the claim was valid. The courts finally made judgments. When evidence of torts and illegal acts was examined by the courts, a legal syllogism was adopted to verify the causal relationship. However, econometric analysis was never adopted to verify the causal relationship. To develop an empirical analysis of law and economics in the future, the judges should recognize statistical causal relationships and use the results of claims for damages estimated from econometric models, using the empirical results as evidence. If the current legal system is an inconvenient means for resolving such disputes, the legislature should amend the existing law or enact a new law in the policy block.

2.5.2 Flow chart of empirical analysis of law and economics

Figure 2.8 shows in more detail the procedure for performing the empirical analysis of law and economics relative to empirical economic analysis. Here, the damage compensation block occupies an important position. The introduction of this block represents a big difference from empirical economic analysis.

The study examined in detail the cases where torts and illegal activity did not occur ① and the cases where torts and illegal activity occurred ② in the cartel price agreement and the bid-rigging. When a tort or illegal act is confirmed by the court, the victim involved in the case will start the procedure for claiming damages. The empirical analysis of law and economics employs materials such as trial decisions and judgments. Proving the existence of a causal relationship is an important point in court. There, beyond legal syllogisms used in law, one can also give suggestions for the use of statistical causal relationships. Specifically, there is a Granger causality test in time-series analysis in Chapter 3. Moreover, the estimation results from econometric analysis can be used to estimate the amount of compensation for damages.

The study considers the collection of actual trial decisions and judgments as the starting point for the damages block. Whether the legal community recognizes statistical causal relationships regarding causal relationships and the results of econometric analysis as reliable evidence is an important factor in the future development of empirical analysis in law and economics.

In the empirical analysis of law and economics, the study finally enters the policy block. As noted, it considers that Weber's perspective is the most appropriate solution. The optimal policy obtained from economics is to create a

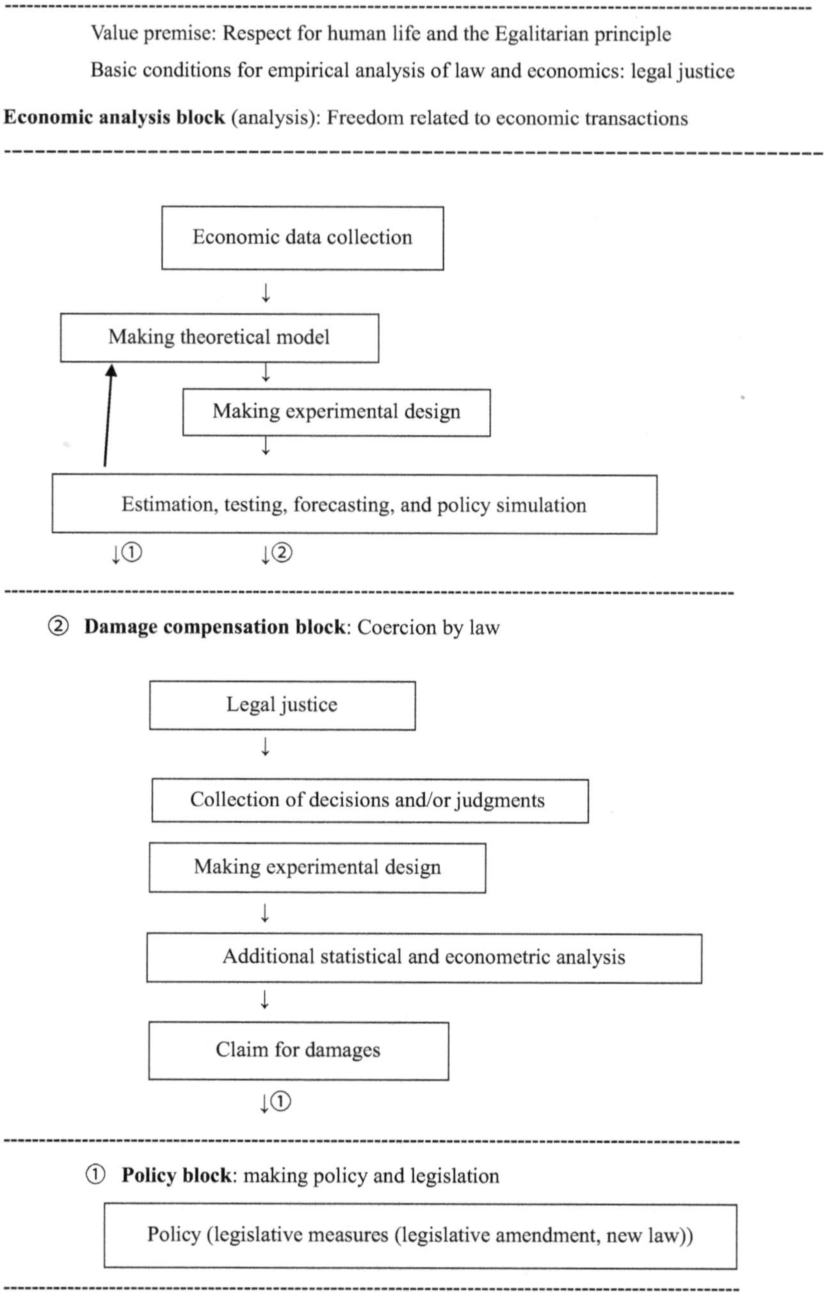

Figure 2.8 Empirical analysis methodology of law and economics

competitive market based on the fundamental theorems of welfare economics. However, as will be discussed in Chapter 11 of this book, the specific means of *pro-competition policy* is ideal *deregulation policy* through revision of laws or new legislative measures. However, in some cases, the ideal *pro-competition policy* and the actual *deregulation policy* do not match their policy objectives. In other cases, the actual deregulation policy resulted in a setback from the pro-competition policy. Moreover, the fundamental theorems of welfare economics and the Coase Theorem do not provide a unique solution to the redistribution problem among the individuals in society.

To solve the distribution problem, the new perspectives on the value premise of the *egalitarian principle* proposed by Myrdal (1969) and the separation of analysis and policy proposed by Weber (1904), rather than the traditional economics perspectives, are essential. The redistribution problem in society is not a problem for economists to solve on their own. However, it is a problem to be discussed and resolved by the people of the nation. That is the work of politics.

2.5.3 Specific facts of empirical analysis of law and economics

Consider briefly an overview of consumer (or inhabitant) damages claim cases in this book. First is the case of price-fixing among oil-refining companies and the case of consumer damage claims against it. The oil-refining companies agreed with the price-fixing for kerosene at a price higher than the competitive price without the agreement. When consumers bought kerosene, they did not know whether the retail price was illegally priced. However, the accusation of the JFTC revealed that the kerosene prices purchased by consumers were illegally priced at retail prices. Finally, the Supreme Court approved that the cartel price agreement by the oil-refining companies was illegal. Consumers then filed a claim for damages on the grounds of the court-approved decision. The question at stake was as follows: Could plaintiffs prove a causal relationship between the illegal increase in wholesale prices and the rise in retail prices? Moreover, could the plaintiffs estimate the difference between the cartel price and the competitive price by a reasonable method?

The following is a description of the cases of bid-rigging. A local government planned the public works and decided the property to bid on the contractors. The general contractors planned a bid-rigging among the contractors for the public works regarding the winning bid of the bid property. The bid-rigging was then accused by the JFTC. Thus, the bid-rigging was found to be illegal. The residents as taxpayers then learned that the bid-rigging wasted taxes and filed a lawsuit for damages. The issue here is whether the residents can prove the existence of a basic agreement among general contractors.

2.6 Conclusion

When conducting an empirical analysis of law and economics, one must clarify the difference between economics and law and the difference between normative and empirical analysis in economics. This chapter explains the empirical analysis of law and economics from a philosophical perspective and reviews them from an empirical economic analysis viewpoint.

It was not until the 20th century that empirical economic analysis began. During the last century, scholars have developed economic theories that enable empirical economic analysis, prepared economic statistics, and developed econometric methods necessary for model estimation and testing. Beyond their contributions to the development of empirical economic analysis, it is necessary to reexamine the basic assumptions of law and those of economics in conducting empirical analysis of law and economics. Thus, this study began with the British empiricism and the Continental rationalism. After examining Kant's philosophy of law, the addresses Weber (1904) and Myrdal (1969) to establish the philosophical and methodological foundation of empirical analysis of law and economics.

The study found an important point in Weber's methodology on social science. Given the optimal economic policy based on economic theory, it may not be the economic policy people want. Though the model used in the theoretical economic analysis is mathematically correct and maintains logical consistency, it can be challenging to detect in actual society. Weber required the separation of economic analysis and policy to avoid such challenges. Policy implementation requires comprehensive consideration, considering the diverse values of the people. The final decision maker of the economic analysis is the economic researcher, while the final decision maker of the economic policy is the policy maker mandated by the people. When policymakers implement deregulation and privatization, they should make sure that the rationale for the measures accords with market competitiveness.

This book presents the model of law and economics with the views of Weber and Myrdal and explores the possibility of verifying the model based on economic statistics and legal materials. To establish economics as an empirical science, it is necessary to enhance the empirical economic analysis and verify the practical validity of the theory with many empirical results. Furthermore, by accumulating empirical analysis of law and economics, it is necessary to accumulate empirical analysis that can be convincing not only in the field of economics but also to researchers and practitioners in the field of law.

3 Case of petroleum product price-fixing and cases related to damages

3.1 Introduction

This chapter examines the role of the courts in adjudicating lawsuits alleging price gouging by Japanese firms for kerosene during the 1970s when oil prices rose sharply in global markets and draws on econometric analysis to ascertain the extent of damages suffered by consumers given this behavior.[1] Crude oil replaced coal as the key source of energy in the world economy after World War II, enjoying advantages in terms of energy efficiency, ease of transportation, and waste disposal. In 1973, key oil-producing countries collectively decided to improve their terms of trade, causing the first Oil Crisis. In October 1973, the Organization of Petroleum Exporting Countries (OPEC) increased crude oil prices by 21% while ten Organization of the Arab Petroleum Exporting Countries cut production to support the price hike and preserve oil resources for the future.

The Japanese government took urgent countermeasures in December 1973.[2] The Cabinet approved an increase in the standard price of oil products by 62% on average in March 1974 (oil product prices were regulated by the government), and this came into effect in April. Though the price of kerosene for household use was pegged for two months, after June, kerosene prices increased further.

The Japanese economy was devastated by the oil price increase, which sparked hoarding by consumers worried about inflation and shortages of daily products such as laundry detergent and toilet paper. The CPI compiled by the Statistics Bureau increased by 30% relative to 1972 prices, signaling hyperinflation. The era of high economic growth, the so-called "economic miracle," ground to a halt as the combination of hyperinflation and recession resulted in stagflation.

1 Despite a few econometric analyses on the estimation of compensation for damages to consumers based on court documents in Japan, there are a couple of empirical studies in the US and Europe, such as Porter and Zona (1999) and Hüschelrath, Müller, and Veith (2016).
2 The proclamation was removed in August 1974.

DOI: 10.4324/9781003370444-3

Here, the study is concerned with accusations of collusion in price-fixing and how the oil price increases were implemented in Japan. The JFTC prosecuted the Petroleum Association of Japan (PAJ) for adjusting supply and the oil-refining companies for manipulating prices. The Supreme Court acquitted the PAJ regarding supply adjustments but judged it guilty of negotiating a cartel price for the 12 oil-refining companies. The Supreme Court ruled on the cartel price agreement among 12 oil-refining companies in 1984.

In response to the Supreme Court rulings, some consumers claimed compensation for damages from the cartel price agreement made by the oil-refining companies. They claimed damages over price-fixing related to the difference between the cartel price and the ostensible market price. As there was a cartel price agreement among the 12 oil-refining companies that were also the principal wholesalers, the retail price paid by consumers was higher than what it would have been in the absence of such an agreement; thus, there is a case for awarding damages to consumers given price-fixing.

The Supreme Court issued subsequent rulings on two kerosene cases, one in Tokyo and one in Tsuruoka. Regarding the Tokyo kerosene case, the High Court in Tokyo and the Supreme Court dismissed the plaintiffs' claims. The Supreme Court ruled on the Tokyo kerosene case in 1987. In the Tsuruoka kerosene case, groups of consumers in Tsuruoka City in Yamagata Prefecture sought compensation for damages suffered from July 1973 to March 1974 for kerosene purchased from Tsuruoka Co-op and from March 1973 to April 1974 for kerosene purchased from other retail stores in Tsuruoka City.[3] Regarding the Tsuruoka case, the District Court in Yamagata dismissed the plaintiffs' claims, but they successfully appealed the case to the High Court in Sendai. However, the 12 oil-refining companies appealed this verdict to the Supreme Court, which overturned the High Court decision that favored consumers.[4] It ruled on the Tsuruoka kerosene case in 1989.

Section 3.2 examines alleged violations of the AMA by the PAJ and the 12 oil-refining companies that act as oil-refining firms and principal wholesalers and examines the cases of compensation claims for losses suffered by consumers. Section 3.3 conducts an econometric analysis to check the causality between the rise in the wholesale price and the rise in retail prices by the Granger causality test. Based on the estimated results, the study calculates the amount of compensation for damages to consumers. After specifying the model and evaluating the empirical results, the study concludes that the

3 The number of plaintiffs who purchased kerosene at the Tsuruoka Co-op was 1,581 while 53 plaintiffs purchased it at other retail stores. There were five cartel price agreements between November 1972 and November 1973 among oil-refining companies; the relevant agreement for this study was the September 1973 cartel price agreement.

4 The study employs the following Supreme Court judgments: Case number 1980(A) 2153, Date of the Judgment February 24, 1984, Keishu vol 38, no. 4; Case number 1981(Gyo-Tsu) 187, Date of the Judgment February 7, 1987, Minshu vol 41, no. 5; Case number 1985(O) 933, Date of the Judgment August 12, 1989, Minshu vol 43, no. 11.

Supreme Court decision should have awarded damages to consumers. The decision was flawed because it denied justice to consumers who were harmed by the cartel's price-fixing, an arrangement that enjoyed the government's blessing. Section 3.4 evaluated the estimated econometric model regarding the causal relationship between wholesale and retail prices of kerosene and the compensation for damages consumers deserved. Section 3.5 concludes the chapter.

3.2 The Japan Fair Trade Commission and the legal process

Figure 3.1 explains the distribution channels of kerosene from drawing crude oil from a well to purchasing refined oil products by final consumers. Crude oil is mainly produced in the Middle East and is traded in international oil markets. The increase in kerosene prices in the early 1970s stemmed from the OPEC orchestration of oil supplies and prices. The oil-refining companies in Japan purchased crude oil on the international market and refined it into various products, such as gasoline, light oil, heavy oil, and kerosene. The Japanese government oversaw the distribution and prices of oil products.

As indicated by the evidence presented in the Tsuruoka kerosene case, the oil-refining companies have the power to control prices in the secondary wholesale markets organized by the oil guilds in each Prefecture. This situation indicates that there is vertical control over prices from the principal wholesalers to the secondary wholesalers. The JFTC acted on the evidence that oil guilds made horizontal agreements on wholesale prices in the secondary wholesale market. Within the oil guilds, members agree to fix wholesale prices in the secondary wholesale market. Regarding such agreements by the oil guilds, the JFTC issued warnings and recommended the prosecution of several branches for violation of the AMA.[5]

Retailers of oil products are the Co-ops and small-scale retailers. The scale of retail stores for kerosene is small; therefore, there is little power to negotiate prices with the oil commercial guilds. Gas stations are retailers of kerosene and are also affiliates of the oil-refining companies. Accordingly, oil-refining companies directly control the retail price for kerosene, and this price is determined by the cartel price agreement among oil-refining companies with government support.

In 1974, the JFTC notified the PAJ and 12 oil-refining companies that they should abolish the cartel price agreement of November 1973 aimed at increasing the retail price of oil products and rescind the October 1973 agreement on

5 This included the JFTC recommendations no. 14 (Hachioji branch, Tokyo Metropolitan Area), no. 15 (Minami Tama branch, Tokyo Metropolitan Area), and no. 16 (Machida branch, Tokyo Metropolitan Area) in 1970; no. 8 (Yamagata branch, Yamagata Prefecture), no. 29 (Nerima branch, Tokyo Metropolitan Area), and no. 28 (the 4th liaison council, Tokyo Metropolitan Area) in 1971; and no. 30 (Suginami branch, Tokyo Metropolitan Area) and no. 44 (Tsuruoka branch, Yamagata Prefecture) in 1973.

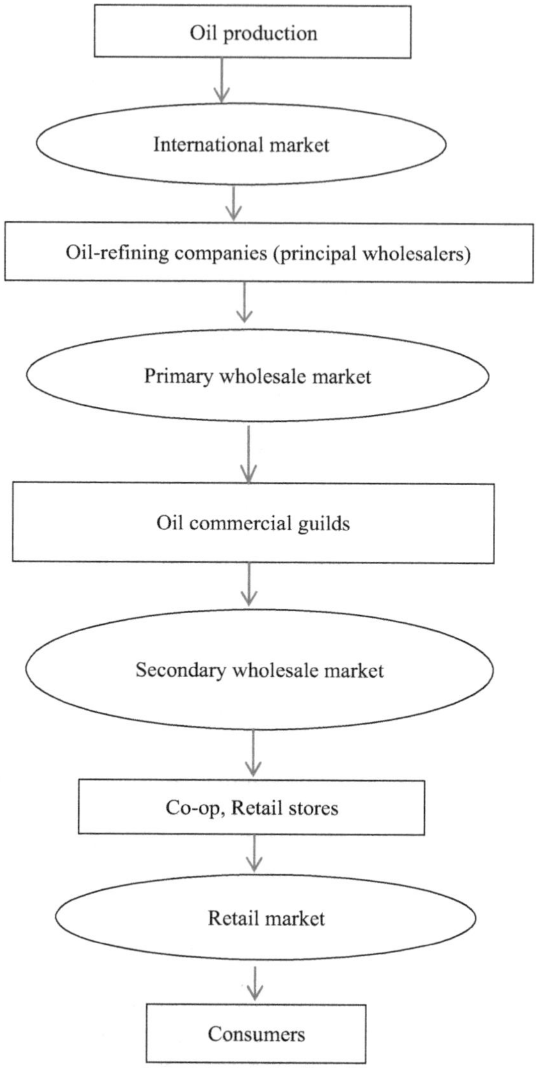

Figure 3.1 The channel from oil production to the final consumers

coordinating the supply of oil products. The 12 oil-refining companies and the PAJ appealed the JTFC action to the High Court in Tokyo. The High Court in Tokyo in 1980 declared the PAJ not guilty of production adjustment but declared the 12 oil-refining companies guilty of fixing prices. The oil-refining companies appealed this latter ruling to the Supreme Court, but the appeal was dismissed in 1984.

Meanwhile, consumers in Tsuruoka City in Yamagata Prefecture and Kawasaki City in Kanagawa Prefecture, including the Greater Tokyo Metropolitan Area, filed lawsuits seeking damages for price-fixing from the oil-refining companies. They argued that if there was no cartel price agreement, the retail price of kerosene for household use might be cheaper than the cartel price for kerosene. The Tokyo High Court (1981) and Supreme Court (1987) rejected the compensation claims. In Tsuruoka, however, in 1985, the Sendai High Court overturned the district court's dismissal of the plaintiffs' case and awarded damages. Subsequently, however, in 1989, the Supreme Court overturned this ruling and the award of damages. In such cases, the burden of proof is on the plaintiffs to prove there was price-fixing and to what degree this disadvantaged consumers.

3.2.1 The Sendai High Court's logic

The case under consideration is a dispute about whether there was a causal relationship between the cartel price agreement among 12 oil-refining companies and the rise in retail prices of kerosene. The purpose of the agreement made by the oil refiners and wholesalers of oil products aimed at fixing prices for their benefit, adversely affecting consumers. The counterargument focuses on whether the cartel price agreement increased retail prices because secondary wholesalers and retailers may not have passed along price increases, thus undermining the impact.

Evidence was presented that oil-refining companies effectively controlled retail prices through strict guidance and intervention in distribution channels. The Ministry of International Trade and Industry (MITI) conducts strong price monitoring of the oil industry and relevant distribution channels. The JFTC could, thus, present evidence that the retail price increase in kerosene resulted from a violation of the AMA.

From a legal perspective, it is sufficient to prove a high probability and establish causality. It is possible to use the estimating method to demonstrate this high probability and prove causality. Given that the market share of oil products of the 12 oil-refining companies exceeded 85%, the High Court in Sendai concluded as follows:

(1) The oil-refining companies increased the agreed prices through the cartel price agreement.
(2) The retail price of kerosene increased in the period of the agreement.
(3) The amount of compensation for damages is the difference between the observed retail price and the observed retail price realized before the cartel price agreement.

The logic of the High Court in the Sendai ruling placed the burden of proof on the oil refiners to prove that the increase in the retail price of kerosene occurred given factors other than the cartel price agreement.

3.2.2 The Supreme Court's logic

The Supreme Court's decision was based on a different logic, placing the burden of proof on consumers as follows:

(1) The injured party had to prove a direct causal relationship existed between the increase in the agreed price of oil products based on the cartel price agreement and the increase in the retail price.
(2) Moreover, they must prove the amount of damages suffered given the illegal price agreement among oil-refining companies. Accordingly, the injured party had to estimate the expected retail price if there was no cartel price agreement and prove that it was cheaper than the cartel-manipulated retail price. According to the Supreme Court, this "expected retail price" is not the retail price realized before the cartel price agreement noted by the High Court in Sendai but is the price without the cartel agreement that reflects fluctuations in the Japanese economy.

The Supreme Court ruled that these points were not proven and that the overall Japanese economy experienced great changes in market conditions that influenced retail prices of kerosene and all other commodities and services and, thus, could not rule out the influence of other economic factors aside from the cartel agreement. Given the apparent proof of price-fixing by oil refiners and primary wholesalers, there were many critiques of the Tsuruoka kerosene ruling in legal journals. The Supreme Court decision required the injured party to estimate the expected retail price without the cartel price agreement based on economic theory and econometric techniques that were not sufficiently developed at that time. Kaneko (1990) and Shoda (1990) concluded that, in any future cases, it would be impossible for consumers to estimate and ask for damages based on this precedent.

Ito (1990) suggested using an econometric model to ascertain the causal relationship between the price rise given the cartel price agreement among oil-refining companies and the rise in the retail prices of kerosene and to estimate the amount of damages suffered by consumers to calculate compensation for damages. This chapter attempts to do just that.[6]

3.3 Constructing an econometric model to evaluate the compensation for damages

In building an econometric model, it is vital to consider the following four points to address the Supreme Court decision. First, when there are macroeconomic

6 Regarding the robustness of the econometric model, even in the period of great changes in retail prices of commodities and services, the study introduces an econometric analysis of consumer behavior. In the period of the first Oil Crisis beginning in 1973, the CPI compiled by the Statistics Bureau increased by 30%. However, this significant increase seemed to downplay public perceptions of inflation, undermining confidence in the CPI. Maki (2005) conducted an empirical analysis to check whether there is a gap between the official CPI and the cost of living index based on consumer preference theory. After estimating the parameters of the econometric model, he found the following: (1) Even in a period of drastic change in relative prices in the Japanese economy given the oil price shock, the change in consumer behavior is well explained by consumer demand theory; and (2) there is little gap between the CPI and the cost of living index derived from the theory.

fluctuations that affect prices for kerosene and other commodities and services in the economy, it is essential to incorporate such effects into the econometric model. Hence, this study incorporated the price of imported crude oil in the econometric model because the main source of the drastic changes in the Japanese economy at that time was the spike in global oil prices. The second point regards the expected retail price used for calculating the amount of compensation for damages to consumers. It is the notional price that would have prevailed without the cartel price agreement, one that would have been affected by the economic fluctuations in the Japanese economy. Further, to get the expected retail price of kerosene, it is essential to estimate the econometric model, excluding the effect of the cartel price agreement while including the impact of the global price surge for oil on the Japanese economy.

Third, it is crucial to examine whether there is a causal relationship between the wholesale price increase given the cartel price agreement among oil-refining companies and the retail price increase for consumers, though there are middlemen between the oil-refining companies and final consumers. When wholesale and retail markets stand between oil-refining companies and final consumers, it is challenging to prove directly that there is a causal relationship between the rise of wholesale prices and that of retail prices.[7] The JFTC exercised its discretionary authority to investigate the situation. However, normally, consumers have limited means to gather such direct evidence and information and must rely on what is available in the public domain and information private firms are willing to provide. Accordingly, this study develops an econometric model to test whether the cartel price agreement affected the increase in retail prices. It warrants conducting the Granger causality test to determine whether there is a relationship between the wholesale price increase and the retail price increase given the cartel price agreement.

The fourth point regards whether the retail price would have been cheaper if there was not a cartel price agreement. Thus, the study constructs and estimates an econometric model imposing the restriction that the cartel price control was not implemented based on the idea of the Lagrange Multiplier (LM) testing. The conditions necessary for building an econometric model is as follows:

(A) On the characteristics of the model, the econometric model includes
- (1) the imported crude oil price variable as the explanatory factor of drastic economic fluctuations in the Japanese economy in the period of the first Oil Crisis in the 1970s in addition to influencing wholesale and retail prices of kerosene, and

7 In lawsuits, usually the source of dispute directly connects plaintiffs and defendants. For example, in the case of compensation for losses from a traffic accident, the plaintiff and the defendant are directly involved. Meanwhile, in the present case, wholesale and retail markets stand between plaintiffs and defendants. An econometric analysis based on economic theory and statistical methods shows that this case presents significant challenges.

(2) the null hypothesis that there is no cartel price agreement among the 12 oil-refining companies to calculate the expected price of kerosene without the cartel price agreement.

(B) On the qualitative testing,

(1) the study applies the Granger causality test irrespective of whether there exists a causal relationship between wholesale and retail prices in the econometric model.

(C) On the quantitative testing, the study will check that

(1) the observed wholesale price of kerosene, including the effect of the cartel price agreement, is greater than the estimated wholesale price based on the null hypothesis of no cartel price agreement in the econometric model and that

(2) the observed retail price of kerosene is greater than the estimated retail price of kerosene without the cartel price agreement in the econometric model.

3.3.1 Geographic variation in retail prices of kerosene

Prices for commodities are not uniform across Japan given different elements such as transaction and labor costs. Regarding the price difference of kerosene in Japan, there are regional differences in retail prices in the *Report on the Price Survey among 66 Cities in Japan* compiled by the Statistics Bureau. The Survey reports monthly data on retail prices in the major 66 cities, including Kagoshima City, Kobe City, Nagoya City, Osaka Metropolitan Area, Sapporo City, Sendai City, Tokyo Metropolitan Area, and Yamagata City. The Survey shows the monthly retail price of kerosene per 18 liters, the typical capacity of one jerry-can.[8] As the Survey does not include the monthly data of kerosene in Tsuruoka City in Yamagata Prefecture, the study employed Yamagata City in Yamagata Prefecture as a proxy in the econometric model, as it is in the same Prefecture and, therefore, is in the same oil commercial guild. The observation period for the econometric estimation covers 96 months from January 1970 to December 1977. Table 3.1 shows the variation in retail prices of kerosene among 65 cities from December 1972 to August 1974.

From Table 3.1, the retail price of kerosene is not uniform across Japan. For example, the retail price per kilo-liter in the Tokyo Metropolitan Area was 20,889 yen, while that in Yamagata City was 15,444 yen. The average retail price in 65 cities was 18,689 yen. The maximum retail price was 21,833 yen in Niigata City and the minimum retail price was 15,167 yen in Akita City. Therefore, the maximum range in retail prices was 6,666 yen per kilo-liter

8 The study changed the unit of 18 liters into 1 kilo-liter for the present econometric analysis. As the Survey did not include the retail price of kerosene at Higashi-Osaka City in June 1974, this study excluded Higashi-Osaka City from the observations.

Table 3.1 Standard Error and Range (Maximum – Minimum) of the retail price of kerosene per 1 kilo-liter (65 Cities in Japan)

	Standard error	*Range*
Dec 72	1,238	6,666
Jan 73	1,282	6,666
Feb 73	1,146	6,000
Mar 73	1,072	5,777
Apr 73	1,129	6,055
May 73	1,139	5,333
June 73	1,107	5,555
July 73	1,563	9,722
Aug 73	1,602	9,722
Sep 73	1,574	9,722
Oct 73	1,339	7,666
Nov 73	1,153	5,555
Dec 73	957	4,722
Jan 74	928	3,722
Feb 74	530	2,333
Mar 74	631	2,333
Apr 74	637	3,055
May 74	776	4,888
June 74	3,752	16,944
July 74	2,198	15,000
Aug 74	1,558	8,888

(120 yen per jerry-can) among the cities. Though Niigata City, Yamagata City, and Akita City are located in adjacent Prefectures and are known for being some of the coldest districts during winter in Japan, they have a high difference in retail prices for kerosene. Overall, the price ranking of kerosene by city appears somewhat random across Japan.

3.3.2 Estimation of an econometric model

Retail prices reported in economic statistics are the going rate for commodities in the market and serve as a yardstick for consumers and retailers. Considering that transactions in the real world are negotiated and that the retail price has a distribution with mean and variance, it is essential to develop a model including stochastic distribution of price. The fundamental model of the present analysis is as follows:

Observed price = theoretical price + stochastic disturbance.

As an equation, it is as follows:

$$y_t = y_t^* + \varepsilon_t$$

where y_t is the observed price at the t-th period, y_t^* is the theoretical price, and ε_t is the stochastic variable with mean 0 and variance σ^2. The stochastic variable includes the factors of transportation conditions, transaction costs, and terms of contract. y_t^* is specified as follows:

$$y_t^* = f(\text{set of predetermined and exogenous variables}).$$

The study specifies the retail and wholesale prices simultaneously to estimate the vector auto-regression (VAR) model (cf. Sims, 1980; Greene, 2012). The general form of VAR is as follows:

$$Y_t = B_1Y_{t-1} + B_2Y_{t-2} + \dots + GX_t + E_t$$

where Y_t is endogenous variables of order n, B is n by n parameter matrix, G is n by m parameter matrix, X_t is exogenous variables of order m, and E_t is random variables of order n. Y_t includes the wholesale price (p^w) of kerosene, the retail price (p^r) at Yamagata City, and X_t is the oil imported price (p^o) in the previous period.

Despite the desire to use the monthly retail price of kerosene in Tsuruoka City in Yamagata Prefecture, it was not compiled by the Statistics Bureau. Therefore, the study employed the monthly retail price of kerosene in Yamagata City in Yamagata Prefecture as a proxy, given its proximity to Tsuruoka City in Yamagata Prefecture.

Usually, the quantity of kerosene is included with its prices in the list of endogenous variables in the VAR model. On examining the monthly variation of the quantity of kerosene, there are cyclical movements, while the monthly variation of the retail price is stable. Thus, oil-refining companies and oil commercial guilds keep the retail price stable by adjusting the amount of inventory. This situation is evident from the seasonal variation of kerosene purchases in the Tokyo Metropolitan Area, Yamagata City, and the national base; prices remain stable year-round even during the winter peak demand season. To keep the retail price stable, they adjust inventory. Therefore, this study did not introduce quantity variables in the VAR.

Data used for the estimation are the monthly series of 96 samples from January 1970 through to December 1977. The study employed December 1977 as a cutoff because the second OPEC-engineered oil price shock took place in 1979–1980. Japan introduced a new price system for oil products after April 1974 under the guidance of MITI to manage price fluctuations and attendant economic disruption. As the kerosene price drastically changed in June 1974, this study introduced a dummy variable that indicates 0 before June 1974 and 1 after June 1974. As a preliminary test of each time series, the study conducted a Dicky-Fuller test and found that the characteristics of the time series changed before and after June 1974; therefore, it introduced a parameter dummy that indicates the change in the parameters of imported oil prices.

Regarding the Supreme Court decision, the retail price of kerosene increased greatly given the fourth cartel price agreement among oil-refining companies in September 1973. However, the study did not introduce any treatment with before and after effects in October 1973. Accordingly, it is possible to calculate the expected retail price if there was no cartel price agreement in September 1973. To determine the best lag in the VAR model, the study applied the Bayesian Information Criterion (BIC) and determined the lag of order 1 as the best.[9] The estimation results for the wholesale and retail price equations are as follows:

$$\begin{aligned} p^w = {} & -25.4376 && + 1.09683p^w(-1) && - .069571p^r(-1) && + 10271.4dum \\ & (.06) && (28.14) && (2.50) && (18.47) \\ & [.952] && [.000] && [.014] && [.000] \end{aligned}$$

$$\begin{aligned} & +.036150p^o && - .498889dump^o \\ & (4.13) && (15.40) \\ & [.000] && [.000] \end{aligned}$$

Std. error of regression = 498.958
R-squared = .997236
Adjusted R-squared = .997068

$$\begin{aligned} p^r = {} & -743.616 && + .306400p^w(-1) && + .838646p^r(-1) && + 12054.1dum \\ & (.92) && (4.13) && (15.87) && (11.39) \\ & [.359] && [.000] && [.000] && [.000] \end{aligned}$$

$$\begin{aligned} & + .00512072p^o && - .653232dump^o \\ & (.12) && (10.59) \\ & [.901] && [.000] \end{aligned}$$

Std. error of regression = 949.827
R-squared = .989814
Adjusted R-squared = .989193

where the value in the round bracket indicated under each parameter shows the *t*-value, and that in the square bracket shows the P-value. In the retail price equation, the *t*-value of the coefficient of $p^w(-1)$ indicates 4.13. It is significantly different from 0, indicating that there is a causal relationship between wholesale prices and retail prices in the sense of the Granger causality. The standard error of the equation in the wholesale price is 498. The value is almost half that of the retail price. Thus, the participants in the wholesale

9 The study employs BIC because it is consistent in selecting the true model for estimating the regression function (see Yang, 2005).

market are professionals; they know the market condition better than consumers, and the variation of wholesale prices is smaller than that of retail prices.

3.4 Assessment

Figure 3.2 shows the observed and estimated values of the wholesale price derived from the VAR model and the band of ±2(standard error) in the July 1973 to March 1974 period. From the figure, observed values stay within the ±2(standard error), and observed values are higher than estimated values. Thus, despite the cartel price agreement among the oil processing companies in the wholesale market, the wholesale price realized in the wholesale market was not abnormally high but was greater than the expected price derived from the model.

Similarly, Figure 3.3 indicates the observed values of the retail price of kerosene consumers purchased at the Tsuruoka Co-op, the estimated values derived from the VAR model in the period from July 1973 to March 1974, and the band between ±2(standard error) regarding the retail price of kerosene. The observed values for the retail price of kerosene sold by Co-op in Tsuruoka City stay within the confidence interval of ±2(standard error). Although the retail price of Tsuruoka Co-op was lower than the estimated values in March 1974, the observed retail price is the same or a little bit higher than the estimated value derived from the VAR.

The estimation results indicate the following. (1) The increase in retail price was affected by the cartel price agreement among the oil-refining companies. (2) The observed retail price of kerosene at Tsuruoka Co-op remained within ±2(standard error). Considering the variation of retail prices in the retail market, the retail price at Tsuruoka Co-op was not necessarily higher than what it might have been in the absence of a cartel price agreement in the retail

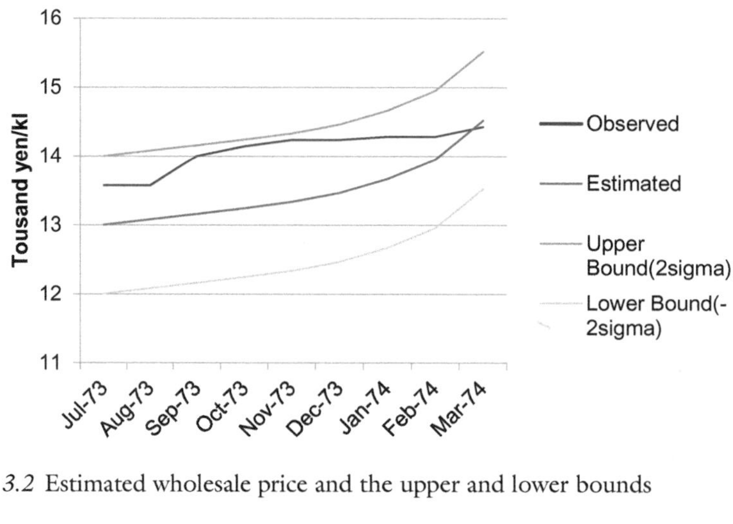

Figure 3.2 Estimated wholesale price and the upper and lower bounds

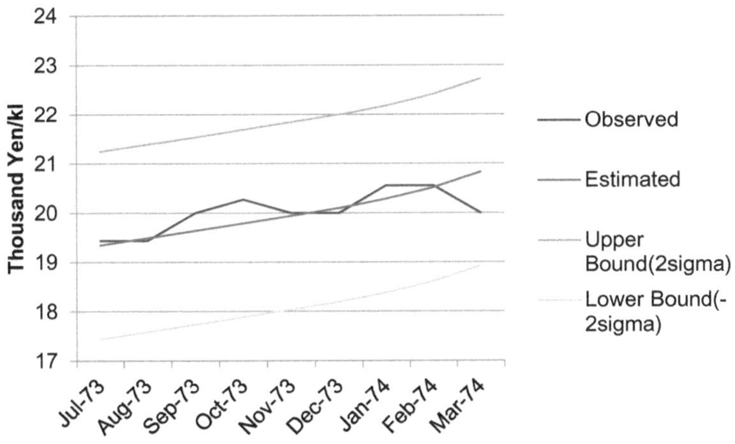

Figure 3.3 Retail price at Tsuruoka Co-op and estimated value (vector auto-regression) and its bounds

markets.[10] (3) Although the difference between the observed retail price and the expected retail price derived from the VAR model was not significantly large, it can be used to calculate the amount of compensation for damages awarded to consumers. Table 3.2 depicts the difference between the purchase price at Tsuruoka Coop and the estimated price derived from the econometric model in the July 1973 to March 1974 period.

The study evaluates the result of the amount of compensation for damages using the confidence interval in Figure 3.3 and the gap between the estimated and observed values in Table 3.2. Regarding the transaction between the Tsuruoka Co-op and consumers in Tsuruoka City in the retail market for kerosene, the difference between the observed price and estimated price is statistically insignificant because the estimated price stays within ±2(standard error). If the court recognized the amount of compensation to consumers based on the results of this econometric model, the amount would have been less than that awarded by the High Court in Sendai. The court awarded approximately 80 yen per jerry-can, while the findings suggest damages of approximately 1 to 3 yen per jerry-can.[11]

As denoted in footnote 3, 1,581 plaintiffs purchased kerosene at the Tsuruoka Co-op while 53 others purchased it at the other retail stores. Although the

10 The retail price of kerosene at the Tsuruoka Coop was cheaper than that in Yamagata City used as a proxy for other retail stores in Tsuruoka City (cf. Figure 3.8 in this chapter). This situation stems from a lump-sum payment contract between Tsuruoka Co-op and secondary wholesalers; thus, wholesalers discounted the price of kerosene.

11 From Table 3.2, the study calculated the sum of the estimated price of a jerry-can (18 liters) during the July 73 through March 74 period as 24 (5) yen, ignoring (including) the negative values.

Table 3.2 Difference between the retail price at Tsuruoka Coop and the estimated price obtained by the econometric model

	Yen/1kilo liter	*yen/18 liter (jerry-can)*
July 1973	95	2
Aug 1973	–51	–1
Sep 1973	359	6
Oct 1973	487	9
Nov 1973	59	1
Dec 1973	–101	–2
Jan 1974	270	5
Feb 1974	43	1
Mar 1974	–828	–14

data for the 53 plaintiffs is scarce relative to the data for the plaintiffs regarding the Tsuruoka Co-op, the study estimated the compensation for damages using the appendix table included in the High Court decision. Figure 3.4 indicates the distribution of retail price per the quantity purchased measured by jerry-can during the March 1973 to April 1974 period. Although it is not feasible to identify the month of purchases for each plaintiff from the appendix table, the price level has three modes: approximately 351 yen (the first mode; 19,500 yen per kl), 405 yen (the second mode; 22,500 yen per kl), and 450 yen (third mode; 25,000 yen per kl).

Comparing the tri-modal distribution to the observed retail price of kerosene at Yamagata City, the study determined that the first mode corresponds to March 1973; the second mode, the April 1973 through October 1973 period; and the third mode, the November 1973 through April 1974 period.

Figure 3.5 shows the retail price in Yamagata City as a proxy of that in Tsuruoka City and the retail prices of the first, second, and third modes, in addition to the estimated price (expected price without the cartel price agreement) and upper and lower bounds (±2(standard error)) of the estimated price. Examining the relationship between the three modes and the upper and lower bounds showed that the first mode (351 yen per jerry-can) in March 1973 is included within the upper and lower bounds. However, the second mode (405 yen per jerry-can) from April 1973 through October 1973 and the third mode (450 yen per jerry-can) from November 1973 through April 1974 are not included within the upper and lower bounds, indicating that the retail price of kerosene purchased at retail stores other than the Co-op is statistically different from the expected retail price derived from the model.

Table 3.3 estimates the compensation for damages at other retail stores than the Co-op in Tsuruoka City given price-fixing by the oil-refining cartel, using the expected price derived from the econometric model. The study proposes two alternatives regarding the compensation for damages. The first

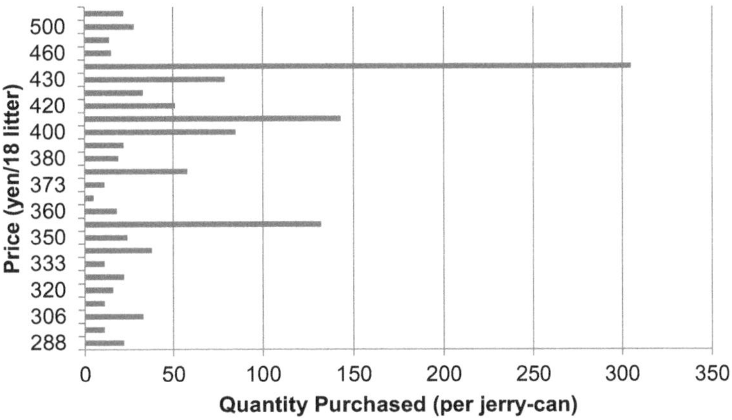

Figure 3.4 Retail price of kerosine outside of Tsuruoka Co-op

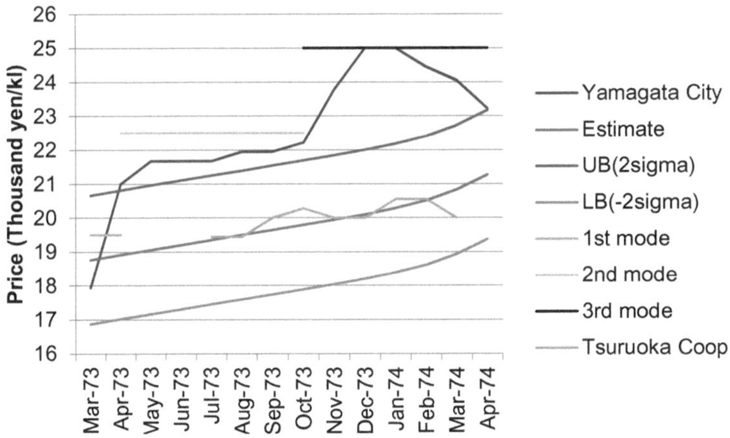

Figure 3.5 Retail price (Yamagata City, High Court in Sendai, Tsuruoka Co-op, and the Model)

is based on the retail price of kerosene in Yamagata City as a proxy to that at other retail stores in Tsuruoka City; the other is based on the information in Figure 4, reported in the High Court decision.

The court awarded between 100 yen and 150 yen per jerry-can, while the findings suggest damages of between approximately 40 yen and less than 90 yen per jerry-can using the retail price of kerosene in Yamagata City as a proxy for that at other retail stores in Tsuruoka City (see Table 3.3 column (a')) and approximately 50 yen and less than 100 yen per jerry-can using the data reported in the High Court decision (see Table 3.3 column (b')). Although the amount of compensation given to each consumer is not large, consumers suffered damage from the cartel price agreement among the oil-refining

Table 3.3 Compensation for damages to Consumers

	Retail price at Yamagata City	*Expected retail price other than the Co-op*	*Expected retail price from the model*	*Compensation for damages per 1 kilo-liter jerry-can*			
	(1)	*(2)*	*(3)*	*(a)*	*(b)*	*(a')*	*(b')*
Mar 1973	17,944	19,500	18,765	–821	735	–14	13
Apr 1973	21,000	22,500	18,914	2,086	3,586	37	64
May 1973	21,666	22,500	19,060	2,606	3,440	46	61
June 1973	21,666	22,500	19,204	2,462	3,296	44	59
July 1973	21,666	22,500	19,349	2,317	3,151	41	56
Aug 1973	21,944	22,500	19,495	2,449	3,005	44	54
Sep 1973	21,949	22,500	19,641	2,308	2,859	41	51
Oct 1973	22,222	22,500	19,790	2,432	2,710	43	48
Nov 1973	23,777	25,000	19,941	3,836	5,059	69	91
Dec 1973	25,000	25,000	20,101	4,899	4,899	88	88
Jan 1974	25,000	25,000	20,285	4,715	4,715	84	84
Feb 1974	24,444	25,000	20,512	3,932	4,488	70	80
Mar 1974	24,055	25,000	20,828	3,227	4,172	58	75
Apr 1974	23,222	25,000	21,270	1,952	3,730	35	67

Note: The table presents two alternatives of the difference between the retail price at retail stores in Tsuruoka other than Tsuruoka Co-op and the estimated price obtained by the econometric model (unit: yen). The retail price in the first mode is 19,500 yen; in the second mode, it is 22,500 yen; and, in the third mode, it is 25,000 yen. The difference is calculated by the gap between (a) the retail price of Yamagata City ((1) in the table) as a proxy of the retail price of Tsuruoka City other than the Co-op at Tsuruoka and (b) the retail price estimated by the author based on that reported in the High Court decision ((2) in the table) and the estimated price derived from the model ((3) in the table). (a') and (b') are the amount of compensation for damages per 18 liters (jerry-can).

companies. Estimating the total compensation for damages to consumers in Japan, with some 38 million households, shows that it is no small amount of money; every one yen increase in the retail price of a jerry-can of kerosene translates into a 38 million yen per jerry-can consumed in Japanese households.

3.5 Conclusion

In theory, this study analyzes consumer behavior under the condition that consumers behave to maximize their utility under the condition of given prices and total expenditure.[12] In the empirical analysis of consumer behavior, whether the observed price stems from cartel price-fixing is immaterial.

12 The study is not concerned with characteristics of the prices, for example, in the theory of consumer behavior, nor the difference between the retail price in a competitive market, an imperfect market, or that as the result of a cartel price agreement in an imperfect market.

However, considering consumer behavior as a part of the general equilibrium model, prices determined in imperfect markets harm consumers and, therefore, the economy based on the two fundamental theorems of welfare economics.

The JFTC accused the PAJ and the oil-refining companies of violating the AMA during the first Oil Crisis, and consumers filed lawsuits to demand damages from the oil-refining companies. The Supreme Court ruled that the oil-refining companies were guilty of fixing prices through their cartel price agreement. Oddly, despite acknowledging this wrongdoing, the Supreme Court failed to award damages to consumers. In the present analysis, although the estimated amount of compensation due is small, the econometric model demonstrates that oil-refining companies should pay damages to consumers to realize justice. As Chalmers Johnson argues, Japan's Iron Triangle of cozy and collusive relations between big business, the bureaucracy, and the Liberal Democratic Party represents a significantly different model of capitalism than the Anglo-American model, drawing on Adam Smith's laissez-faire, market-oriented variant (cf. Johnson, 1982). In Japan's system, he asserts that there is a systematic bias in favor of producers over consumers. The judiciary's negligence toward consumer interests in the kerosene case supports Johnson's thesis concerning government bias.

This chapter is an effort to demonstrate the power and relevance of econometric analysis in legal decisions related to economic theory. A better understanding of market forces and the impact of regulations, policies, and cartels is essential to informed judicial decisions on economic matters. As the law and courts exercise extensive influence over economies and markets, econometrics is an essential tool of analysis to enhance the judicial process.

4 Case on price-fixing of bearings and the particular field of trade and market

4.1 Introduction

Semiconductors are said to be *industry necessities*. However, they are not limited to semiconductors. Bearings are also industry necessities as mechanical parts that transmit power without friction in rotating parts of electric appliances, machines, and automobiles. As described in Section 4.5, various petroleum products meet the conditions of the industry necessities as an energy source.

The Japanese bearing industry is in a leading position at the global level. At the beginning of the 21st century, the top five companies worldwide were two companies in Europe (SKF in Sweden and Schaeffler in Germany), one in the United States (Timken), and two in Japan (NSK and NTN). The Japanese companies have established sales companies and production plants in Europe, the United States, and Asia. The bearing industry forms an oligopoly market in the domestic market while facing the competitive market in the global economy backed by advanced technology.

Kuznets (1966) listed industrialization, urbanization, and technical innovation as the conditions for *modern economic growth*, and the bearing industry embodies industrialization and technological innovation. Evaluating these two from the market perspective, a few companies with technological superiority dominate the international market, while the industry becomes oligopolistic companies in the domestic market. As the destination of *modern economic growth*, the companies producing industrial products with technological innovation often become the global companies in the international market and the oligopoly companies in the domestic market.

The rise and fall of the manufacturing industry supported the strength of the Japanese economy, as clearly reflected in the bearing industry. Consider the history of the bearing industry since 1945, divided into domestic and international markets. The domestic market was protected by the industrial policy implemented by the government. In the mid-1950s, the JFTC approved a rationalization cartel for five bearing companies by restricting the types of bearings they could produce. The goal was to avoid excessive competition in the industry. The four accused companies this time have continued to be the leading companies in the industry given their technological superiority and have maintained the typical oligopoly in the domestic market for the specific

DOI: 10.4324/9781003370444-4

products. They have created an environment conducive to mutual cooperation by holding public and private meetings. This situation is similar to the relationship between primary distributors of petroleum products.[1]

Considering the international market until the 1990s, investigations and lawsuits related to export dumping of Japanese products were conducted in Europe and the United States. However, at the end of the 1990s, the EU Commission agreed that all anti-dumping measures had ended and the problem with Europe was resolved. After the 1990s, the Japanese companies set up factories in China and Southeast Asia and created joint ventures. In the 2000s, trade friction arose in the form of countermeasures against counterfeit products in China and Southeast Asian countries. Regarding China, the 1st to 7th counterfeiting missions had been dispatched by 2007.

The study summarizes the situation surrounding the Japanese bearing industry circa 2008 when the price-fixing case occurred. The oligopoly market was formed in the domestic market. In the international market, the dumping lawsuits in Europe and the United States ended; instead, it was a period in which countermeasures against counterfeit products were being pursued in China. Under such circumstances, it was necessary for Japanese companies to improve their technology to survive in the international market. However, the easiest way for the companies to secure corporate profits was to take advantage of the oligopoly in the domestic market. Therefore, they concluded a cartel price agreement.[2]

Section 4.2 explains the outline of the case. Section 4.3 presents the court's decisions. Section 4.4 considers the different concepts of the market in economics and the particular field of trade defined by the AMA. Section 4.5 discusses several issues raised in this case and the evaluation. Section 4.6 concludes the chapter.

4.2 History of the bearing industry and overview of the bearing price agreement

Section 4.2.1 describes the history of the bearing industry in Japan for more than a century from the 1910s regarding the international market. Section 4.2.2 explains the outline of the present case.

4.2.1 History of the bearing industry

The history of Japan's bearing industry embodies *modern economic growth*. It was founded at about the same time as that in Europe and the United States. The founding companies have merged repeatedly and survived the Japanese

1 The rationalization cartel was a cartel exempted from the application of the AMA. It was concerned with restrictions on technology and production varieties along with the recession cartel and, thus, was excluded from the application of the AMA. After January 1982, the rationalization cartel was not implemented and was abolished in 1999.

2 See Komiya, Okuno, and Suzumura (1988) for industrial policy related to postwar Japan's economic growth.

economy. NSK was established in 1916. NTN (formerly Toyo Bearing), JTEKT (Koyo Seiko and Toyoda Machine Works merged in 2006), and Fujikoshi were founded in 1918, 1921, and 1928, respectively. Worldwide, Europe and the United States were the major manufacturing bases at the beginning of the 20th century. Schaeffler in Germany was founded in 1883, and SKF in Sweden was founded in 1907. In the United States, Timken was founded around the turn of the 20th century because the need for bearings increased with the emergence of the automobile industry represented by the Ford Model T.

The Japan Bearing Industry Association (JBIA) plays an important role in unifying the companies implementing the effective industrial policy by the government and as a source of information on the bearing industry worldwide. In the tri-polarization of Japan, the United States, and Europe, making up the world market, Japanese companies were exposed to international competition and cooperation. The leaders of the Japanese bearing industry exchanged information with those of SKF and Timken.

4.2.2 Overview of the case of the bearing price-fixing

This study examines the outline of the present case via judgments, newspaper articles, and industry information. In July 2011, the JFTC conducted an on-site inspection of NSK, NTN, JTEKT, and Fujikoshi. In June 2012, it accused three of them, except JTEKT, and seven executives; JTEKT made a voluntary declaration before the investigation began. Thus, it was not subject to the charges under the surcharge exemption measures stipulated by the AMA.

In this case, the object was ball and roller bearings manufactured and sold. The products manufactured by each company were less likely to have technological differences among them, and it was easy for each company to manufacture substitutes for their products. Given the standardization of products based on the Japan Industrial Standard and international standardization, it is challenging to establish technological superiority of its own. Steel manufacturers are the raw material suppliers of the products, while manufacturers of automobiles, construction machinery, railway vehicles, and agricultural machinery are the main demanders for the products of the bearing companies. These are the major manufacturers with strong bargaining power regarding price in the Japanese economy.

The bearing companies divided the sales department into two major divisions: industrial machinery and automobile. Each division existed independently.[3] Regarding the bearings for industrial machinery, the combined sales share of NSK, NTN, JTEKT, and Fujikoshi from April 2010 through March 2011 was 78.8%. Individually, the share of NSK, NTN, JTEKT, and Fujikoshi

3 Regarding the particular field of trade (market in economics) in the AMA, this case has two particular fields of trade. The main reason to define two particular fields of trade in the ruling comprises the two divisions in the actual observation of the corporate system.

was 30.8%, 29.2%, 13.4%, and 5.4%, respectively. The total market share of the four companies in the automobile bearings was 86.7%; individually, their shares were 32.3%, 28.4%, 24.9%, and 1.1%, respectively. Thus, the four companies had large market shares for industrial machinery and automobiles.

This study considers the role of the JBIA as the trade association for the industry and examines the contributions and collaborations of the four companies in the JBIA. The JBIA collected information on the bearing technology on the international standard and considered industrial policies related to the industry through the policy committee in the JBIA. The policy committee had the secretariat as a subordinate organization to the committee, and employees of four companies participated as staff. As part of the consensus-building process, the secretariat first discussed specific details. After that, the agreement was reached at the policy committee attended by executives from the four companies. The agreed items were passed on to each company, and the branches of each company communicated with each other to implement the agreement. Figure 4.1 summarizes this structure.

In the background of the agreements to raise the price of bearing products, there was a sharp rise in that of steel, which is the main raw material in producing the bearings. According to the ruling, there were four price agreements, beginning in 2004 up until the fifth price arrangement in 2010. The fifth one is directly related to the case. Figure 4.2 shows the trend in the producer price index (PPI) for steel compiled by the Bank of Japan and its year-on-year changes.

Considering the PPI of steel on the left axis, the rising trend continued from January 2002 until February 2008. There was a rapid increase in March 2008, followed by a peak in August 2009. Then there was a downward trend until January 2010. After that, it had an upward trend until August 2011, but, after peaking in August 2011, it has been on a downward trend.

Price agreements were held five times from 2004 to 2010, excluding 2006 and 2009. Of the five times, the year-on-year rate of price increase was large, except for 2010. The actual increase in steel prices in 2010 was lower than in previous agreement years, which may explain why there was a large difference between the agreed prices in 2010 and the prevailing prices.

Considering the year-on-year rate of change shown on the right axis of Figure 4.2, at the time of the first price agreement in 2004, the annual year-on-year rate of increase was 13.7%. In November 2004, the rate was particularly high at 19.1%. Considering the year-on-year figures for the 1st to 5th price agreements, the maximum, minimum, and annual average values for the first, second, and fourth price agreements show almost the same trends. Table 4.1 summarizes the results.

Table 4.2 shows two figures for each month of 2010: the PPI for steel and its year-on-year change (%). In general, when forecasting the price trends of raw materials, they often take seasonal fluctuations into account and refer to year-on-year comparisons. Therefore, the price change (%) relative to the same month of the previous year is displayed.

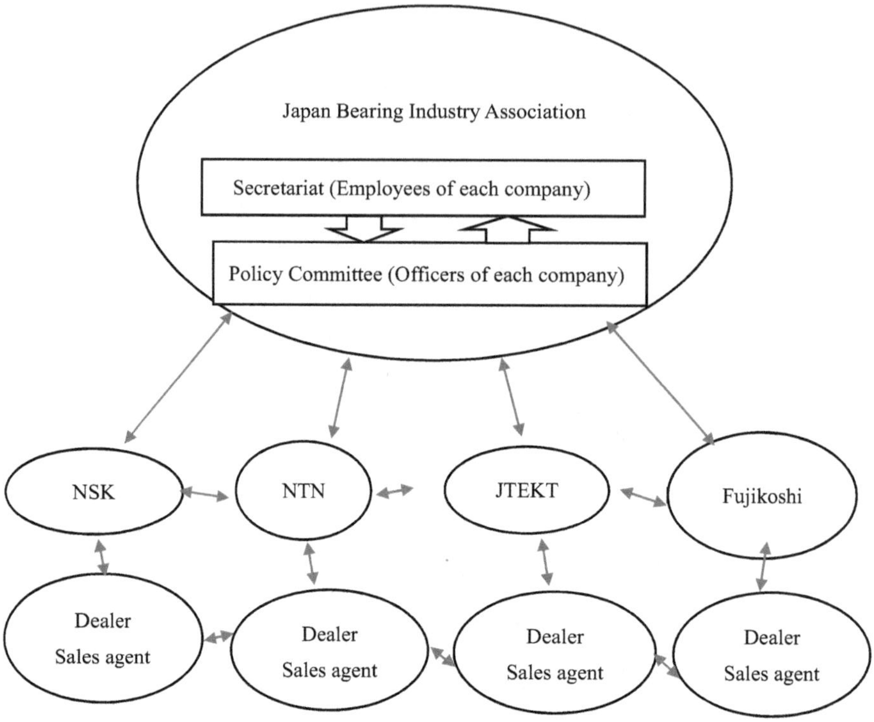

Figure 4.1 Relationship between Japan Bearing Industry Association and companies

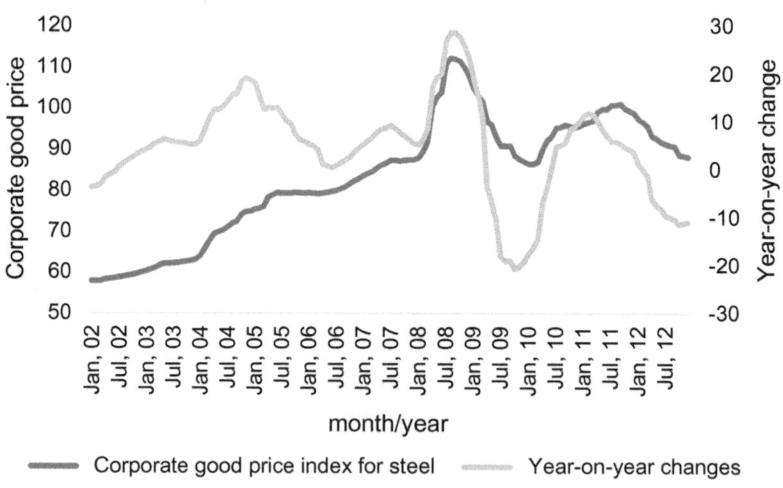

Figure 4.2 Trends in the producer price index for steel and its year-on-year comparison (%)

Table 4.1 Rate of change in the steel producer price index at the time of the first to fifth price agreements

	Maximum (month)	*Minimum (month)*	*Annual average*
2004 (1st agreement)	19.1% (November)	5.9% (January)	13.7%
2005 (2nd agreement)	18.0% (January)	5.8% (December)	11.2%
2006	5.3% (January)	0.3% (June)	2.6%
2007 (3rd agreement)	9.1% (July)	5.2% (January)	7.2%
2008 (4th agreement)	28.6% (September)	5.1% (January)	19.8%
2009	19.2% (January)	−20.7% (October)	−7.6%
2010 (5th agreement)	9.8% (December)	−17.5% (January)	−1.3%

Table 4.2 Producer price index of steel in 2010 and changes in year-on-year prices (%)

	Producer price index of steel	*Changes year-on-year prices*
January	86.3	-17.6
February	86.3	-16.3
March	86.8	-14.5
April	89.9	-7.0
May	92.0	-4.0
June	93.1	0.3
July	95.1	4.9
August	95.3	5.1
September	95.8	5.6
October	95.5	8.2
November	95.2	8.8
December	95.5	9.9

Regarding the consensus-building process for the price agreement on industrial machinery bearings between the four companies in 2010, a newspaper article suggested the steel price hike in February. This was the impetus for the 5th price agreement. The JBIA policy committee meeting was held in March, and they discussed the issue of steel price hikes. At the policy committee meeting held in May, NSK proposed to raise prices by the same amount as the rise in the steel price, and they agreed to it. Therefore, at the secretariat meeting in June, a draft of the price increase rate was prepared. The figures were determined as 8% for general bearings and 10% for large bearings. The basis for the 8% is as follows: 5.6% (steel price increase rate of 20% by material cost composition ratio in a product of 28%) + indirect cost increase. The basis for 10% is as follows: 8% (20% (Steel price increase rate) by 40% (material cost composition ratio in a product)) + indirect cost increase. Thus, at the end of June, the secretariat decided to raise the price of general bearings by 8% and large bearings by 10%. They reached the price agreement at the JBIA policy committee meeting in late July.

The agreement of price increase on the industrial machinery bearings was 8% for general bearings and 10% for large bearings, but the prevailing prices were neither 8% nor 10%. Considering the manufacturers' suggested price increases of each company, NTN applied a uniform 6% increase for general and large bearings. NSK and Fujikoshi applied the standard to 8% of the general bearings and 10% of the large bearings. At JTEKT, the standard price was set at 8.3% for the general bearings and 10.6% for the large bearings.

Steel prices were on an upward trend in 2010, but the increase in the prices was not the 20% initially expected. Moreover, the prevailing rate of increase in the sales prices for industrial machinery bearings in 2010 was significantly lower than expected. According to the verdict of the High Court in Tokyo, the actual price increase of compromise contents was 0.74%, 1.82%, 2.11%, and 1.21% for NTN, NSK, JTEKT, and Fujikoshi, respectively. The rate of increase in product prices for industrial machinery was significantly lower than expected. The agreement on the automobile bearing was concluded in July 2010. It was agreed that the price increase for the automobile bearings would be 20 yen per kilogram. They followed the agreement.

4.3 Judgment of the courts

On June 14, 2012, the JFTC accused the three companies and seven people involved, excluding JTEKT. With the materials provided by JTEKT, there was solid evidence of the agreement on the prices, which is the essential point of contention in the cartel case. There were two issues in the case. One of the points of contention was whether the actual transactions fell under the *particular field of trade* stipulated in the AMA.[4] Another was whether there was any agreement that would mutually bind the business activities of the four companies and substantially restrain competition or collusion regarding the actual sale of the bearings for industrial machinery and automobiles.

In criminal cases, there is an arraignment process on the facts of the charges. If the defendant pleads guilty, the trial is contested on sentencing. However, if the defendant denies the allegation, the point of dispute will be clarified and will be contested in court. In this case, Fujikoshi pleaded guilty and did not contest the sentence. NSK pleaded guilty but contested the sentencing. NTN denied and fought the charges. In particular fields of trade, the bearings are challenging to technologically differentiate, even for custom-made products. Thus, companies can manufacture substitutes without any challenges. Between bearings for industrial machinery and those for automobiles, the market structure and transaction mode differ because the demanders for industrial machinery and those for automobiles differ, and the particular field of trade (market) is different. The court ruled that a particular field of trade corresponds to the bearing sales for industrial machinery and automobiles.

4 Actual transactions are negotiated transactions but not market transactions defined by economics.

Fujikoshi was found guilty at the Tokyo District Court on December 28, 2012, and NSK was found guilty at the Tokyo District Court on February 25, 2013. On February 4, 2015, NTN was found guilty at the Tokyo District Court. It was dissatisfied with the judgment and appealed to the Tokyo High Court. It was dissatisfied with the judgment at the Tokyo High Court as well and appealed to the Supreme Court. The Supreme Court decision on December 5, 2017, confirmed the guilty verdict.

Consider the surcharge payments. After the District Court decision on NSK in February 2013, the JFTC issued a cease-and-desist order and a surcharge payment order to these companies on March 29, 2013. As Fujikoshi did not appeal against the orders, the decision was finalized. NSK did not appeal against the cease-and-desist order, and the order became final. However, an appeal was filed against the surcharge payment order. NTN filed an appeal against the cease-and-desist and surcharge payment order. NTN withdrew the appeal for the exclusion order on December 22, 2017, and the order became final.

4.4 Market in economics and particular field of trade on AMA

Experts on AMA interpret that the particular field of trade in the AMA is the same as the market in economics. However, from the perspective of economics, the particular field of trade is not necessarily the same as the market in economics. Accordingly, the commodity market such as bearings will be analyzed on the assumption that the market is global. The commodity market such as tradable and durable goods (e.g., bearings) has no boundary between domestic and international markets. In reality, tariffs and quantitative restrictions have been enforced given the protection of national interests. In such a case, it is possible to analyze only the domestic market, using the framework of industrial organization theory.

However, the market in economics has a wide scope relative to the particular field of trade in law. The market is treated as a place to collect all kinds of information such as technology, price, quantity, and domestic and overseas industry information. Of course, price is a big concern as an important signal, but if there is price coordination or price agreement between market participants, the action is a violation of AMA. In law, it is common to regard a particular field of trade as a market. The main reason is that the law has a domestic characteristic.

Regarding homogeneity and substitutability, economics assumes that the commodities and services traded in the market are homogeneous. However, doubts will arise as to whether the homogeneity of products is ensured in actual transactions.[5] Hence, the court's decision is also interesting from the economics perspective. It refers to the substitutability of the bearings between

5 Especially, in an oligopoly market, product differentiation is one of the powerful corporate strategies.

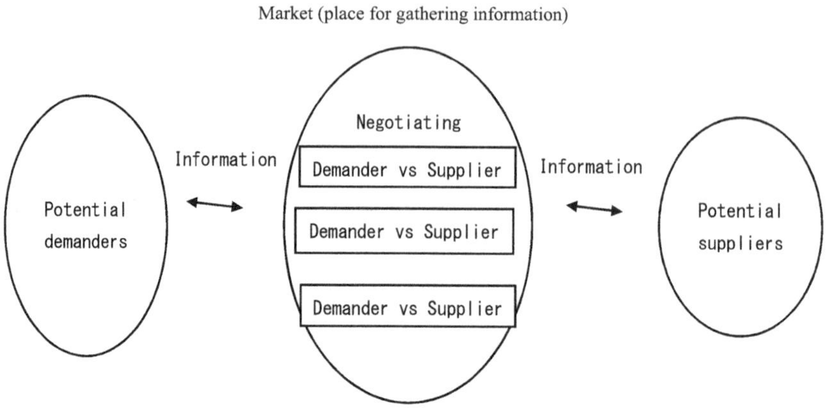

Figure 4.3 Potential users and suppliers and bilateral transactions in the market

companies. The definition of homogeneity in economics is that if demanders perceive the commodity to be the same (homogeneous), the homogeneity of the commodity produced by each company is ensured even if the commodity is a custom-made product. When demanders recognize the commodity as homogeneous, substitutability is also recognized.

Moreover, there are potential transactions before actual transactions are made for specific goods. One of the important factors to recognize collision is whether there is communication of intention between the supplying party. Economics places importance on results, while law places importance on intention. Though there was price-fixing among the companies, it did not affect the actual market prices. Considering the results, economics considers that there may be no effect on price agreement. However, the law judges that there is price-fixing through communication of intention, indicating that the companies violated the AMA regardless of the actual business results.

Finally, as the defendant's defense counsel asserted in this case, the transaction is basically a negotiated one, and this should be distinguished from the transaction through the market. Figure 4.3 is a diagrammatic representation of the allegations of the defendant's defense counsels.

Attorneys focus only on the actual transaction and do not consider the potential demanders and suppliers behind it. As described above, the demanders select an arbitrary supplier from potential suppliers by competitive quotations or the like. That is, demanders recognize that there is no difference in the products produced by the suppliers.

4.5 Several points of discussion through the case and its evaluation

Bearings, as industry necessities, are as indispensable as machine parts. Bearing manufacturers produced high-quality products by international standards.

This case must not be treated as a mere price-fixing case in the domestic market. However, consider it from the perspective of the rise and fall of Japan's bearing industry in the global economy. The perspectives are divided into (1) the hollowing out of industry, (2) the catch-up of emerging countries, and (3) the possibility of technological progress.

In the 20th century, the industry repeatedly filed dumping lawsuits with Western countries because Japanese bearings had a comparative advantage over Western countries in terms of labor costs. Entering the 21st century, dumping lawsuits with Europe and the United States have disappeared. Given the differences in labor costs, manufacturers moved their factories to China and Southeast Asia. Along with this, though parts manufacturers still have some of their factories in Japan, it has become popular to move their factories overseas. To maintain the quality of overseas production, it is necessary to transfer technology overseas; it is also necessary to have high-quality employees.

This case has revealed the strengths and weaknesses of Japan's economic system. The strength lies in manufacturing. The products were of high quality with little variation in quality, and the reliability of individual products was high. In-house training supported employees' desire to improve their skills. It supported the high quality of the products with small variations of the products. Based on these foundations, the government's industrial policy functioned effectively.

The MITT (currently the Ministry of Economy, Trade and Industry) collected information worldwide and distributed information to promising industries through industry groups. Thus, the industry was strengthened and contributed to the growth of the Japanese economy. A peculiarity of the Japanese economy is that it is strong in its ability to improve upon the basic design but weak in the basic design of products that require creativity.

The influence of the government via industrial policy was strong in the bearing industry. The corporate managers were highly dependent on the government and lacked strategies for the future of the industry. Specifically, they lacked the perspective of globalization, the knowledge of technology, and the outlook for future demand. Such government-led industrial policy created an environment that facilitates price agreements among domestic companies. A major factor behind this incident is the administrative guidance by the government, along with recession cartels and rationalization cartels. A typical case of cartel price-fixing was that between petroleum product wholesalers during the first Oil Crisis, which is the same as the bearing price-fixing.

The characteristics of the Japanese economy comprised an advantage for the manufacturing industry and a disadvantage for the service industry, requiring originality and creativity. Knowledge of the law is indispensable for resolving trade frictions between foreign countries. Lawsuits against dumping and those against counterfeit goods will be one of the solutions in addition to the official negotiations between the governments. Regarding the interdependence of the industrial structure within Japan, it was necessary to leave the industry necessities in Japan even if the productivity was not high to make the domestic economic cycle run smoothly without external frictions. It is impossible to create high value-added industries based on the foundation of industry necessities.

4.6 Conclusion

This case was one of the typical price-fixing cases. The JTEKT's self-declaration made it easy to clarify the cartel structure. Therefore, the courts proved the illegality of price-fixing relatively easily. A feature of this case was the complexity of the surcharge payment. There were various cases, such as companies not paying the surcharge, those that paid reduced surcharges, and those that paid it in full. However, this case showed the industry's inward-looking nature or defensive stance to the global economy. Companies must grow in the midst of globalization. The bearing companies did not pursue the profits by means of price-fixing in an oligopoly market within a closed domestic market. The industry backed by technological capabilities would challenge the global market, improving technology and enhancing legal capabilities against economic friction between countries.

5 Case of water meter bid-rigging

Scattering of winning bids given changes in contract methods and claiming for damages

5.1 Introduction

A water meter is a device that measures how much water each household uses; it is situated between the water faucet and the water pipes laid on the road. Standards for water meters are stipulated by the Measurement Act. Water meters are legally obliged to be inspected when new water meters are shipped and re-examined every eight years. For ordinary household use, there are three types of calibers: 13 mm, 20 mm, and 25 mm, called three small caliber meters. There are two types of products ordered by the Bureau of Waterworks: new and recycled products. As water meters must be replaced every eight years by the Measurement Act, there is also a market for recycled products. Most of the water meters ordered by local governments are small-diameter water meters for ordinary household use with 20 mm being the main force.

The Bureau of Waterworks of the Tokyo Metropolitan Government (TMG) is the largest ordering party in all the local governments in Japan. Its orders for the water meters range from the volumes of 800,000 to 900,000 per year. The average unit price of the water meter with a diameter of 20 mm was approximately 4,000 to 7,000 yen during the period when bid-rigging existed, and 2,500 yen per the latest data. Assuming that the price of the water meter is 4,000 yen and the order quantity is 800,000, the total amount for the water meter of the TMG is approximately 3.2 billion yen per year.[1]

Under the AMA, a market is called a particular field of trade. Market participants include the local governments as demand entities, and water meter manufacturers and distributors as supply entities. The local governments decide the target price of the water meters and the method of ordering contracts. Transactions were made through a discretionary contract between the local government and a specific company. However, since the discretionary contract hindered the competitiveness of the market, it was gradually changed

1 As will be described later, Nabari City in Mie Prefecture has spent about seven million yen per year, and Yokohama City has spent 388 million yen per year. Thus, the scale of orders differs greatly for each local government. From the ruling, the contract price of the TMG serves as a guideline for the market price for the local governments throughout the country.

DOI: 10.4324/9781003370444-5

to a bid-based transaction. There are two types of bidding methods: designated competitive bidding (selective tender) and general competitive bidding (tender).

Comparing the designated competitive bidding and the general competitive bidding from the local government standpoint, there were advantages to the designated competitive bidding. When the bidding property requires a certain level of technical skill, the local government would feel more at ease with contractors doing business in the past. In the case of the designated competitive bidding, even if there was a preliminary investigation by the local government, the complexity of the contract documents could be avoided. On the general competitive bidding, there is a possibility that a wide variety of companies participate in bidding and the amount of paperwork to deal with it would be enormous. However, the disadvantages of the designated competitive bidding are also clear. The contract price becomes higher than the competitive bid price; therefore, the ordering party must purchase goods and services at a higher price.

The series of the water meter rigging described here comprises three separate cases. Regarding the first case, the JFTC issued a cease-and-desist order to the companies for water meters ordered by the local governments in Tokyo, Fukuoka, and Osaka in 1992. The number of contractors was 24 in Tokyo, 11 in Fukuoka, and ten in Osaka. Seven contractors are commonly included in Tokyo, Fukuoka, and Osaka. However, the collusion culture in the water meter industry did not go away after the surcharge payments in 1994.

In the second case of the water meter collusion, the JFTC filed criminal charges against 25 contractors in connection with bid-rigging for water meters in Tokyo. The 25 companies include 24 companies that were the target of the trial decision in the first case. The decision by the Tokyo High Court was issued in 1997, imposing fines and suspending imprisonment on the accused company and the accused. The two companies and one person filed an appeal against the judgment. However, the Supreme Court dismissed the appeal in 2000. The local governments and residents had filed lawsuits (e.g., the Nabari City, Tokyo, and Utsunomiya City lawsuits) claiming damages related to the collusion.

The third incident was in 2003. The JFTC issued the trial decisions to the 19 companies. Criminal charges were also filed against four leading companies and their employees, and four companies and five of their employees had been convicted by May 2004. In connection with the series of water meter collusion cases, lawsuits claiming damages were filed by the local residents and the local government in Yokohama City, Kanagawa Prefecture, and Kawasaki City.

Section 5.2 describes the content and results of the cases. Section 5.3 addresses the damage claim cases. Section 5.4 observes the actual changes in the successful bid prices, depending on the changes in bidding methods. Section 5.5 uses simulation analysis to examine changes in successful bid prices with regime changes such as discretionary contracts, designated competitive bidding, and general competitive bidding. Section 5.6 concludes the analysis.

5.2 Cases of the water meter collusion

5.2.1 The first case

For many years from 1973 to 1991, the TMG adopted a discretionary contract for ordering water meters of all diameters. In this contract method, at first, the nominated contractors presented a desirable unit price for the contract to the TMG. The TMG concluded the discretionary contract of the unit price between the suppliers, who offered the lowest unit price within the target price set by the TMG and agreed to receive the orders at that lowest unit price. The suppliers of the water meters were interested in keeping the desired contract price close to the target price made by the TMG. The mechanism of collusion was simple. The prospective contractor and the contract prices were decided among the nominated contractors decided by the local government. Although the official meeting was dissolved in February 1992 given the on-site inspection by the JFTC after December 1991, the meeting was continued in practice, and collusion was carried out in the same way as before in Tokyo.

In Fukuoka Prefecture, the period of bid-rigging was from October 1987 to April 1992. In the case of Osaka Prefecture, the period of bid-rigging was from April 1990 to December 1991. In the case of Fukuoka and Osaka, when the nominated contractors were decided by the local government, they reported it to the managing company and followed the decisions regarding the name of the prospective contractor and the contract price. In December 1992, the JFTC issued a cease-and-desist order to the companies that received contracts for water meters from Tokyo, Fukuoka, and Osaka. With the suppliers' acceptance, the trial decisions were issued in January 1993.

The JFTC issued the surcharge payment order in 1994. The surcharges were imposed on 23 out of 24 suppliers in Tokyo, eight out of 11 suppliers in Fukuoka, and nine out of ten suppliers in Osaka. Regarding the amount, the total amount of the surcharges was 138 million yen for the case regarding the TMG, and they ranged from 620 thousand yen to 25 million yen per supplier. In Fukuoka, the total amount of surcharges was 26 million yen, with a range of 540 thousand yen to six million yen. The total amount related to Osaka was 16 million yen, with a range of one to three million yen depending on the companies.

5.2.2 The second case

In the early 1990s, the bidding system to procure water meters changed from discretionary contracts to designated competitive bidding and general competitive bidding. The TMG partially revised the ordering method. This act was influenced by the first case in which the JFTC issued the trial decision in January 1993. The suppliers anticipated the change in the contract method and held a meeting of sales executives to discuss countermeasures against the change in ordering method from around October 1993. In 1994, the TMG put all meters into the designated competitive bidding. The managing company determined the prospective contract price and the prospective order recipient for each bidding period, and each contractor agreed to follow the agreement.

Given the on-site inspection by the JFTC in July 1996, the content of the bid-rigging could not be conducted. Since then, the successful bid price has fallen significantly below the target price in Tokyo. The period from April 15, 1994, to July 11, 1996, corresponds to the execution period of the violation. The JFTC issued a cease recommendation to 25 water meter companies in March 1997, and the companies agreed to it, resulting in the trial decision in April. The 24 out of 25 companies were ordered to pay the surcharge. The total fine was 386 million yen. The surcharge in 1997 was approximately three times higher than in 1994 given the July 1991 revision of the AMA concerning surcharges payment.[2] This case was filed as a criminal complaint and tried as a criminal case at the Tokyo High Court. There were 25 defendant companies and 34 defendants. Each defendant was fined five to nine million yen, and each was sentenced to six to nine months in prison with a suspended sentence. Two companies and one person appealed the judgment to the Supreme Court. The appeal was dismissed in September 2000.

5.2.3 *The third case*

After the JFTC conducted an on-site inspection in July 1996, the successful bid price ordered by the TMG dropped. Four major companies selected the properties to be ordered and decided on the prospective order recipients. Moreover, the companies selected the properties for which small- and medium-sized companies should receive orders and decided on the prospective order recipients. Accordingly, four major companies and 15 small companies received orders for most of the water meters of the three small diameters for household use.

Since 1997, the TMG has stopped the designated competitive bidding and changed to general competitive bidding. General competitive bidders were solicited by public notice, and all applicants who met the prescribed application conditions were invited to participate in the general competitive bidding. In February 2005, the JFTC issued the surcharge payment orders to 13 companies. Further, four major companies and their related persons were criminally charged. The Tokyo High Court handed down guilty verdicts for each of them.

5.2.4 *Public interests: Good or bad bid-rigging*

The topic of *good bid-rigging or bad bid-rigging* is one of the themes of small- and medium-sized enterprise (SME) theory in economics. In the theory, collusion, a characteristic of the Japanese economy, has been a necessary evil. When large-scale companies and SMEs coexist in a market and must compete

2 From half of 4% (2%) to 6%.

with each other, large-scale companies would have a competitive advantage given differences in capital and technological capabilities, pressuring SMEs. Moreover, a wage gap existed between employees of large-scale companies and those of SMEs. Hence, to protect SMEs and their employees, it was necessary to segregate large-scale companies and SMEs in the market through collusion. Bid-rigging can redistribute profits and earnings between large-scale companies and SMEs. This logic had a certain degree of persuasive power in industries with a high ratio of SMEs, especially during the high-growth period of the Japanese economy in the 1960s.

However, the court rejected this view. The court weighed the interests of the public and those of the industry and declared that the economic interests of the public take precedence over those of the industry. Even if the profits of the industry are to be redistributed, it should be done via the market by the related law, not by industry intentions. The goal of the SME Basic Act at that time was to correct the disadvantages of SMEs given economic and social constraints by improving the productivity and trading conditions of SMEs and improving the economic and social status of SME employees. The ruling declared that the TMG understood the current state of the water meter industry and had devised bidding properties by size, considering the disparity between SMEs and large-scale companies.

The second fundamental theorem of welfare economics regards income redistribution. Pareto-efficient resource allocation can be achieved via a perfectly competitive market by income redistribution through taxes and subsidies. The key points are through government economic policies and through the perfectly competitive market. The redistribution of income by industry does not satisfy the condition of the second fundamental theorem of welfare economics. Therefore, the redistribution of income through bid-rigging has no logical economic reason.

5.2.5 A bridge between the market in economics and a particular field of trade defined by AMA

The number of transactions between the TMG and the supplier of water meters was the largest among the local governments in the country, and the TMG had a significant impact on the price formation of bidding by other local governments. The contract price in Tokyo serves as an indicator of the standard price nationwide. When a contract can be made at a certain price in Tokyo, other local governments can accept orders at the contract price. The reason is that the companies that participated in the bidding of the TMG and other local governments are almost the same.

Regarding the demarcation of a particular field of trade, there is a diffusion effect of the contract price from the TMG to the local governments other than Tokyo, but there is no diffusion effect from the local governments to the TMG. Therefore, regarding a particular field of trade in the case of bid-rigging related to Tokyo, this study does not consider the diffusion effect on the successful bid price from the local governments. In the case of bid-rigging regarding the TMG, the particular field of trade (market) of water meters is limited to the administrative district of TMG but does not include other areas. However, regarding local governments, the price of water meters was affected by the winning bid price in Tokyo. In this way, the definition of the particular field of trade differs between TMG and other local governments. In the local governments other than Tokyo, the particular field of trade for water meters is not the administrative district of the local government but the nationwide areas.[3] Figure 5.1 shows this relationship.

The consensus-building process for order coordination was possible through communication of intentions among suppliers without the people in charge meeting in one place. This was handled by the managing company based on the background of the strong mutual binding force between major companies. According to the ruling, the collusion in the present case has a unique composition (see Table 5.1).

From Table 5.1, the TMG places orders for water meters, and bid-rigging takes place between major companies as usual in ordinary bid-rigging. This procedure is indicated in Tokyo. However, for other local governments, the successful bidding price for the successful bidder is determined as an extension of bid-rigging that occurred in Tokyo. Table 5.2 summarizes the results of the bid-rigging in the cases related to the TMG.

5.3 Cases of the damages claim

The direct victims of bid-rigging by water meter suppliers were the water-works bureaus of the local governments that ordered the water meters because they purchased water meters at a higher price than if there had been no rigging. However, payments to water meter suppliers were made from the budgets of the local governments, which did not directly hurt the pockets of the

3 As water meters are standardized products regulated by the Measurement Act, residents and local governments outside of the administrative district of the TMG face a nationwide water meter market as a particular field of trade defined by the AMA. Each local government exists as a cluster in the nationwide market, and the cluster of the TMG has a large proportion of the number of water meters purchased in the nationwide market. Therefore, the trend of the contract price of the TMG plays an important role as a guideline for forming the winning bid price of other local governments. For example, the TMG purchased water meters worth three billion yen per year; the Local Government of Nabari City purchased water meters worth six million yen (i.e., the ratio is 500 and 1 between Tokyo and Nabari City). Therefore, price trends in Nabari City do not affect price trends in Tokyo. However, water meter companies are spread all over the country, and all the contract price information of each local government is obtained from their own network. Instead of holding a meeting to discuss bidding prices with successful bidders, the managing company of collision communicates with the person in charge of bidding for local water meter suppliers with a single phone call while watching trends in Tokyo. There is communication of intention in the industry. This situation falls under Article 2, Paragraph 6 (unreasonable restrictions on trade) of the AMA.

(1) Particular field of trade: TMG (The winning bid price in Tokyo defuses nationwide)

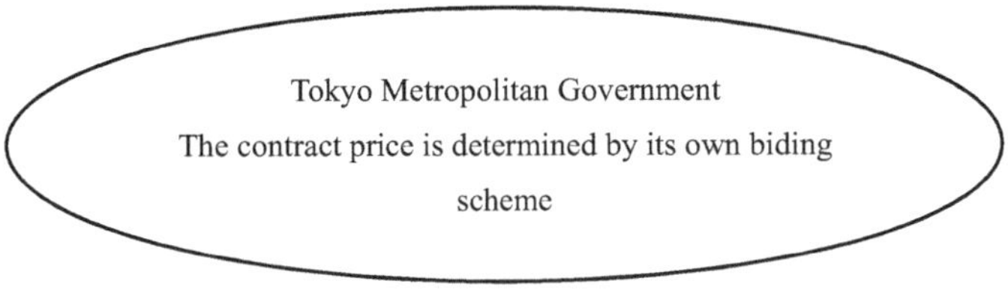

(2) Particular field of trade: Nabari City, Yokohama City (there are differences in the order scale relative to TMG, and there exists asymmetry of information between the companies and local governments)

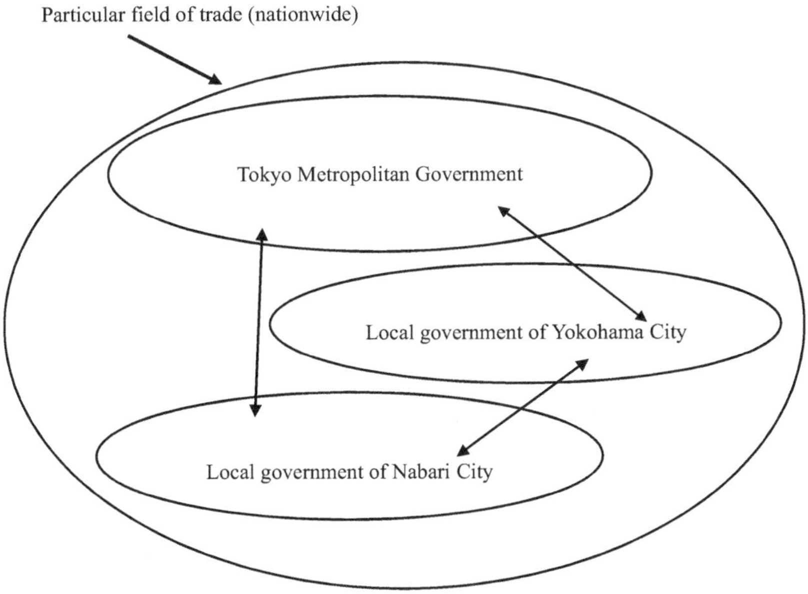

(Note) (a) The TMG creates the market price for the contract price nationwide, and water meter suppliers share this information; (b) Water meter suppliers have a nationwide network (communication of intentions among water meter suppliers); and (c) There is no network (interruption of information) between local governments.

Figure 5.1 The demarcation of particular fields of trade

local governments and civil servants. The essential victims are local residents. They pay taxes and receive public services such as water supply from the local governments. When water meters are purchased at a higher price than without collusion, the budget of the local governments has not been used properly.

Table 5.1 Composition of the water meter collusion case

Tokyo	*Other than Tokyo*
1) Ordering plan (target price)	1) Bid-rigging influenced by the trend of Tokyo
2) Tender announcement	2) Order plan (target price)
3) Bid-rigging among contractors	3) Tender announcement
4) Bidding	4) Bidding
5) Successful bid	5) Successful bid

Table 5.2 Main data of Case 1, Case 2, and Case 3

	Case 1	*Case 2*	*Case 3*
Trial Decision by JFTC	1992	1997	2003
Judgment by the court	1997, Tokyo High Court	2000, The Supreme Court	2004, Tokyo High Court
Number of companies	24	25	19
Main method of orders	Discretionary contract	Designated competitive bidding	General competitive bidding
Surcharge payment:			
Target companies	23	24	13
Penalty (yen)	134 million	386 million	76 million
Resident lawsuit:		1997 Tokyo District Court (Rely on the Local Autonomy Act) 1998 Tokyo High Court (Rely on the AMA) 2002 Settlement between TMG and businesses 2003 Withdraw	
Compensation (yen)		Two billion	

Formally, two possible entities seek compensation for damages against the water meter suppliers: the claim for damages by the local governments and local residents. When the latter claim damages, they also employ lawsuits against the local governments and the water meter companies as defendants.

5.3.1 Case related to the Tokyo Metropolitan Government

The claim for damages stemmed from a civil lawsuit where local residents were the plaintiffs, and the director of the Waterworks Bureau and water meter suppliers were the defendants. In June 1997, 24 residents in Tokyo filed a lawsuit with the Tokyo District Court against the Director of the Bureau of Waterworks, TMG, and 28 contractors, demanding compensation for damages on behalf of the TMG based on Article 242-2 of the Local Autonomy Act. In April 1998, the TMG filed a suit for damages against 25 water meter suppliers with the Tokyo High Court based on Article 25 of the AMA.

The settlement was reached between the TMG and 25 defendant companies in June and October 2002, and the water meter suppliers paid approximately two billion yen in settlement money. The period for claiming compensation for damages was three years, from 1994 to 1996. In those days, the ordered amount by the TMG was three billion yen per year; therefore, the settlement amount was equivalent to approximately 20% of the annual scale of orders. As per the settlement between the TMG and 25 defendant companies, the resident lawsuit was withdrawn in January 2003.[4]

Usually, resident lawsuits of the claim for damages are filed first, and local governments take action while observing the trial decisions and judgments of the criminal cases. In the case of the bid-rigging in TMG, the claims for damages by residents were indirectly declared by the courts as the settlement between the local government and water meter companies. However, few judgments had claims for damages granted in resident lawsuits when local governments were not active in lawsuits. Generally, it would resemble the following case by Nabari City in Mie Prefecture.

5.3.2 Case of claiming damages by Nabari City in Mie Prefecture

In 1997, the JFTC issued a trial decision on the case of bid-rigging for water meters in Tokyo from 1994 to 1996. In response to the decision, the residents of Nabari City in Mie Prefecture filed a lawsuit against the Nabari City Water Supply Business Administrator for neglecting to claim damages and for damages against five companies with the Tsu District Court. In September 1999, the decision to dismiss the claim was issued.

There was a lot of indirect evidence of collision. For example, water meter prices dropped significantly after the JFTC filed a complaint. Moreover, after changing the method of procuring water meters, prices fell in Yokkaichi City in Mie Prefecture. Considering these facts, the court also doubts whether the purchase price in Nabari City in 1996 was appropriate. However, the residents in Nabari City did not prove the fact that the defendant companies engaged in bid-rigging when Nabari City purchased water meters in 1996 and unfairly

4 Regarding the case of the second water meter collusion (Bureau of Waterworks, TMG), a criminal case related to violation of the AMA was the cause of the case of claiming damages. A claim for damages is a civil case. In the case of claims for damages, the lawsuits of residents rely on the Local Autonomy Act. The claim for damages by the TMG is based on the AMA. In chronological order, the accusation by the JFTC triggered a lawsuit by residents seeking damages in 1997. Judicial decisions regarding criminal cases such as the Tokyo High Court decision in 1997 and the Supreme Court decision in 2000 were major turning points. The TMG as the administrative agency acted to claim damages in 1998, and the case of the damage compensation between the TMG and the water meter suppliers was solved in the form of the settlement in 2002. Given the settlement, the resident lawsuit was withdrawn in January 2003.

inflated the price using the evidence. The District Court in Tsu declared that the plaintiffs' allegation and substantiation merely surmised that the defendant companies had repeatedly violated the AMA regarding orders for water meters in Tokyo and that they must have engaged in collusion in Nabari City as well. As long as the plaintiffs could not prove the fact that the defendant companies unfairly inflated the price given collusion in Nabari City, the court did not accept awarded damages to residents in Nabari City.

Dissatisfied with this ruling, the residents of Nabari City appealed to the Nagoya High Court. The decision to dismiss the appeal was issued in August 2001. The Nagoya High Court declared that there was much circumstantial evidence such that the companies were members of the Water Meter Manufacturers Association and engaged in bid-rigging in Tokyo. Thus, it is possible to engage in bid-rigging at Nabari City. However, such evidence did not specifically clarify the existence or content of bid-rigging by the appellant companies regarding the purchase of water meters in Nabari City. The courts needed direct evidence specifying such as dates and places of collusion.

The District Court in Tsu admitted that the winning bid price fell relative to the prior contract prices in Nabari City since June 1997. However, regarding a decrease in the successful bid prices, the courts declared that there was no objective evidence of the causal relationship between collusion and the decrease in the successful bid prices. There was also no objective evidence to rule out the possible decrease in prices: it was caused by an increase in inventories of the suspended companies or an increase in production by not suspending companies, resulting in an excess supply of water meters.

5.3.3 Cases of claiming damages by Utsunomiya City, Kanagawa Prefecture, Yokohama City, and Kawasaki City

First, the study explains the case of claiming damages by Utsunomiya City. Residents of Utsunomiya City sued the former director of Waterworks Bureau of Utsunomiya City and 12 designated bidders to the Utsunomiya District Court on the grounds that the residents in Utsunomiya City suffered damages from the bid-rigging. The Waterworks Bureau conducted the designated competitive bidding in August and September 1996. The Bureau set the target price between 8,180 yen and 8,230 yen for the new water meters with a diameter of 20 mm for household use. However, after the case of water meter collusion in February 1997 by the TMG came to light, the successful bid price in Utsunomiya City was 3,180 yen, falling sharply to 2,900 yen in October.

The settlement was reached at the Utsunomiya District Court in the lawsuit for damages in May 2003. The condition was that five successful bidders had to pay one million yen to Utsunomiya City, and 12 designated bidders had to pay 9,000 yen each to the plaintiffs. However, the settlement document between plaintiffs and defendants did not include the word "collusion." One of the winning bidders commented that though the plaintiffs had not proven wrongdoing, the settlement was accepted to try to settle the matter as fast as possible.

In the case related to Yokohama City, the residents claimed damages of 228 million yen for the contracted order of 776 million yen. The basis for estimating the amount of damages claimed was the difference between the successful bid unit price immediately before the bid-rigging and the successful bid unit price during the bid-rigging period. One out of four defendant companies agreed to the settlement. In September 2010, the plaintiffs lost the case at the Yokohama District Court because there was no direct evidence to support the existence of the basic agreement.

Dissatisfied with the decision of the Yokohama District Court, the plaintiffs filed an appeal to the Tokyo High Court in September 2010. The second trial was also defeated in October 2012. The court decided that there was insufficient evidence to support the existence of the bid-rigging in Yokohama City. Finally, the residents abandoned their appeal.

In the case of Kanagawa Prefecture, the residents claimed damages of 126 million yen for the contracted order amount of 563 million yen. Of the ten defendant companies, two went bankrupt and two agreed to the settlement in 2007. The proceedings of the trial were filed in July 2009, and the plaintiffs lost at the Yokohama District Court in July 2009. The court ruled that there was insufficient evidence to prove collusion. The plaintiffs filed the appeal to the Tokyo High Court in July 2009. The court ruled in May 2010 that there was no objective evidence to support the exchange of price information relative to the bids. The appellants then abandoned the appeal to the Supreme Court.

In the case of Kawasaki City, the residents claimed damages of 82 million yen regarding the contracted amount of 381 million yen against eight defendant companies. Of these, one company went bankrupt, one company agreed to the settlement in July 2008, and one company was deemed to have confessed because it did not disclose the dispute and was ordered to pay the full amount claimed. In January 2011, the case was lost at the Yokohama District Court. The court judged that though the defendant companies grasped the nationwide order situation and made adjustments, there was insufficient evidence to prove collusion directly. The plaintiffs then dismissed the appeal.

In many cases, the plaintiffs lost the case when the judgment was made in court, although a partial settlement was made in many other cases. A common point in the judgments of the courts is that the plaintiffs could not specify the specific date and place of the bid-rigging. Thus, the direct facts of the bid-rigging have not been proven. In the case of claims for damages in lawsuits by residents, it is a fatal flaw that residents do not have the official investigative powers the police, public prosecutors, and the JFTC have. Though the residents indirectly identify the dates and meeting places of collusion from the rulings of criminal cases and investigations by the JFTC, it would be too much of a burden to require them to identify specific dates and places of meetings from their own investigations for the courts. It is almost impossible for citizens to overcome this condition. Moreover, it is challenging to specify the specific date and place of the meeting because the means of information transmission are not limited to meetings. In today's internet society, telephones and e-mails are frequently used. Further, it is quite conceivable to consult orders by small local governments with major companies in conjunction with bid-rigging related to the TMG.

5.4 Movement of the successful bid prices

The peculiarity of this case is that the bidding items are standardized products and are of the same quality nationwide. As the contractors have a nationwide network, there is information asymmetry between the local governments and the contractors. Data on the contract prices of each local government are fragmentary. However, from the ruling text, it is possible to extract a part of the chronological changes in the contract prices circa February 1997, as shown in Table 5.3.

Table 5.3 Changes in contract prices before and after February 1997 (correspond to the second case)

(1) Utsunomiya City (from Mainichi Newspaper)

	Contract price
August/ September 1996	8,180 yen to 8230 yen
August 1997	3,180 yen (257%)
October 1997	2,900 yen (282%)

(2) Nabari City, Ueno City, and Yokkaichi City: Before and after February 1997

Nabari City (judgment by the Tsu District Court in 1999)

8,900 yen → 3,170 yen (280%)

Ueno City (neighboring city to Nabari City, judgment of the Tsu District Court in 1999)

→ 3,100 yen (287%)

Yokkaichi City (neighboring city to Nabari City, Judgment of the Tsu District Court in 1999)

8800 yen → 3100 yen (283%)

(3) Tokyo: Before and after February 1997

Tokyo (1999 Tsu District Court decision, 1998 Yokohama District Court decision)

7,100 yen → 5,500 yen (129%)

(4) Yokohama City: Before and after February 1997

Yokohama City (judgment of the Yokohama District Court in 1998)

New type	About 8,000 yen → 5,900 yen → 3,000 yen in August 1997
Type A	About 7,000 yen → 5,815 yen
Type B	4,000 yen → 3,420 yen

(Note) Figures in parentheses are ratios (before February 1997 and after February 1997). If this ratio is 200% or more, it indicates that the successful bid price before February 1997 was more than double the successful bid price after February 1997. Figures in parentheses for other cities are the same.

The figures in parentheses show that the contract price before February 1997 was more than double that after February 1997. Before February 1997, it was 7,100 yen in Tokyo but 8,180 yen in Utsunomiya City, 8,900 yen in Nabari City, and 8,800 yen in Yokkaichi City, over 1,000 yen more expensive than Tokyo. After the change to the bidding system from discretionary contracts in February 1997, the Tokyo price decreased to 5,500 yen.

5.5 Simulation analysis: Prerequisites and results

A comprehensive review would reveal the importance of competition. The water meter has little technological change, and the quality is uniform during the period of three cases. The contract prices have been lowered in stages in response to the change in the contracting regime of discretionary contracts, designated competitive bidding, and general competitive bidding. Thus, the importance of competition is evident. Hence, to verify the hypothesis of changing the degree of competition given changes in the bidding method, the study will conduct a simulation analysis.

Figure 5.2 shows the changes in contract prices from 2012 to 2018 for household use observed in Tokyo. This time series of contract prices is obtained when the TMG adopts a bidding method of general competitive bidding. Hence, the TMG bids for 20 mm water meters every time. The successful bid amount changes along the level of 2,000 yen. The average price of this series is 2,370 yen, and the standard deviation is 180 yen. However, sometimes, the 15 mm and 25 mm calibers saw no orders.

The empirical observation of the trends of the contract price showed a gap before and after the changes in the contract methods (see Table 5.3). However, within the same contract method, the trend of the contract price

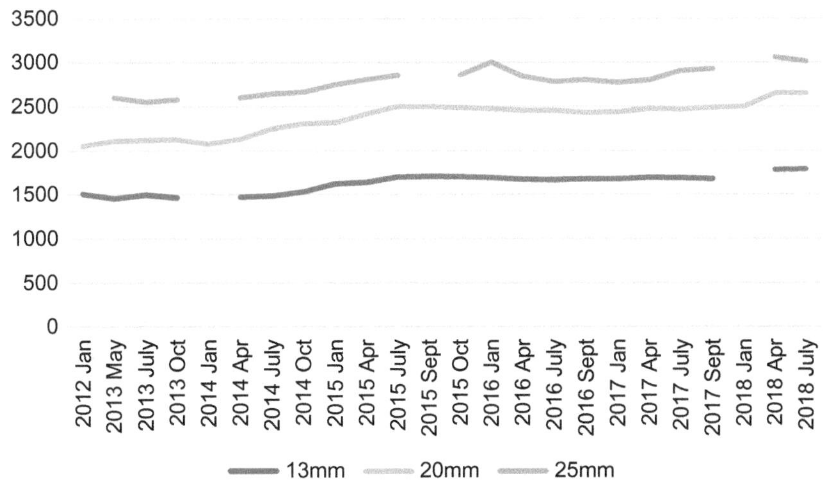

Figure 5.2 Changes in contract prices for household use in Tokyo since 2012

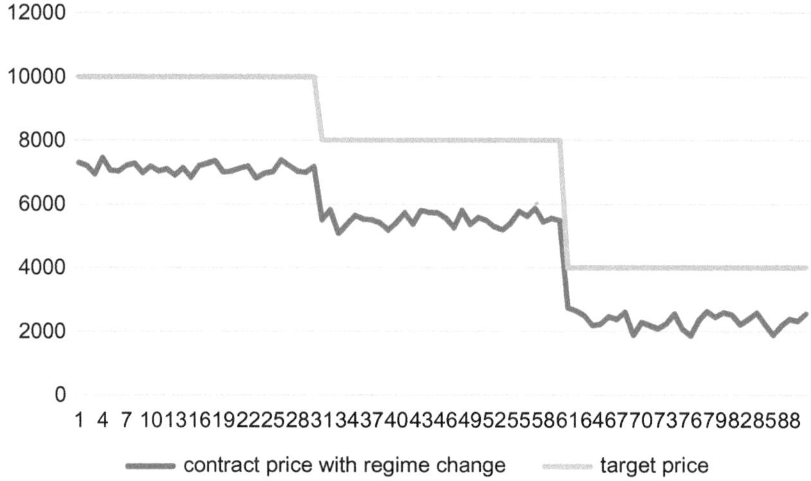

Figure 5.3 Movement of the target price and simulated contract price with regime change

was stable relative to the gap generated by the changes in the contract methods indicated in Figure 5.2. The study conducts two types of simulation: the first is the average changing three times with a small and stable standard deviation, and the second is the conditions of average and standard deviation being constant, where the volatility denoted by the standard deviation is larger than the first simulation. Based on the observation, the first simulation examines the effect of changing the contract methods. However, the second simulation does not care about the effect of changing contract methods; thus, the discrepancy from the change in the contract method is explained by other factors such as supply-side fluctuations during the period. If the second simulation is true, there are large fluctuations in the contract price within the period.

Figure 5.3 shows the movement of the simulated contract and target prices. It is divided into three periods: discretionary contract, designated competitive bidding, and general competitive bidding. The target prices for the first, second, and third terms are 10,000 yen, 8,000 yen, and 4,000 yen, respectively. Potential contract prices are followed by the normal random numbers with an average of 7,100 yen with the standard deviation of 200 yen in the first period, an average of 5,500 yen with the standard deviation of 200 yen in the second period, and an average of 2,370 yen with the standard deviation of 200 yen in the third period.[5] The target price is the upper bound of the contract price; if

5 The first simulation considers fragmentary information that the target price has decreased, as the contracting method of the TMG has changed from discretionary contract, through designated competitive bidding, to general competitive bidding per the actual contract price move-

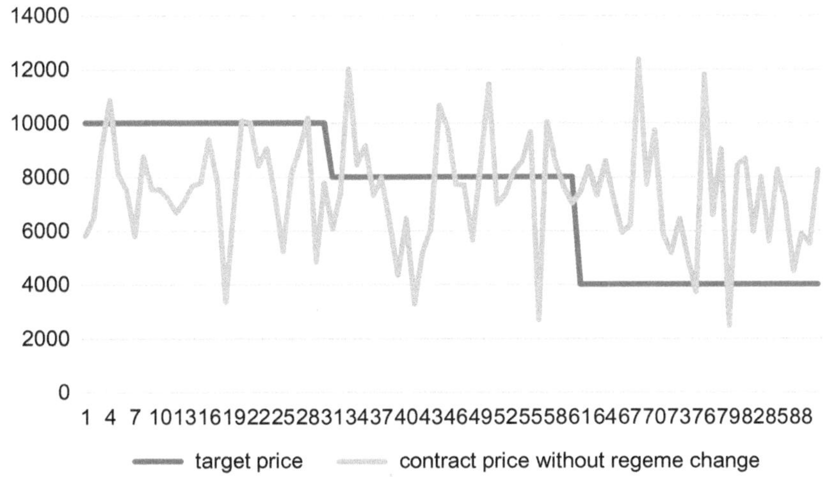

Figure 5.4 Movement of the target price and simulated contract price without regime change

the bidder presents a price higher than the target price, the bidder is disqualified, and the contract price cannot be determined as a successful bid.

In the real world, the successful bid price does not fluctuate drastically. The simulation does not contradict the observation in the real world. In the second simulation, normal random numbers are generated under the condition that the average contract price for the entire period is constant at 8,000 yen and the standard deviation is 2,000 yen. If the standard deviation were fixed at 200 yen, the result would be similar to the first period in Figure 5.3 (average of 7,100 yen and the standard deviation of 200 yen). Figure 5.4 emerges from the simulation.

Fluctuations in Figure 5.4 are not realizable in the real world. By the second simulation, it is not possible to follow the observation of the actual contract price. Further, explaining the discrepancy caused by the changes in the contract methods is not feasible. From the two types of simulation, the change in the contract methods from discretionary contract through designated competitive bidding to general competitive bidding certainly lowers the contract prices given the increasing competitiveness.

5.6 Conclusion

Exchanging information in the industry has merits such as the sharing of current market conditions and technological knowledge. It is generally not a bad

ments. The first simulation employed the value of the standard deviation of 200 yen, which is close to the calculated standard deviation of 180 yen.

thing. However, problems arise when the industry thinks only of its interests and conducts selfish activities. It becomes a problem when the interests of the industry adversely affect the economy and society as a whole and go against the public interests. Here, it would be possible to list improvements for local governments, bidders, residents, and the judiciary in the cases of water meter collusion.

For local governments, it is necessary to collect professional and technological information before setting target prices. Specifically, they can expand the collection of data such as costs of the factors of production and distribution services. As clarified in this analysis, it is important to change the bidding method from discretionary contracts and designated competitive bidding to general competitive bidding to expand the possibility of competition. When the bidding method is changed to general competitive bidding, it would be necessary to take measures such as checking the applicants and clarifying claims for damages in the contract terms. Once an illegal act is committed, it would be necessary to promptly take measures such as suspending bidding and claiming damages. It is also important for local governments and businesses to promote information disclosure. For example, local governments require bidders to submit quotations that serve as the concrete basis for bidding prices at the time of bidding, and contractors are obliged to disclose property financial statements (contractor expenses) in their business reports.

For residents, government oversight would be one of the important themes. In the field of public economics, *government failure* along with *market failure* is the subject of research. Finally, the judiciary may be necessary to consider respecting the right of residents to audit bid-rigging cases. Meanwhile, there is room for reconsideration of the possibility of the plaintiffs' direct proof in relation to the materials prepared by administrative agencies such as the JFTC.

6 Government bid-rigging

Cases of the Central Procurement Office of the Defense Agency and the Hokkaido Development Agency

6.1 Introduction

In a typical bid-rigging scheme for public works, designated contractors collude with each other to determine the successful bidder and win the bid at a price higher than the fair price. This act hurts the ordering party. The theme of this chapter, government bid-rigging, is that the ordering party (central government or local governments) or a person belonging to the ordering party decides the successful bidders for government-procured goods and public works.

This chapter addresses two cases. The first is a bid-rigging set in the CPO of the Defense Agency. National defense is one of the key areas in which the government has a responsibility to the people. The implementing agency was the Defense Agency (which became the Ministry of Defense in 2007). For national defense, it is necessary to prepare goods and services through the market, such as aircraft, transport vehicles, fuel, and equipment for people involved in national defense work. The CPO was the organization of the Defense Agency. It procured goods and services through the market by bidding. In this case, the defense attorney for the petroleum product suppliers claimed government collusion, posting that the defendants were innocent. However, the court did not rule that the case was a government bid-rigging, and the defendants were found guilty.[1]

1 Meanwhile, there was another incident involving the CPO. It was a criminal case involving breach of trust and bribery. The chief, deputy chief, and contractor at the time of the incident were indicted and ultimately convicted. The case involved a contract between the CPO and a communications equipment affiliate. Given that the contractor arbitrarily overestimated the price at the time of the successful bid, the contractor had to return the excess public money. However, as the CPO neglected audits for many years, there was a possibility that it would be held responsible for supervising the contractor. Therefore, it colluded with the contractor and forced the contractor to understate the amount of public money returned, hurting the country. Moreover, the Deputy Director General was forced to rehire the contractor's company after retirement given the relationship with the Agency. Just around this time, the long-standing puss of the CPO came to the surface at once.

DOI: 10.4324/9781003370444-6

Consider the second case of bid-rigging involving the Hokkaido Development Agency. This bid-rigging concerned the harbor and fishing port constructions for which the Hokkaido Development Bureau (HDB) of the Hokkaido Development Agency planned to place an order based on the Hokkaido Comprehensive Development Plan in 1997 and 1998.

This chapter expands on the range of considerations to the macroeconomic perspective of public finance and the price analysis of microeconomics. It examines the issue of government procurement and taxes. The government procurement sources are taxes and government bond issuance, which are the national debt. The government budget has indicated a deficit since the 1990s, and the cumulative total is at the level of over 100 trillion yen in Japan. Thus, tax revenue is 40 to 50 trillion yen every year, and the rest hinges on government bond issuance of almost the same amount as tax revenue. This is a case of fraud that happened in the government sector (or public sector). The root of these cases lay an essential problem almost inconceivable in the private sectors such as household and business sectors. It is the loosening of financial discipline.

Regarding the collision by the government, the court acquitted it in the case of the CPO of the Defense Agency, but it pleaded guilty in the case of the HDB of the Hokkaido Development Agency. Section 6.2 considers the case of CPO regarding the procurement of oil products used as an energy source for vehicles, and Section 6.3 denotes the case of HDB of the Hokkaido Development Agency.

6.2 Case of the bid-rigging on the Central Procurement Office of the Defense Agency

The study describes the circumstances of the bid-rigging of the CPO using the decisions of the JFTC and the judgments by the courts.

6.2.1 Beginning of the case of bid-rigging at the Central Procurement Office

The JFTC conducted on-site inspections of oil wholesalers and interviewed the person in charge at each company in March 1999. It found that the total bid shares of each petroleum refining company were close to the previous year's shares in the procurements of the Self-Defense Forces ordered by the CPO. Moreover, the JFTC recognized that the bidding procedure conducted by the CPO was different from ordinary bidding. From bidding to successful bids, in the initial bidding, the CPO nominated contractors, applying for each property at the bases of the Self-Defense Forces. The public notice included delivery date, delivery location (base), delivery conditions, procurement quantity, and nominated contractors. The number of bidding properties was 400 to 500 each year.[2]

2 The total number of properties subject to bidding each year was obtained by the product of the number of types of petroleum products (five types), the number of bases, and the number of bids in a year.

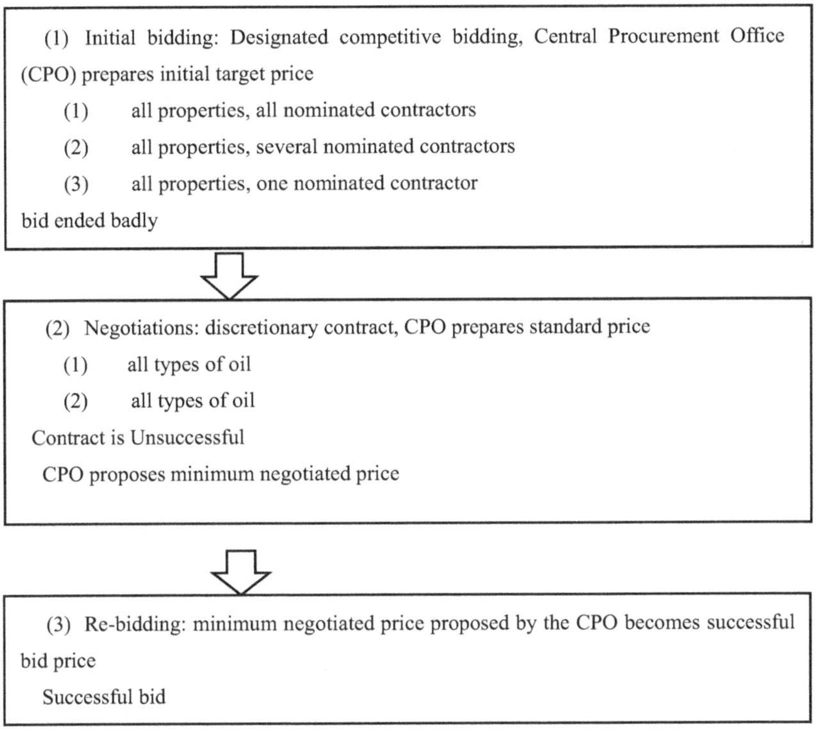

Figure 6.1 Flow of the bid

As the process from the bidding to the successful bid is somewhat complicated, Figure 6.1 briefly summarizes the outline of the process. The CPO calculated the target prices for the five types of petroleum products, considering the lowest market prices. The CPO nominated bid applicants for each property to conduct the designated competitive bidding. The initial bids were made three times, as shown in Figure 6.1. As the bid prices presented by the oil wholesalers exceeded the target prices for all properties, all properties ended in failure. In the first out of three bids, the bidders all nominated oil wholesalers. However, only a few companies participated in the second bid, and there was only one bidder for the property in the third bid. Hence, the number of bidders gradually decreased. At the end of the third round, one of the 12 wholesalers always remains the final negotiator for all properties.

The next stage is negotiation. Negotiations with oil refiners were conducted for each type of oil product rather than each property. In this negotiation, the prices (called standard prices) for each of the five types of petroleum products were discussed after deducting the fixed costs for which the calculation method has been disclosed to the oil wholesalers. Fixed costs comprised the transportation and general administrative costs, considering grade differences in elements such as petroleum products, regional differences in transporting products to each base, packaging, and taxes. In the negotiations followed by the initial bidding, the CPO presented the standard price for each oil type, conducting negotiations on the price for each oil type with the oil supplier participating in the third of the initial bidding. The negotiations were conducted twice; in all cases, the prices proposed by the oil wholesalers were higher than the standard prices, resulting in an unsatisfactory situation. At the stage in which a bad condition emerged, the CPO presented the minimum negotiated prices to the wholesalers.

After presenting the minimum negotiated prices, the CPO revised the original target price to a higher minimum negotiated price and recalculated the budget. When the budget measures were taken, bids were made again for each property. Finally, the bid was successful at the minimum negotiated price. In October 1999, the JFTC filed criminal charges against 11 oil wholesalers to the Prosecutor General. The JFTC filed additional charges with the Prosecutor General against nine persons in charge of wholesale companies in November. The Tokyo High Public Prosecutors Office indicted 11 wholesale companies and nine persons in charge. The applicable laws and regulations in this case were the AMA and Criminal Code.

The defendants argued that there was no room for price competition among the nominated companies and that the defendant companies did not substantially restrict competition. Indeed, the CPO decided the successful bid price by turning the designated competitive bidding into a mere formality. The defendant firms simply held order coordination meetings to determine the company responsible for ensuring prompt and reliable delivery of petroleum products. However, they made the schedule for the order coordination meeting and attended it immediately after the bid briefing from the CPO. After mutually confirming the basic agreement with them, they determined the prospective bidder and the successful bid price for each individual property per the basic agreement.[3]

The court acknowledged that the designated competitive bidding in this case had become a mere formality. However, the CPO did not instruct, request, or lead the bidding method. In fact, the defendant companies were hindered from free competition in bidding. That is, they jointly bound and conducted the business activities. Therefore, their acts fall under the unfair trade restrictions stipulated in the AMA.

6.2.2 *Reason for the complicated bidding system: Curse of one price for one commodity*

The petroleum products in this case were five oil types: automobile gasoline, kerosene, light oil, heavy oil A, and aviation turbine fuel. The product of each

3 The basic agreement among the defendant companies was that the successful bid company was determined by considering the order record for each oil type in the previous fiscal year, and the bidders cooperated to get a successful bid for the prospective successful bidder.

grade is homogenous regarding quality among oil wholesalers. A key focus in the present case was the curse of one price for one commodity for each type of oil product. The CPO always gazed at the attitude of the JFTC and the Board of Audit. The JFTC investigates the possibility of collusion in the procurement of elements such as petroleum products, equipment, and aircraft. The Board of Audit inspects the accounts of procured goods. It noted in the financial statements in 1958 and 1963 that there were variations in the unit price for each type of oil per base procured by the CPO, and it also noted that if the CPO purchases procured goods in bulk, it would be possible to purchase them at a lower price.

The CPO was worried that the Board of Audit would re-ascertain whether there were variations in the procurement prices of the same type of oil. The trauma of the one price for one commodity, which was noted more than 40 years ago, had been handed down over a long period to the officers in charge of the CPO.

Assuming Walrasian market equilibrium in economics, the analytical conclusion is that the same commodity has the same price. Next is an examination of what the market is. At the Walrasian market, demanders and suppliers gather at a marketplace, and an auctioneer presents and decides the price. Initially, the auctioneer offers a price to the market participants. The demanders and the suppliers report the quantity demanded and supplied to the auctioneer per their demand and supply schedules. The auctioneer then totals the individually presented demand and supply to obtain the market demand and supply. If the market demand is greater than the market supply (excess demand), the auctioneer raises the presented price, and if there is excess supply, the auctioneer lowers the price. The proposed price by the auctioneer changes until the market demand and supply become equal. In the Walrasian market, commodities are not traded until market supply and demand are met. Finally, transactions are made at the market price where market supply and demand match. Therefore, in the Walras market, one commodity for one price is inevitably realized. The actual transaction differs from the Walras market. The conclusion that prices should be the same for the same commodity is inconsistent with actual observations.

The following is an explanation for the observed fact that transactions in the real economic society are not of one price for one commodity, using an example of automobile gasoline. When one drives along the road, one finds and passes by gas stations. The price of each type of oil is displayed on the signboard at the gas station. Even if one limits one's self to the price of regular gasoline, the price varies from station to station. The price of regular gasoline spreads over a wide range around a certain value (say, the average price reported by economic statistics). Transactions between consumers and oil retailers are established at different prices. In this case, the price of gasoline does not indicate one price for one commodity. Even if gas stations along the road are regarded as a particular field of trade or market for automobile gasoline, actual gasoline prices are in a range (see Figure 6.2(a)). After noting

(a) Automobile gasoline and gasoline station (GS)

Market or a particular field of trade for gasoline

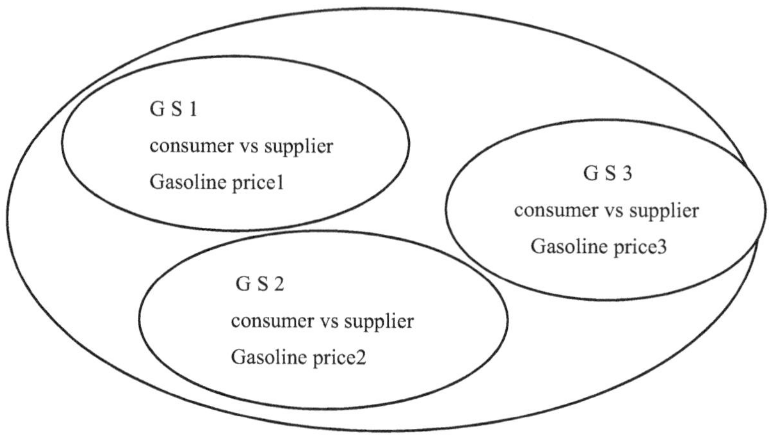

(Note) Gasoline prices are different between GSs

(b) successful bid prices for the properties by base using designated competitive bidding

Market or a particular field of trade for gasoline

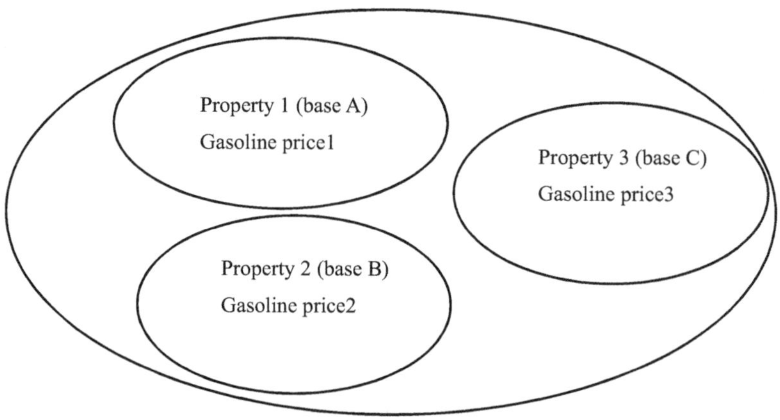

(Note) Gasoline prices are different between properties

Figure 6.2 (a) Actual transaction of automobile gasoline. (b) Successful bid prices for the properties by base using designated competitive bidding

this situation, consider the present case of designated competitive bidding for individual properties by base, not oil type. There is no guarantee that the unit price of the successful bid price for each property at the bases is the same. Rather, unit prices naturally scatter (see Figure 6.2 (b))

As long as the CPO bids for petroleum products for each property at the bases, the probability of realizing one price for one commodity is zero. The person in charge of the CPO was unfamiliar with economics and believed one commodity for one price should be the truth in the real world. He probably failed to logically explain the divergence from one commodity for one price. Thus, he recognized that it was unavoidable to purchase petroleum products by adding a premium to the market price to clear the condition of one commodity for one price. He then devised the procurement method that formally realizes one commodity for one price. However, it was inconsistent with the purpose of the Accounting Act and the AMA.

The practices and conventions were devised within the CPO. Moreover, the oil wholesalers took advantage of the trauma of the CPO. When wholesalers can sell petroleum products at a price higher than the market price, they get excess profits. Furthermore, by selecting a prospective contractor through bid-rigging, they established a stable profit structure within the industry.

6.2.3 Estimates of wasted amounts of public money

The section calculates the tax waste on government procurement in the case recognized by the court. The basic materials are Tables 2 and 3 in the judgment of the High Court. The tables show the initial target prices and successful bid prices for four oil types for the 1st period (provisional), 1st period (supplementary), and 2nd and 3rd periods. Table 6.1 shows the gap ratio between the contract price and the initial target price.

The gap rate is a figure obtained by dividing the successful bid price by the initial target price and is the figure indicating how much petroleum products were purchased at higher percentages. The average gap rate is 15% when the gap rate is simply averaged because there is no volume data for each oil type. The contract price was 15% higher than the initial target price. The total amount for the bidding was 28.7 billion yen. Therefore, it was an overspending of public money worth 3.7 billion yen. If this is simply extended to the government budget of 127 trillion yen, 19 trillion yen would be an overspending of the public funds.

Table 6.1 Gap ratio of oil products between contract price and initial bid price (contract price/initial bid price)

Types of oil products/period	*1st Provisional*	*1st Supplementary*	*2nd*	*3rd*
1) Automobile gasoline gap rate	1.19	1.21	1.22	1.17
2) Kerosene gap rate	1.17	1.17	1.15	1.06
3) Light oil gap rate	1.15	1.16	1.16	1.17
4) Heavy oil Gap rate	1.14	1.12	1.10	1.07

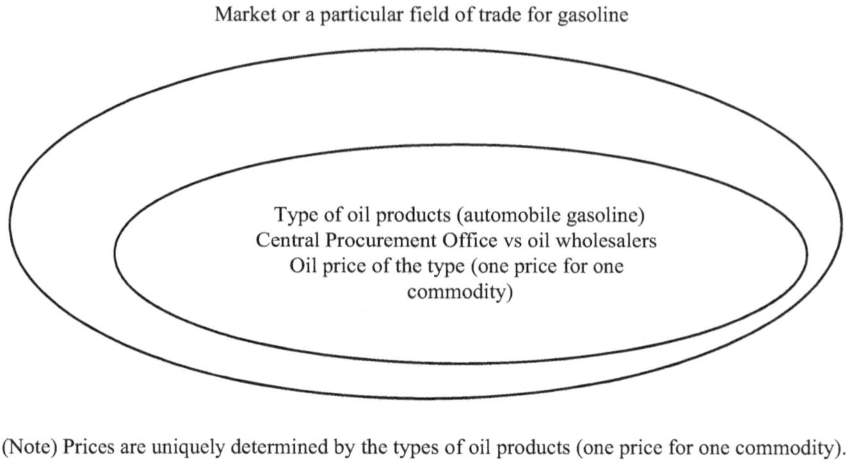

Figure 6.3 Bidding by types of oil products

To avoid the inconvenience that there were variations in the unit price for each type of oil, as the Board of Audit noted, it is necessary to bid not for each property at bases but for each oil type at the initial bidding. The total amount of all properties would be collectively procured at the CPO and would be managed in petroleum product storage tanks throughout the country. For transportation from storage tanks to each base in all areas in Japan, bids for transportation would be made on a property-by-property basis. Thus, it is possible to secure the quantity of petroleum products and transport them separately and introduce competitiveness for petroleum products and the distribution process for transportation of oil products assumed to be a fixed cost. Figure 6.3 shows an image of the market.

6.3 The case of the government bid-rigging in Hokkaido Development Agency

There were several institutional hurdles to overcome for specific people in the governmental agency to decide on a prospective bidder on their own intentions. The first hurdle is that the person suggesting collusion has official authority. The next hurdle is to include an element that simulates a discretionary contract in the bidding process.

Regarding the first hurdle, the bureaucracy has a defined range of responsibilities related to the duties in charge. Therefore, even if it is a request from the supervisor of the person in charge of the project, there is no obligation to comply with the project outside the scope of responsibility. This government bid-rigging began when the Secretary of the Hokkaido Development Agency asked the manager of the Department of Ports and Harbors in the HDB to handle the bidding.

Regarding the second hurdle, bidding involving the Hokkaido Development Agency is governed by the Accounting Act. When the target price of the property is above a certain price level, an order through a discretionary contract is not possible and the successful bidder must be determined by bidding. The two methods of bidding are designated competitive bidding and general competitive bidding. The ordering party decides which method to adopt. Even in designated competitive bidding, the successful bidder, as expected by the ordering party, is not always determined from among the nominated contractors. Therefore, to ensure the bidder wins the bid for the property as intended by the ordering party, it is necessary to create a discretionary contract mechanism within the designated competitive bidding system. The present government bid-rigging is a case of bid-rigging incorporating these two factors into the bidding system.

6.3.1 Progress and judgment of the case

The defendant in the government bid-rigging was a member of the House of Representatives from Hokkaido and served as the Secretary of the Hokkaido Development Agency from September 1997 to July 1998. The duties of the Secretary were to supervise the affairs of the Agency. These include jurisdiction over the investigation and formulation of the Hokkaido Comprehensive Development Plan, the coordination and promotion of affairs related to the implementation of projects, and supervising the duties of the staff. When the defendant was in office in October 1997, the representative and managing director of a construction company visited the office of the Secretary at Kasumigaseki, Tokyo. The main business of the company was to construct a harbor and fishing port ordered by the 11 Departments of Development and Construction per region, such as Abashiri, Obihiro, Kushiro, Muroran, and Rumoi.

Until 1993, the company received orders for harbor and fishing port construction from eight or nine Departments. However, the number of public works decreased after 1994, and the company could only receive orders from three Departments in 1996. From 1995 to 1993, the construction works of the company decreased by 40% in amount from 9.8 to 6.2 billion yen, and ordinary profit also decreased from 700 to 200 million yen. Thus, it had a sense of crisis in management and requested an interview with the defendant. The purpose of the meeting was to ensure that the harbor and fishing port construction at Monbetsu Port was scheduled to be ordered in 1997 and 1998. The Secretary asked the manager of the Department of Ports and Harbors in the HDB to give instructions to the company to receive orders. The defendant received cash compensation of two million yen from the company in October 1997 and August 1998, and one million yen each in March 1998 and June 1998.

At the time of this case, the contractors for port construction ordered by the Department took the form of designated competitive bidding. However, the reality was different. The nomination of contractors was based on the following five processes:

(1) At each Department of Development and Construction circa January every year, the deputy manager in charge of agriculture, water, and transportation prepared a draft plan that listed the favorite contractor that should be awarded bids for each port construction. When he could not decide on the favorite, he drafted a plan with a blank column. The draft plan was submitted to the manager of the Department of Ports and Harbors in the HDB at Kasumigaseki in Tokyo.
(2) The manager examined the proposal and decided on the preferred contractor. The plan was sent back to the deputy manager in charge of each Department of Development and Construction.
(3) Each deputy manager informed the secretary-general of the Local Construction Industry Association of the prospective contractor for each bidding.
(4) The secretary-general shared notice of selecting the prospective contractor of the bidding.
(5) The prospective contractor negotiated the bid price with other bidders and won the bidding.

The above duties of the manager of the Department of Ports and Harbors in the HDB have no legal basis and may rather be contrary to the Accounting Act. The process was only a series of customs conducted by the Hokkaido Development Agency. Figure 6.4 shows the structure.

6.3.2 The judgments of the courts

The court declared that the defendant was fully aware of the fact that the manager of the Department of Port and Harbor in the HDB had decided on the prospective contractor, though the defendant was not authorized to direct and supervise the HDB regarding port construction (the Secretary did not have the official authority). However, the Secretary of the Hokkaido Development Agency has control over the services of the Agency staff (the Secretary has the responsibility of directing and unifying the entire body). The defendant received the request from the company to intervene in the selection of contractors, he sent the request to the manager of the Department of Port and Harbor of the HDB and received compensation. Receiving monetary compensation for such efforts undermines public confidence in the fairness of the preparation of the budget implementation plan, which is the primary duty of the Secretary. Therefore, it is appropriate to recognize the provision of the respective contributions in this case as a bribe and the reward for the duties of the Secretary of the Hokkaido Development Agency.

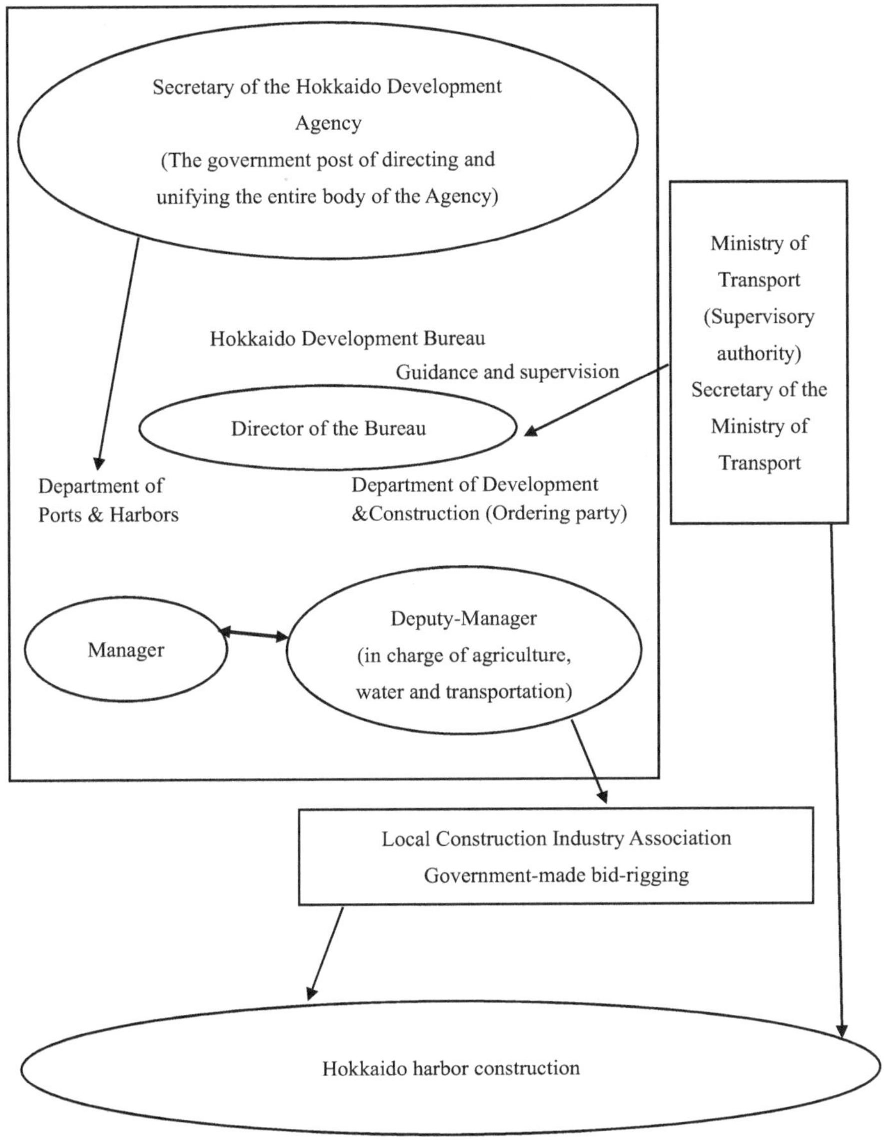

Figure 6.4 Structure of official authority

The first trial concluded with a guilty verdict by the Tokyo District Court in November 2004. The accused appealed. In the second trial, the appeal was dismissed by the Tokyo High Court in February 2008. The defendant appealed to the Supreme Court. However, the Supreme Court rejected it in September 2010. Finally, a retrial appeal was filed, but the request for retrial was dismissed by the Tokyo District Court in March 2019.

In the present case of government bid-rigging, the preconditions for forming a particular field of trade (market) were the problem. When considering the market as a place of actual trading, it becomes necessary to consider that the market is impersonal; that is, it is controlled by the rule of law, not the rule of people. Individual transactions are influenced by individual motivation, but the market is operated under certain rules. The creation of a market environment or system design becomes important. Government bid-rigging occurred because the government distorted the market through human rules and ignored the rule of law aimed at the competitive bidding system.

Hence, consider the District Court, the High Court, and the Supreme Court rulings related to government bid-rigging from the perspective of bureaucrats' reaction to their authority and violation of the Accounting Act in the designated competitive bidding. Regarding the bureaucrat's reaction to the official authority, the manager of the Department of Port and Harbor in the HDB knew that the instructions of the Secretary were based on the official authority. The case reveals the politician's lack of knowledge of the law. However, if there had been communication between the politician and the bureaucrat, such an incident would not have occurred. In the verdict, the courts determined that the bureaucrat's testimony was sufficiently credible. This is the result of the bureaucrat's understanding of the content of the official authority of the Secretary of the Hokkaido Development Agency.

Finally, consider the violations of the Accounting Act in the designated competitive bidding. In the present case of government bid-rigging, the format is formally designated competitive bidding within the framework of the Accounting Act. However, as a matter of practice, it was essentially a discretionary contract.

6.4 Conclusion

The bidding system was a common element in the cases of the CPO and the Hokkaido Development Agency. The objective of adopting the bidding system is to introduce competitiveness into public works projects. Considering the reality of the two cases, the competitive bidding method was formally adopted as the premise. However, while it took the form of competitive bidding, the reality was that the successful bidder was decided in advance. It was no different from the discretionary contract. Looking back at the bidding method from the perspective of government rigging, the person in charge of bidding did not thoroughly understand the meaning of bidding.

In the case of the CPO, there were testimonies that some of the wholesalers were absent from the rigging meetings, and some of the participants were reluctant to participate. The persons in charge of the participating companies might have recognized that collusion was illegal. In the case of the Hokkaido Development Agency, if some sort of internal check between bureaucrats and the defendant had worked, this kind of case would not have happened. The essence of the CPO case lies in how public money was handled and processed.

In the CPO bid-rigging case, four billion yen of public money was overpaid. If the overpayment of public money is extended to the entire government budget, it may amount to more than 10 trillion yen a year.

An urgent policy in Japan is to strengthen fiscal discipline. Some public works via bidding have overpaid public funds. In the CPO bid-rigging case, there was an overpayment of 15% of public funds. It is necessary to change how people think about public money. It is used for the people rather than selfish interests. The process of the government bid-rigging regarding the Hokkaido Development Agency is simple. The politician lacked knowledge of the law. Moreover, the present designated competitive bidding, including the discretionary contract, relied on the low awareness of legal compliance within the government office and the inadequacy of the internal check system.

As a reform of the bidding system, the introduction of comprehensive evaluation instead of conventional price evaluation has been devised. As the source of funds for bidding is public funds, the price is one of the major determinants in winning a successful bid. Accordingly, several points are required. The first is to review the problems of the current designated competitive bidding system. The second is to strengthen the system for checking whether bidding methods are being conducted without any problems per the Accounting Act and the Local Autonomy Act. The third is to enhance the checking of financial statements of national and local governments through internal audits. Fourth, it is important to ensure the transparency of the public scrutiny of budget execution using public funds.

7 Case of stalker furnace bid-rigging

Scattered target prices of the properties and high winning bid rate

7.1 Introduction

This collusion case is a bid-rigging involving contractors in the construction, renewal, and expansion of stoker furnaces ordered by local governments. Garbage is pulverized, incinerated, and rendered harmless at a garbage disposal plant. The bid item for the refuse incineration facility comprises incineration equipment, electrical and instrumentation equipment, construction equipment, and buildings, including exterior facilities. The bidding mechanism in the case of the stoker furnace bid-rigging was simple. A local government set the target price for the bidding property. With the target price as the upper limit, the winning bidder was the lowest bidder among the bidders, participating in the designated competitive bidding.

The purpose of bid-rigging by contractors is to increase the profits of the belonging industry. In rigging, mutual cooperation is necessary among companies within the industry, and the profit of each company is stabilized at a high level through the redistribution function within the industry. Thus, bidders must win the bids at high prices. As the local government sets a maximum price called the target price for each bidding property in accordance with Article 234 of the Local Autonomy Act, it is necessary for the bidders to bring the successful bid price as close as possible to the target price.

The nominated contractors must accurately predict the target price calculated by the ordering party. They prepare their calculation program corresponding to the target pricing manual prepared by the ordering party. The calculation program includes several parameters that must be set; by repeating simulation experiments using many bid properties, it is possible to estimate the target price determined by the ordering party. The nominated bidders participate in the bidding coordinate in advance to determine the winning bidder. Hence, the prospective successful bidder can bring the successful bid price closer to the target price without considering the intention of competitors.

The relationship between major companies and outsiders becomes an issue in establishing bid-rigging concerning the establishment of the basic agreement on cooperation among major firms. The presence of outsiders reduces the possibility of cooperation and increases competitiveness. Competitiveness

DOI: 10.4324/9781003370444-7

would increase as the number of outsiders increases. This point will be considered in this chapter. Moreover, if there is bid-rigging, the successful bid price would be higher, and, therefore, the successful bid rate would be higher than the rate when there is no bid-rigging. This is the subject of consideration regarding the successful bid rate. The three points—the prediction of the target price, the influence of outsiders, and the consideration of the successful bid rate—are where the problem of this chapter resides.

The contractors involved in this case were the major five companies directly involved in the bid-rigging. Moreover, there were seven outsiders related to this case. A lot of direct evidence was presented, such as statement records, employee memos, a list for sharing information on construction work plans, a record of each company's desire to receive orders, the tonnage of orders received from the five major companies, a list of prospective order recipients, internal documents, and bid rate data. As direct evidence is created by human beings, misunderstandings and mistakes are inevitable.

Accordingly, the records that existed as direct evidence were subject to human errors and misconceptions, and the plaintiff and defendant had different emphases and selections per their desire to gain an advantage. Thus, even when considering the same record, there is bias in its interpretation. The judges also have diverse values, and, even if decisions are made based on evidence, there is a bias in how the evidence is taken up among the judges. In the case of claiming damages derived from this bid-rigging case, judgments differ greatly per judge.

Section 7.2 provides an overview of the bid-rigging of the stoker furnaces. Section 7.3 conducts data analysis per the data contained in trial decisions and judgments from the perspective of successful bid rates and the role of outsiders. Section 7.4 examines the successful bid rate, target price, and the role of outsiders from statistical, economic, and legal aspects, using competition as a keyword. Section 7.5 provides an econometric analysis using an economic model and econometric techniques. Section 7.6 addresses the case of a claim for damages by residents related to the stoker furnace bid-rigging case. Section 7.7 concludes this chapter.

7.2 Case of the stoker furnace bid-rigging

Contractors participating in this case were called plant manufacturers. They design and manufacture the stoker furnace and perform installation works. They also construct waste incineration facilities and peripheral facilities, such as factory buildings. There were five major companies, along with outsiders in the construction of stoker furnaces.

From April 1994 onwards at the latest, the five companies made the basic agreements, which is an important requirement for collusion, to equalize the chances of receiving orders for stoker furnace construction works ordered by the local governments through designated competitive bidding. The contents of the basic agreement were as follows:

(1) When some company (or companies) expresses the desire to receive orders for construction project planned by the local governments.
    (1.a) In case there is only one company that wishes to receive the order, the company shall be scheduled to receive the order for the said construction work.
    (1.b) In case there are multiple applicants, they discuss and decide on the prospective recipient.
(2) When the prospective order recipient is decided among the five companies and outsiders participate in the designated competitive bidding, the prospective order recipient asks the outsiders to cooperate.
(3) The successful bid price is determined by the prospective order recipient. The others cooperate such that they can receive the order at the desired price.

In this case, the JFTC conducted an on-site inspection in September 1998 and issued a cease-and-desist order to the above five major companies in August 1999. The bid-rigging was conducted from April 1, 1994, to September 17, 1998. During this period, there were 87 stoker furnace bidding, and 66 were won by the five major companies. The construction work during the period amounted to 1,103.1 billion yen, and the average construction cost per project was 12.6 billion yen. Dissatisfied with the trial decision, the five major companies filed a lawsuit with the Tokyo High Court to request its cancellation. The High Court decision was issued in September 2008, and the appellants' claim was dismissed. The appellants appealed to the Supreme Court. The Supreme Court decided in October 2009 and dismissed the final appeal. After this, a surcharge payment of 27 billion yen was issued by the JFTC to the five companies.

7.3 Data analysis

The basic data are the 87 properties ordered during the period. Of the 87 properties, 66 properties were awarded by the five major companies. Of these, 60 properties were claimed by the JFTC to be violating construction. Six properties were excluded from the violating properties although the five major companies won the bids. Thirty properties were recognized as violating properties by the trial decision, three of which were won in the bid by an outsider. Therefore, 27 properties were recognized as violating properties for the five major companies. Regarding the surcharge payment order for the five major companies by the JFTC, one property was excluded from the 27 properties, and six properties were added to the 26 properties. Finally, the surcharge payment order for the five major companies totals 32 properties.

This section examines the following four problems: (1) Why did the number of violating properties decrease by the trial decision from 60 to 30? (2) Out of the 66 properties won in the bid by the five major companies, why were six properties excluded from the violations? (3) Why were three properties won by an outsider deemed to be violating properties from a legal perspective? (4) Why were six properties included in the surcharge payment order of the 32 properties? The study employs the successful bid rate as the consequence variable in the causal relationship determining the effect of bid-rigging. It does not use the successful bid price as the consequence variable because the target price fluctuates depending on the properties. Using the ratio between the successful bid price and the target price as the standardization escapes the demerit using the actual price. The successful bid rate is defined as

Successful bid rate = successful bid price/target price

The target price is an exogenous variable for the contractors because it is determined by the ordering party based on the law. While the ordering party calculates the target price using the manual in most cases, the bidders easily and precisely anticipate the target price. This is not uncommon in all the bidding regarding public works. The successful bid price is the lowest price bid by the contractors, and the factors that determine the successful bid price are: (1) whether the basic agreement has been reached among the five major companies, (2) the determination of the prospective order recipient, (3) presence of cooperation between the five major companies and outsiders, (4) accurate prediction of target price, and (5) ability to the plant design constrained by technological conditions. Expressing this as a formula, the successful bid price is described by the following function:

> Successful bid price = f (whether a basic agreement has been reached between the five major companies and who is scheduled to receive an order, whether there is cooperation between the five major companies and outsiders, the expected price, and technological conditions)

7.3.1 *Why the initial number of violating properties was halved in the trial decision*

At first, 60 properties were claimed by the JFTC to be violating construction. Now, divide all the properties won by the five major companies into two groups. One is the group that was recognized as violating properties by a trial decision from 60 properties. The number of the violating properties is 28. Another is a group recognized as non-violating properties by the trial decision. The number of the non-violating properties is 32.[1]

A statistical test was conducted to test whether there is a difference in the successful bid rates between these two groups. The hypothesis is that there is no difference in the population means of the two groups, and the alternative hypothesis is that there is a difference between the two groups.

$H_0: \mu_1 = \mu_2$
$H_A: \mu_1 \neq \mu_2$

If H_0 is true, then the following statistics

$$z = (x_1 - x_2 - (\mu_1 - \mu_2)) \cdot \sqrt{(n_1 \cdot n_2 \cdot (n_1 + n_2 - 2)/(n_1 + n_2))} / \sqrt{((n_1 - 1)s_1^2 + (n_2 - 1)s_2^2)}$$

1 The successful bid rate was not indicated for the three properties out of 60. See (Footnote 4).

follows the t-distribution with $n_1 + n_2 - 2$ degrees of freedom.

Below are the statistical characteristics of the successful bid rate of the group of violating properties and that of non-violating properties.

The group of 25 recognized as violating properties

Number of properties (n_1) 25; sample mean (x_1) 98.53; standard deviation (s_1) 1.85.

The group of 32 recognized as non-violating properties

Number of properties (n_2) 32; sample mean (x_2) 98.08; standard deviation (s_2) 2.63

The statistic of z was 0.72. The critical value of the 1% significance level is 2.66, indicating that H_0 is not rejected at the significance level of 1%. There is no statistical difference in the successful bid rates between the two groups. Therefore, the decrease from 60 to 30 properties stems from factors other than the successful bid rates. Significantly, many of the properties not recognized as violating properties were bid before August 1995. Regarding the difference in credibility of evidence obtained from the employee memos and statements of the five companies, the handling of the violating properties before and after August 1995 was clearly divided. All violating properties before August 1995 were removed from the violating properties with one exception.[2]

7.3.2 *Statistical examination of six properties excluded from violating properties of five major companies*

Table 7.1 shows the six properties that the JFTC found not to be infringing.

From Table 7.1, the successful bid rate of property no. 66 is 100%. There are no successful bid rates in the range of 90%, two properties (no. 67 and no. 77) in the 80% range, two properties (no. 28 and no. 40) in the 70% range, and property no. 41 has a successful bid rate of 48.78%. Except for one property (property no. 66), the successful bid rate is relatively low.[3] The study will consider whether it is statistically appropriate to exclude property no. 66 as not subject to violation, using a statistical hypothesis test. It conducts statistical tests for differences in the successful bid rates between the violating property

2 Property no. 26 was the only property whose bid date was before August 1995 and was recognized as a violating property. However, it was excluded from the property subject to the surcharge payment because it was challenging to certify that it falls under the category stipulated in Article 7-2, Paragraph 1 of the AMA regarding the surcharge payment order.

3 Property no. 66 has a successful bid rate of 100% but is not the property subject to violation. In the trial decision, the examiner (public prosecutor at the trial) declared that the bidding situation was not a competition of prices between contractors. However, on the allegations of the trial procedure, the order was not received based on the basic agreement. The trial judge did not raise any doubts about this statement.

Table 7.1 Six properties excluded from violating properties

Property no.	*Successful bidder*	*Success bid rate (%)*	*Bidders (majors and outsiders)*
28	A major company	75.97	Eight companies: 5 + 3
40	A major company	73.69	13 companies: 5 + 8
41	A major company	48.78	Eight companies: 5 + 3
66	A major company	100.0	Seven companies: 5 + 2
67	A major company	80.17	Ten companies: 5 + 5
77	A major company	89.86	Eight companies: 4 + 4

(Note) Regarding bidders, the number below + is the number of outsiders.

group and the non-violating property group. If there is a significant difference in the successful bid rates between the two groups, these two groups would be distinguished by the successful bid rates.[4]

The study employs the sample mean and its standard deviation for each group for the statistical significance test of the mean difference. As a hypothesis, there is no difference in the population average between the two groups. As the alternative hypothesis, the successful bid rate of the violating properties is higher than that of non-violating properties.

H_0: $\mu_1 = \mu_2$
H_A: $\mu_1 > \mu_2$

If H_0 is true, then the following statistics

$$z = (x_1 - x_2 - (\mu_1 - \mu_2)) \cdot \sqrt{}(n_1 \cdot n_2 \cdot (n_1 + n_2 - 2)/ (n_1 + n_2))/\sqrt{}((n_1 - 1)s_1^2 + (n_2 - 1)s_2^2)$$

follows the t-distribution with $n_1 + n_2 - 2$ degrees of freedom. The basic numerical values used for the test are as follows:

The properties identified as violating (57 properties with reported successful bid rates):

Number of properties (n_1) 57; sample mean (x_1) 98.33; standard deviation (s_1) 2.23.

The properties found to be non-violating (6 properties):

Number of properties (n_2) 6; sample mean (x_2) 78.07; standard deviation (s_2) 17.35.

The statistic of z was 8.74. When a one-sided test is performed under the hypothesis that the population means of two groups are equal, the critical value at the 1% significance level is 2.39.

4 The number of properties is 60, but three properties have a blank successful bid rate. The sample size is 57 in total and six for the non-violating property group.

The hypothesis that the mean values of the two populations are equal is rejected at the 1% significance level. Statistically, there is a difference in successful bid rates between the two groups. From a common sense perspective, there is a high possibility that property no. 66 is included in the violating group but not in the non-violating group. This is because it is considered an outlier in the non-violating group.

7.3.3 Why three properties that made the successful bid by an outsider company were considered violating properties

The examiner (public prosecutor at the trial) claimed 60 properties were violating properties, but only 30 properties were recognized as violating properties by the trial decision. These properties include three properties the five major companies failed to bid on. Although the properties were not included in the five major companies, they were found to be the violating properties. Table 7.2 shows the instances in which the successful bidder was an outsider.

The three properties in Table 7.2 are property nos. 46, 52, and 71, respectively. In the trial decision, these properties won by one of the outsiders were marked N (a company in the five major companies), M (a company in the five major companies), and N (a company in the five major companies) in the memo of the prospective bidder possessed by the employee of the major company. Thus, the original prospective successful bidder was intended to be a major company.

The study examines why the three properties won by the outsider are included in the violating properties. Economic transactions employ the process of *intention*, *action*, and *result*. Economics emphasizes results, while jurisprudence emphasizes intention. The three properties were recognized as properties subject to violation because the prospective contractor would originally be scheduled to be one of the major companies based on the basic agreement. However, one of the outsiders won the bid for some reason, such as a change in the successful bidder for the property just before bidding under the cooperation between the five major companies and the outsider or a procedural error during the bidding process.

Table 7.2 Properties that were not included in the five major companies but were found to be in violation

Property no.	*Successful bidder*	*Success bid rate (%)*	*Bidders*
46	Outsider	95.03	11 companies: 5+6, [N]
52	Outsider	96.35	Eight companies: 5+3, [M]
71	Outsider	99.52	Six companies: 4+2, [N]

The study divides the bid-rigging of the five major companies into the stages of intent, action, and result. This discussion will examine the relationship between the definition of competition used in the AMA and competition frequently used in economics. The five major bidders decide the prospective bidder based on the basic agreement. If outsiders other than the five major companies participate, the *intention* corresponds to the stage that the five major companies consult with the outsiders, and the outsiders approve the prospective order recipient decided by the five major companies.

An *action* is a bidding action by the nominees. Notably, when competitive bidding is conducted, cooperation (bid-rigging) between bidders and competition as defined by economics takes place in two cases. In jurisprudence, competition is defined in Article 2, Paragraph 4 of the AMA such that competition is when multiple suppliers supply the same or similar goods or services to demanders. Therefore, there is no distinction between cooperation and competition.

For competition under the AMA to become synonymous with competition in economics, it is necessary to add unfair trade restrictions. The unfair trade restrictions are defined in Article 2, Paragraph 6 of the AMA, which means suppliers jointly determine prices with other suppliers, restrict mutual supply behaviors, and materially restrict competition in a particular field of trade, contrary to the public interests. Competition in economics means that each supplier offers the lowest possible price to the demanders. It is called the price competition among suppliers. Competition in economics is synonymous with the *fighting between companies over price* indicated in the judgment text.

Finally, the *result* is the determination of the winning bidder and bid price. Accordingly, it is possible to observe the successful bid rate as fact.

7.3.4 Examination of six additional properties ordered to pay surcharges

In the surcharge payment order, the six properties classified as non-violating properties were added to the properties subject to the surcharge payments, as shown in Table 7.3.

The successful bid rate for each property is high, with one case in the 98% range and four cases in the 99% range, except for property no. 47, which is 94.68%. This is a typical case for collusion because the bidders were limited to the five major companies, except property no. 47.

Table 7.3 Six additional properties ordered to pay a surcharge

Property no.	*Successful bidder*	*Success bid rate (%)*	*Bidders*
39	A major company	99.66	Five companies
43	A major company	98.59	Five companies
44	A major company	99.97	Five companies
47	A major company	94.68	Six companies: 5 + 1
57	A major company	99.60	Five companies
73	A major company	99.97	Five companies

7.4 Considerations related to target prices, successful bid rates, and outsiders: Statistical consideration

In the bid-rigging case, the main focus regards the basic agreement and the role of outsiders in proving the constituent elements. And the level of successful bid rate would be another focus. Now, examine the issues of the basic agreement, the role of outsiders, and successful high bid rates, using competition as a keyword from statistical, economic, and legal perspectives.

Figure 7.1 shows the number of successful bids by the five major companies and the six outsiders in this case. The number of successful bids was 12, 13, 12, 16, and 13, respectively. That by six outsiders was 6, 7, 3, 2, 1, and 2, respectively. Figure 7.1 shows the number of winning bids by the contractor.

Considering the distribution of the number of successful bids, there is a difference in the number between the five major companies and the six outsiders. Now, focus on outsiders and their successful bid rates in detail. Table 7.4 shows the number of successful bids by outsiders and their successful bid rates. It shows the successful bid rate for each successful bid property of outsiders. There are four underlined numbers in the table, which are properties with a successful bid rate of less than 80%.

The six outsiders were inferred to be divided into two groups: two semi-major companies and four other outsiders. This inference is confirmed by the statistical tests. The successful bid rates for the semi-major outsiders (outsiders 1 and 2) were almost over 90%, indicating that the two semi-major outsiders have a cooperative relationship (not a competitive relationship) with the five major companies. Such a high bidding rate of the two semi-major outsiders does not appear to be the result of competition with the five major companies.

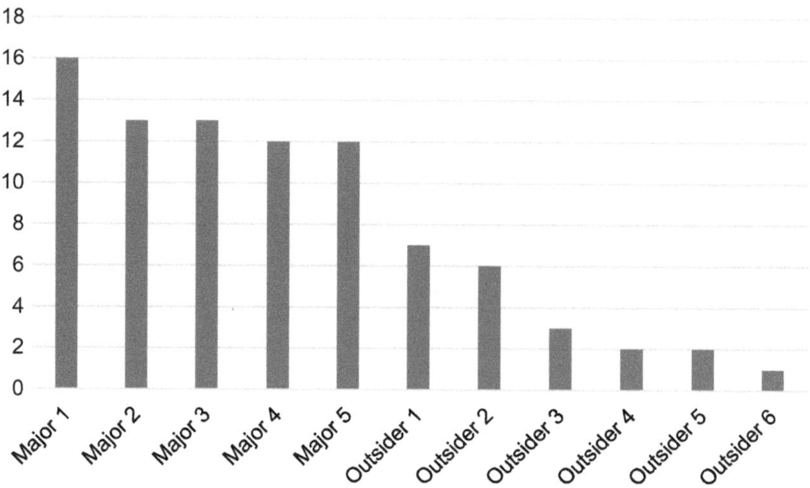

Figure 7.1 Number of successful bids for the five major companies and six outsiders

Table 7.4 Successful bid rate for each property won by outsiders

(a) Outsider 1 (six properties):							
Property no.	8	25	48	63	54	78	
Successful bid rate	86.41	95.65	96.83	93, 85	91.58	89.92	
(b) Outsider 2 (seven properties):							
Property no.	7	23	46	52	69	71	72
Successful bid rate	99.70	100	95.03	96.36	99.80	99.52	99.60
(c) Outsider 3 (three properties):							
Property no.	12	30	68				
Successful bid rate	52.32	92.11	72,40				
(d) Outsider 4 (two properties):							
Property no.	16	37					
Successful bid rate	93.39	84.15					
(e) Outsider 5 (one property):							
Property no.	65						
Successful bid rate	95.60						
(f) Outsider 6 (two properties):							
Property no.	42	70					
Successful bid rate	76.51	74.27					

For the four outsiders, the successful bid rates of 95.60% (outsider 5), 93.39% (outsider 4), and 84.15% (outsider 4) also seem to stem from cooperation with the five major firms. Interestingly, the successful bid rates of outsider 3 are 52.32%, 92.11%, and 72.40%, respectively. It would be reasonable to judge that 92.11% is the result of cooperation, and 52.32% and 72.40% are the result of competition.

Accordingly, even if there is no basic agreement with the outsiders, it would be possible to make a cooperative relationship with the five major companies. Hence, the outsiders would not always be in a competitive relationship with them.

In response to the question of why the bid rate of outsiders is as high as that of the five major companies, the study divides the companies into three groups: five major companies, two outsiders as semi-majors, and four outsiders. At first, the study conducted a significance test of the difference in the bid rates between the five majors and two semi-majors. If there is no significant difference between the two groups, they have a common intention of cooperation through successful bid rates.

The hypothesis is that there is no difference in the population means of the two groups, and the alternative hypothesis is that there is a difference in the population means of the two groups.

H_0: $\mu_1 = \mu_2$
H_A: $\mu_1 \neq \mu_2$

If H_0 is true, then the following statistics

$$z = (x_1 - x_2 - (\mu_1 - \mu_2)) \cdot \sqrt{(n_1 \cdot n_2 \cdot (n_1 + n_2 - 2)/(n_1 + n_2))} / \sqrt{((n_1 - 1)s_1^2 + (n_2 - 1)s_2^2)}$$

follows a t-distribution with $n_1 + n_2 - 2$ degrees of freedom.

The following are the statistical characteristics of the successful bid rate of the group of five major companies and that of two semi-major outsiders.

The successful bit rates for 66 properties of five major companies:

Number of properties (n_1) 66; sample mean (x_1) 96.58;
standard deviation (s_1) 7.94,

The successful bit rates for 13 properties of two semi-major outsiders:

Number of properties (n_2) 13; sample mean (x_2) 95.71,
standard deviation (s_2) 4.31

The statistic of z was 0.38. When a two-sided test is performed under the hypothesis that the two-population means are equal, the critical value at the 1% significance level is 2.64. Therefore, H_0 is not rejected at the significance level of 1%. There is no significant difference between the successful bid rates of the five major companies and the two semi-major outsiders, indicating these two groups have cooperation without basic agreement. Second, the significance test was conducted on the difference in successful bid rates between the five majors and that of the four outsiders excluding two semi-majors. The following are the statistical characteristics.

The successful bit rates for 66 properties of five major companies:

Number of properties (n_1) 66; sample mean (x_1) 96.58;
standard deviation (s_1) 7.94,

The successful bit rates for eight properties of four outsiders:

Number of properties (n_2) 8; sample mean (x_2) 80.09;
standard deviation (s_2) 14.41,

The statistic of z was 5.01. A two-sided test under the hypothesis that the two-population means are equal shows that the critical value of the 1% significance level is 2.64. H_0 is rejected at the significance level of 1%.

Accordingly, the two semi-major outsiders were effectively under the basic agreement of the five major companies. However, the outsiders excluding two semi-majors are highly independent. However, even if they are highly independent, they do not always act competitively.

7.5 Econometric analysis regarding target prices of properties for bidding

7.5.1 Preliminary consideration: Change in the unit prices by plant scale

There are several plants with the same plant scale in the present case. The unit price defined by the target price divided by processing capacity (plant scale) is calculated, as the study examined the difference in the unit price for the same plant scale.[5] Table 7.5 shows the differences in the unit prices for the same plant scale.

On the topic of economies of scale, the study accumulated contributions of econometric analysis using production functions and engineering cost functions. The equipment industry such as the waste treatment plant construction shows economies of scale, where the unit cost decreases as the plant scale increases. However, there was a difference of approximately 30% to 70% in the unit cost evaluated by the target price in the same plant scale in the present case. In the plant construction, though there are own circumstances, the fact that the unit cost was 70% higher for the same plant scale of construction is strange considering the past empirical results on the equipment industry. There is room for ingenuity in estimating the target price calculated by local governments.[6]

In Table 7.5, there is a range in the target price for each plant of the same scale. However, the successful bid rates are over 95% for most properties, and more than half of the properties have a successful bid rate of over 99%. Hence, the contractors have accurately predicted the target price calculated by the local governments, and the amount exceeding the proper price is the company's excess profit. This result leaves room for consideration of the standards for calculating the target price and the harmful effects of bid-rigging.

7.5.2 Quantitative analysis related to the target prices

The econometric analysis estimated the envelope of the unit price by plant scale that expresses the lowest unit price by size. After the expected target price is estimated, the deviation from the actual target price is calculated. Accordingly, the extra budget execution amount by the ordering party is estimated.

The data used for the econometric analysis were the target prices of the property, processing capacity (tons), and construction details (e.g., renewal, expansion, and newly established) for the 87 properties indicated in the trial decision.

5 The present analysis is not an analysis that measures the engineering cost function to test the economies of scale of the equipment industry. Rather, it focuses on the adequacy of the target prices calculated by the local governments. Hence, the study adopted the target price as the numerator of the unit price.

6 In public works such as river construction works and sewage works, construction costs naturally vary per the topography of the construction site. However, in the plant construction, the facility is the main work. Moreover, other issues such as securing the land have already been resolved. In plant construction works, rational design is possible from technological and engineering relationships; therefore, when the plant scale is the same, the unit price would almost be the same.

Table 7.5 Differences in the unit prices for the same plant scale

(a) Processing capacity of 100t per day (four properties)			
Property no.	Unit price (million yen)	Construction details	Successful bid rate
57	47.18	Expansion	99.60
62	44.31	Renewal	95.90
81	60.47	Renewal	98.88
82	57.18	Renewal	99.51
Average unit price 52.28			
(b) Processing capacity of 150t per day (two properties)			
Property no.	Unit price (million yen)	Construction details	Successful bid rate
53	71.31	Expansion	96.28
87	42.38	Expansion	97.53
Average unit price 56.84			
(c) Processing capacity 210t per day (two properties)			
Property no.	Unit price (million yen)	Construction details	Successful bid rate
44	33.81	Renewal	99.97
49	57.25	Renewal	99.75
Average unit price 45.53			
(d) Processing capacity 600t per day (two properties)			
Property no.	Unit price (million yen)	Construction details	Successful bid rate
61	29.00	Renewal	100.0
80	49.28	Newly established	94.68
Average unit price 39.14			
(e) Processing capacity 900t per day (three properties)			
Property no.	Unit price (million yen)	Construction details	Successful bid rate
43	29.86	Renewal	98.59
54	32.18	Newly established	99.97
60	38.53	Newly established	99.62
Average unit price 33.52			

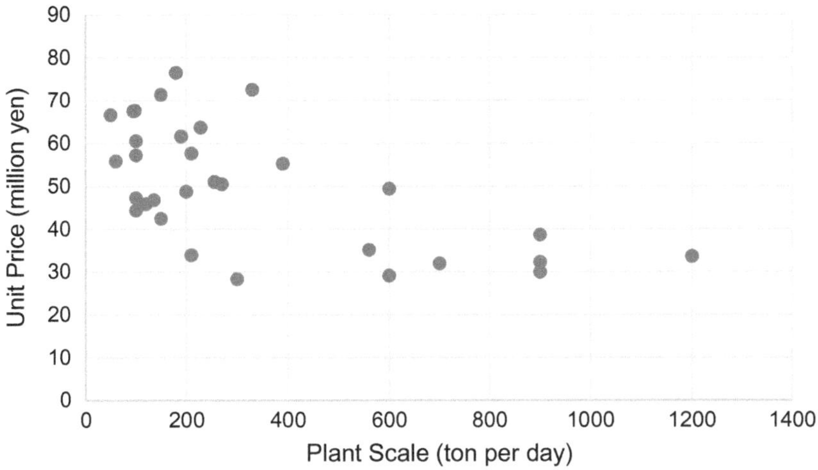

Figure 7.2 Scatter diagram between the plant scale and the corresponding unit price

Regarding the plant construction, there is a relationship between the plant scale and the unit price. Figure 7.2 is the scatter diagram between the plant scale and the unit price of the plant. The plant scale is indicated on the horizontal axis, and the corresponding unit price obtained by dividing the target price by the plant scale is plotted on the vertical axis. From this scatter diagram, the unit prices tend to be relatively high in small-scale areas, and unit prices decrease as the scale increases.

Based on the empirical fact that there are economies of scale in plant construction, the study specified the following estimating equation of the unit price:

$$y = a/x + b$$

where y is the unit price obtained by dividing the target price by the scale, x is the plant scale, and a and b are parameters to be estimated. Mathematical characteristics of the specification are that the unit price decreases as the plant scale increases, and the unit price converges to a constant value as the plant scale increases. The study expresses the characteristics in mathematical form as follows:

$$dy/dx = -a/x^2 < 0 \text{ (downward-sloping curve)}$$

$$x \to 0 \text{ then } y \to \infty$$

$$x \to \infty \text{ then } y = b \text{ (unit price converges to b).}$$

In the first stage of determining the parameters a and b, the study conducted a test of whether there was a difference in unit price among the construction details (e.g., renewal, expansion, and newly established) in the plant construction works. If there is a significant difference, it is necessary to explicitly specify the construction details for these properties. The estimated equation is as follows:

$$y = a/x + b + d_1 dum + d_2 dum_2$$

where dum is a newly established dummy for 1 as newly established and 0 for other construction details, and the value of 1 is for eight properties. Further, dum2 is the expansion dummy for 1 as expansion work and 0 for other construction details, and the value of 1 is for one property. The estimation result is as follows:

Variable	Estimated Coefficient	Standard Error	t-statistic	P-value
C	41.0051	4.67228	8.77626	[.000]
X	1469.16	605.635	2.42582	[.022]
DUM	.228890	5.70569	.040116	[.968]
DUM2	2.72129	8.90617	.305551	[.762]

Std. error of regression = 13.0456
R-squared = .250554
Adjusted R-squared = .167282

The t-values of the coefficients dum and dum_2 were low and were not significantly different from zero. From the result, there is no significant difference in the content of the construction details, and there is no need to consider the difference in the content of the construction details. The estimated result after removing the two dummy variables is as follows:

Variable	Estimated Coefficient	Standard Error	t-statistic	P-value
C	40.8958	3.71972	10.9943	[.000]
X	1542.13	498.738	3.09207	[.004]

Std. error of regression = 12.6097
R-squared = .247943
Adjusted R-squared = .222010

Using this estimating equation, the study estimated the optimal unit price function related to plant scale as an envelope. Figure 7.3 shows the estimation results obtained by the ordinary least squares (OLS) method and the envelope obtained by fixing the parameter a and varying the value of b.

As the second step, the study estimated the parameter value of a after the value of b is fixed in the following equation:

$y - b = a/x$.

The study estimated the value of a by the nonlinear (NL) estimation method. The result is as follows:

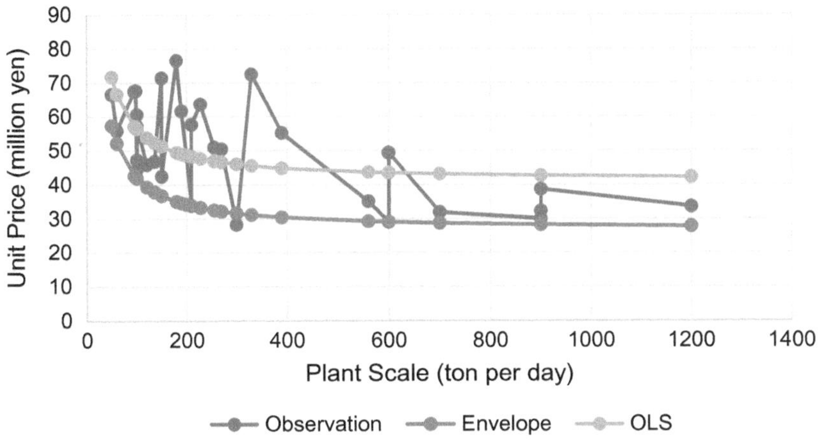

Figure 7.3 Ordinary least squares (OLS) estimated value and the envelope

Parameter	Estimate	Standard Error	t-statistic	P-value
A	3232.85	381.135	8.48218	[.000]

Standard errors computed from quadratic form of analytic first derivatives (Gauss)
Std. error of regression = 15.8270
R-squared = .247943
Adjusted R-squared = .247943

Figure 7.4 shows the envelope derived by the NL estimation and that derived by the OLS method.

From Figure 7.4, the OLS-based estimating equation follows the envelope of the observed values. It is possible to compare the observed and theoretical unit prices for each scale using the envelope. By focusing on the difference between them, the study calculates the overestimation of the target price relative to the estimated target price. That amount exceeds 116.5 billion yen for 32 properties subject to the surcharge payment, equivalent to 10.5% of the total target price of 1.1031 trillion yen. Thus, there is room for improvement in the estimation of the target prices by local governments. Moreover, if a target price is calculated in anticipation of a profit rate of 10%, the expected target price will be as shown in Figure 7.5.[7]

7.6 Claim for damages

There were cases of claiming damages from local residents. After the cease-and-desist order was issued against the five major companies in June 2006, cases

7 This calculation uses the equation of profit rate = (target price – cost)/target price, and the target price is obtained by the term, cost/0.9.

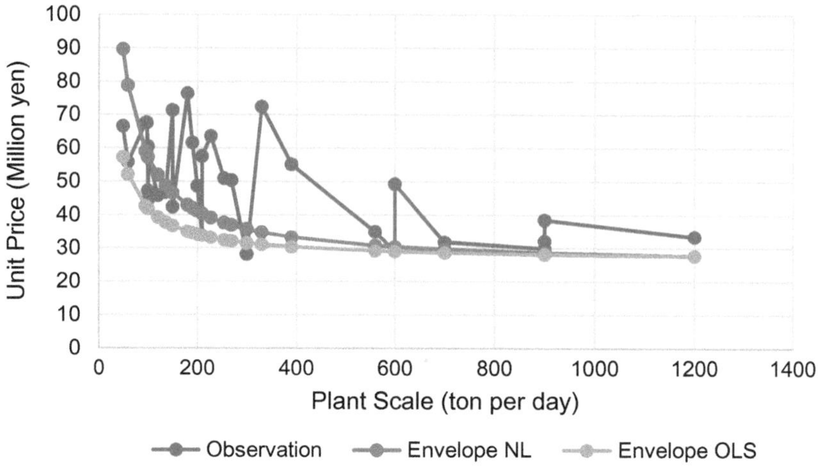

Figure 7.4 Two types of envelopes (ordinary least squares [OLS] and nonlinear estimations)

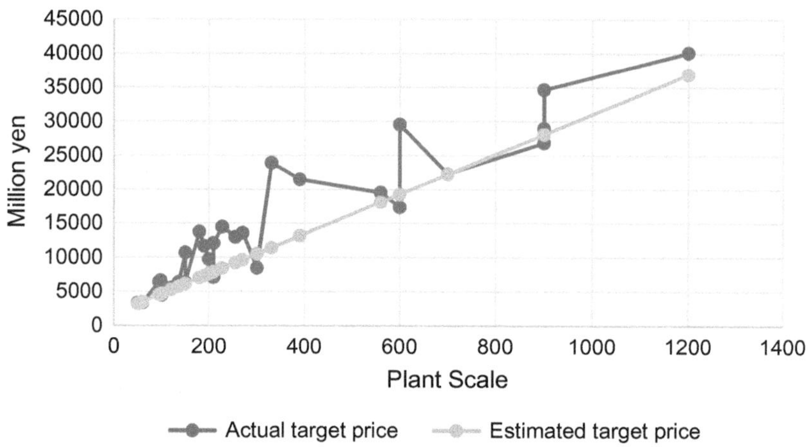

Figure 7.5 Actual target price and estimated target price

of damage claims for stoker furnace bid-rigging occurred in various places. The lawsuits for residents were based on Article 25 of the Local Autonomy Act. Some of the confirmed cases can be seen on the website of the National Citizen Ombudsman Liaison Conference. This was compiled in January 2013. Table 7.6 summarizes the confirmed results.

Beyond the National Citizen Ombudsman Liaison Conference materials, some cases ended without being appealed to the Supreme Court before 2013, cases that were settled, and cases that are currently pending. Search the LEX/DB Internet database, such as property nos. 5, 9, 10, 19, 26, 29, 32, 33, 34, 47, 49, 55, 57, 59, 62, 75, 79, 84, and 87.

Table 7.6 Results of the Supreme Court's decision on the claim for damages (partially as of January 2013)

Property no.	*Allocation*	*Date*	*Compensation amount (Million yen)*
3	Tama New Town	April 2007	1286.47
17	Ageo City	May 2009	0
18 (39)	Yokohama City	April 2009	3017.9
22	Toyosaka County	December 2007	48.925
43	Kobe City	April 2009	1637.7
53	Amagasaki City	July 2011	336.0
55	Atami City	April 2009	0
58	Kyoto City	April 2007	1831.2
83	Yonago City	January 2009	1140.72

Considering the series of rulings, various cases, such that the claim for damages, was finally accepted, and the claim for damages was dismissed. In some cases, judgments are reversed during the transition from the District Court through the High Court to the final appeal to the Supreme Court. The stability of the judgment is not ensured.

7.7 Conclusion

The study examined the cases of stoker furnace bid-rigging and the accompanying damage compensation cases. Regarding the general tide, there are variations in the judgments of claims for damages, and there are several reasons such claims for damages cannot be recognized by the courts. This situation directly regards legal certainty and would require a direction toward less judgmental swings in the future.

Regarding the successful bid rate, it will become a high figure given collusion because the contractors' forecast of the target price has a certain degree of accuracy. Moreover, when there is competition, the successful bid price is inevitably lowered. However, does the high bid rate prove the existence of collusion? Even without bid-rigging, when the target price set by the local governments is lower than what the contractors expected, the bidding price of the contractors may approach the target price even in the case of competition, and the successful bid rates may reach near to 100%.

Even so, a high successful bid rate would be a necessary condition for collusion. Considering the current situation, a high successful bid rate is probably the first indicator to check when suspecting the existence of bid-rigging. Finally, regarding the target price, there is a range of target prices even for the same scale. There is room for the local governments to consider whether the current methods for calculating the target price are appropriate.

8 Tama district in Tokyo bid-rigging case

A bid-rigging case in which the winning bid was polarized

8.1 Introduction

Considering the rulings related to the bid-rigging case, the study finds the date and place in the bid-rigging process, the actions of the parties to the rigging, and the agreed items. However, few judicial precedents record the target price and the details of bidders and include information such as the bid prices presented by each bidder and the successful bid price. The judgment analyzed in the present chapter includes economic statistics that can withstand economic analysis.

One characteristic of this case is that there are two restrictions regarding the boundary of the successful bid price. Usually, the target price calculated by the ordering party is the upper bound for the successful bid price. In this case, other restrictions regarding the lower bound include the ordering party that sets up the minimum limit price for the property. It is defined as the 80% of the target price. Therefore, in this case, bidders suffer upper and lower bounds, and the successful bid price must exist between the target price and the minimum limit price.

The general contractors engaged in the collusion were subject to administrative penalties for violating the AMA and to the surcharge payment. Moreover, they must respond to claims for damages from residents (consumers). Judicial rulings have been relatively harsh on such claims for damages from residents as plaintiffs for bid-rigging and price-fixing cartels. One of the reasons is the challenge for the plaintiffs to prove the existence of bid-rigging and a causal relationship between bid-rigging and higher successful bid prices in courts.

In this case, the plaintiffs took a different method of claiming damages from the conventional procedure. For example, the Tsuruoka kerosene case in Chapter 3 was a class action suit by consumers based on Article 3 of the AMA. However, this time, it is a lawsuit by residents based on Article 242-2 of the Local Autonomy Act. This point will be discussed in the next chapter.

Section 8.2 describes the Tama area bid-rigging case and proposes a theoretical model called the perfect forecasting target price model. Section 8.3 evaluates the model. Section 8.4 denotes comprehensive consideration, and section 8.5 concludes this chapter.

DOI: 10.4324/9781003370444-8

8.2 Case of Tama district in Tokyo bid-rigging

8.2.1 Overview of the case

This case is a violation of the AMA, where general contractors cooperated to negotiate the successful bid price for public works. The period covered by the case is from October 1, 1997, to September 27, 2000. The ordering is the Public Corporation for New City Construction in Tokyo (abbreviated as Public Corporation) linked to the TMG. The Public Corporation engaged in urban infrastructure development projects, and it placed orders for public sewerage construction works in the Tama district in Tokyo, including Hachioji City, Hino City, Machida City, Tachikawa City, and neighboring cities and towns, to general contractors and local contractors. When placing an order for a construction project with a target price of five million yen or more, the Public Corporation must decide on the contractor through designated competitive bidding.

The Public Corporation adjusted the nominated bidders to participate in the designated competitive bidding among qualified contractors who had the human resources and facility capacity to perform the construction. It usually nominated ten bidders or ten JVs, comprising two companies. There were 80 general contractors and 165 local contractors involved in this case.

When a property is put up for bid, the Public Corporation must calculate the maximum price of the property called the target price. The target price was determined by considering the cost of completing the property and the profit of the successful bid winner, which was not disclosed. The price equivalent to 80% of the target price was set as the minimum limit price. Therefore, the upper limit as the target price and the lower limit as the minimum limit price were considered the price range of the successful bid price. The lowest bid price among the bidders was considered the successful bid price.

The social organization for the general contractors in the Tama district, called San-Tama Kenyukai, was the background that made bid-rigging possible. It was a social gathering of sales managers of the general contractors with the sales offices in the Tama district. There were 80 general contractors on the list, and the general contractors were divided into two groups (34 and 46) regarding this case. The former 34 general contractors were accused of being parties to the violations.

There was a basic agreement to prevent the order price from falling among the 80 general contractors. The contents of the basic agreement to receive the order from the Public Corporation among the bidders include the following: (1) The winning bidder for the property would perform the construction in question in the past. (2) The winning bidder for the property would relate to the construction site of the construction in question. (3) When only one company wishes to receive an order for the construction works, it is regarded as the prospective bid winner. Moreover, if there are multiple applicants for the order, the prospective order recipient should be decided through negotiation among them. (4) The winning bid price is determined by the prospective bidder, and other bidders cooperate such that the order can be received at the price determined by the prospective bidder.

Such a basic agreement aimed to secure the profits of the industry and technological and economic aspects. As for the technological aspect, if the public works have already been done once or are in the adjacent area, the prospective contractor understands the technical challenge of each process because of the accumulation of past construction know-how at the property. Further, the contractor can easily address unforeseen situations such as groundwater gushing and ground subsidence. On the economic aspect, as basic surveys have already been completed, the contractor needs no costs incurred before starting construction works or no costs in transporting newly ordered machinery. As the absence of such costs leads to cost savings, the prospective contractor would get higher profits consequently.

Of the 80 general contractors, 34 were accused in the case. The violating general contractors were limited among the group involved by the basic agreement. The JFTC recognized that the other 46 general contractors were cooperators and not the group members covering the basic agreement.[1]

In the process of deciding on the successful bidder, there was a bid-rigging. After issuing a notice of tender, the Public Corporation decided on bidders to participate in the designated competitive bidding. If a general contractor selected by the Public Corporation hoped to win the bid for the property, it expressed the desire to receive the order to the Director who was the employee of the major general contractor at the Tama sales office and also the chairman of the social organization called San-Tama Kenyukai. He advised on whether the bidder could get a successful bid and gave suggestions for future sales policies to become the prospective contractor.

The prospective general contractor informed the other general contractors involved in the bidding of the successful bid price. Receiving this, the other general contractors bid at a price higher than the successful bid price or bid at a price lower than the minimum limit price. Figure 8.1 illustrates these processes.

The accused were 34 general contractors (38 properties), and 30 general contractors (31 properties) were ordered to pay surcharges. There are three litigation issues:

1 Here is a summary of the basic numbers. The total number of bids for the properties in the case is 72. During the bid-rigging period, general contractors won the bids for 40 properties. Therefore, the number of properties won by the local contractors is 32. Thirty-four companies were accused, and 38 properties were the target of bid-rigging. Four of the accused companies (four properties) were not fined. Among the four contractors who received orders for multiple properties, three properties were not subject to violations. Therefore, seven properties were not subject to the surcharge payment. Thus, 30 general contractors and 31 properties were, ultimately, subject to the surcharge payment.

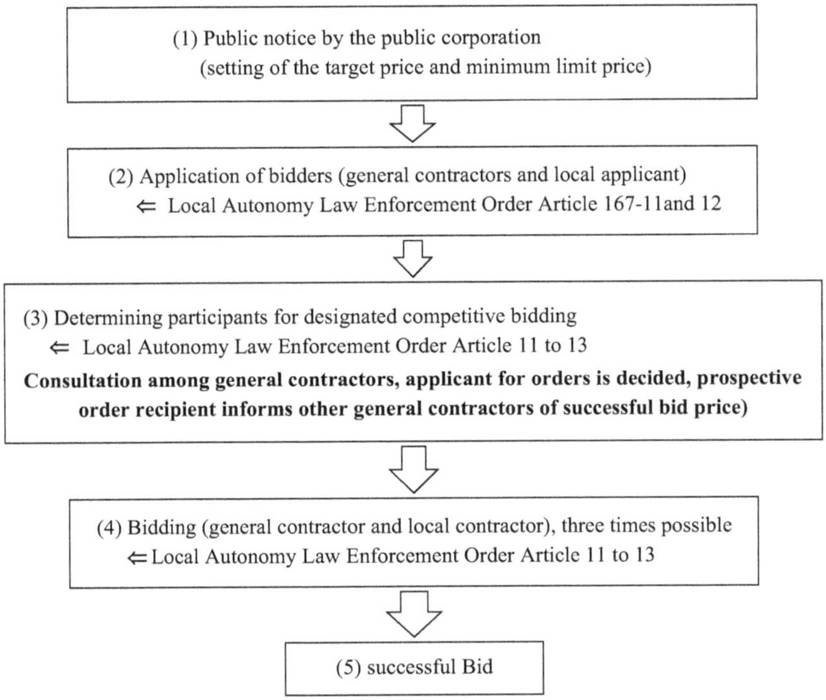

Figure 8.1 The process from the public notice to the successful bid

(1) Existence or non-existence of the basic agreement.[2]
(2) Whether the basic agreement imposes substantial restrictions on competition.
(3) Whether the 38 properties are subject to a surcharge.[3]

Regarding issue (1), the court acknowledged that the general contractors had agreed to mutually cooperate, and the illegal general contractors cooperate for the prospective general contractor to receive the order. Therefore, the court ruled that the existence of the basic agreement was recognized.

Regarding issue (2), the criteria used for judgment at the court were the number of illegal general contractors and collaborators (other general contractors) expected to cooperate at the bidding. The larger the number of general

2 One of the points at issue in the trial decision is whether there is a basic agreement on bid-rigging. Generally, there may be no document agreed upon between the general contractors. The existence of the basic agreement depends on whether the examiner can prove that the bid-rigging practiced for many years is based on the basic agreement that does not exist as the document.

3 Concretely, the examiner must prove that there was an adjustment act between the contractors regarding the property and that this resulted in the effect of restricting competition.

contractors participating in the bidding, the more likely the illegal general contractors would be influenced to get the bid by the prospective contractor and the proposed successful bid price. Moreover, the court considered the bidding behavior of outsiders (local contractors) in bidding. According to this standard, the 34 general contractors were examined, and the 33 general contractors were finally declared illegal.

Regarding issue (3), Article 7-2, Paragraph 1 of the AMA stipulates that the basic data for calculating surcharges is the sales amount of the relevant goods or services. Therefore, the surcharge was set as the cost related to the completion of the successful bid. The contractors subject to the surcharge include (1) illegal general contractors based on the basic agreement, (2) the prospective general contractor based on the basic agreement, and (3) illegal general contractors who are subcontractors of the JV. However, when the number of outsiders is relatively large, the court considered the condition of whether the outsiders engaged in competitive behavior.

The basic agreement is not a legally binding agreement like a contract. However, such a practice existed as content regarding coordinating orders and cooperating in bidding. Moreover, it was widely known among the general contractors in the Tama district because of the succession from their predecessors. Thus, the 33 general contractors respected and complied with the basic agreement, and it functioned effectively as a rule for order coordination. According to this rule, prospective bidders obtained the cooperation of other general contractors belonging to 33 illegal general contractors and collaborators and made successful bids for the desired properties.[4] Twenty-five out of the 30 companies appealed the decision to the Tokyo High Court. Ultimately, the Supreme Court rejected the claim of the general contractors. In this way, they imposed the surcharge.

8.2.2 Statistical data related to the present case

Based on the materials included in the trial decision and the judgment, the study examined the distribution of the successful bid rates (ratio of the successful bid price and the target price), individual bid status and winning bid price for individual properties, and the characteristics of contractors who bid but were not successful.

8.2.2.1 Successful bid rates

The general contractors won the bids for 40 out of the 72 bidding properties. First, consider the successful bid rates of all 72 properties using a histogram.

4 The Supreme Court certified that this basic agreement satisfies the requirement of binding the business activities stipulated in Article 2, Paragraph 6 of the AMA. With the establishment of this basic agreement, a communication of intentions was formed between the general contractors, in which they mutually recognized and accepted to act based on the agreement and were in step with each other. Therefore, the basic agreement can also satisfy the requirement in the same paragraph jointly and mutually.

Figure 8.2 indicates three histograms. Figure 8.2(a) plots the successful bid rates for the 72 properties. They are polarized and concentrated in two intervals near 80% and near 100%. In the figure, they are plotted as an increment of 2.5, with 8 levels from 80% to 100%. Fifteen properties (approximately 20%) in the interval (section Y^3) have a successful bid rate of 80 to 82.5%, and 49 properties (approximately 68%) in the interval (section Y^1) have a successful bid rate between 97.5% and 100%. Thus, 64 out of 72 properties (almost 90% of the total) are concentrated near the target price or the minimum limit price. Regarding the intervals of Y^1 and Y^3, the section is further narrowed: Y^{1+} is set an interval from 99% to 100%, and the number of properties belonging to this interval is 39 properties. When the interval from 80% to 81% is set as Y^{3-}, the number of properties belonging to this interval is 15, which is the same as Y^3. The number of properties included in Y^{1+} and Y^{3-} is 54 or 75% of all properties.

Figure 8.2(b) is a histogram of 40 properties won by the general contractors. Seven properties (approximately 17%) are in the lowest class (Y^3), and 30 properties (75%) are in the highest class (Y^1).

Figure 8.2(c) is a histogram of 32 properties won by the local contractors. There are eight properties in the lowest class (Y^3, 25% of the total) and 19 properties in the highest class (Y^1, approximately 59% of the total).

In the graph divided into general and local contractors, as with the overall histogram, the bidding rates are polarized, indicating that the successful bid rates are concentrated in the two intervals near 80% and 100%. From these figures, regardless of whether they were general or local contractors, the winning bidders predicted the target price accurately. Moreover, when prospective bidders foresee the existence of strong competitors for a certain property, the prospective bidders aim to win the bid even at the minimum limit price equivalent to 80% of the target price.[5]

Table 8.1 shows the successful bid rate frequency by interval for all the properties, for the 40 (32) properties won by the general (local) contractors. This table provides the basic data for testing the validity of the economic model described later.

8.2.2.2 Individual bid status and winning bid price

Consider the individual bid status for the individual property to examine the characteristics of the bid status for the successful bidder and other unsuccessful bidders. This material is attached to the High Court ruling, which shows all the bid prices and the successful bid price for the 15 properties.

5 There are three possibilities to get the bid at the minimum limit price. First, the successful bidders make a profit even if they receive the order for the property; second, they can cover the fixed cost even if they do not make a profit; and they get the successful bid for the property at risk of loss as a stepping stone for the future.

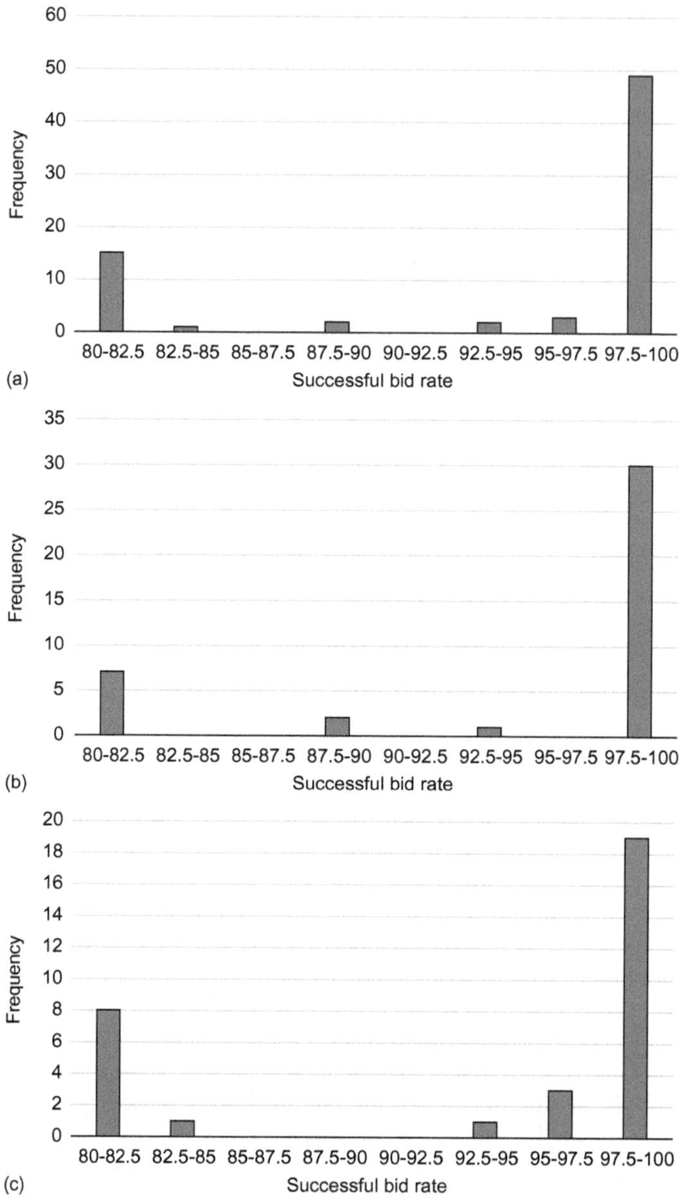

Figure 8.2 (a) Successful bid rates for 72 properties. (b) Successful bid rates for the general contractors. (c) Successful bid rates for the local contractors

Table 8.1 Bid rate frequency table for general contractors X_1 and local contractors X_2

	Y^3 *(80.0–82.5%)*	Y^2 *(82.5)–97.5%)*	Y^1 *(97.5–100%)*	Total
General contractors X_1 Properties bided by illegal general contractors	1 (A)	2	28	31
Properties bided by not Illegal general contractors	6 (B)	1 (C)	2 (D)	9
Total Number (Note)	7 [7]	3	30 (22)	40
Local contractors X_2	8 [8]	5	19 (17)	32
Total Including number	15 [15]	8	49 (39)	72

In the ruling, the target price, the bid prices of ten bidders or ten JVs, and the successful bid prices of violating general contractors were reported for the 15 properties. Figure 8.3 indicates the status of bid prices. The study classified the status of bid prices into three types in Figures 8.3(a), 8.3(b), and 8.3(c), respectively.

In Type I, only the successful bidder submitted a bid price lower than the target price, and the other nine bidders presented bid prices higher than the target price. In this type, the prospective bidder encourages other bidders to bid at a price higher than his bid price, thereby disqualifying the other bidders. This is a typical case type. Eight properties out of the 15 properties correspond to the Type I.

In Type II, the bid prices of multiple violating general contractors are included between the target price and the successful bid price. For this type, several general contractors appear to be competing in bid price between the target price and the minimum limit price. Accordingly, the judgment regarding competitiveness was divided per whether the successful bid price of the illegal general contractor was close to the target price or the minimum limit price. If the successful bid price was close to the target price, cooperation was suspected, and if it was close to the minimum limit price, there was a high possibility of competition. There are three properties of this type.

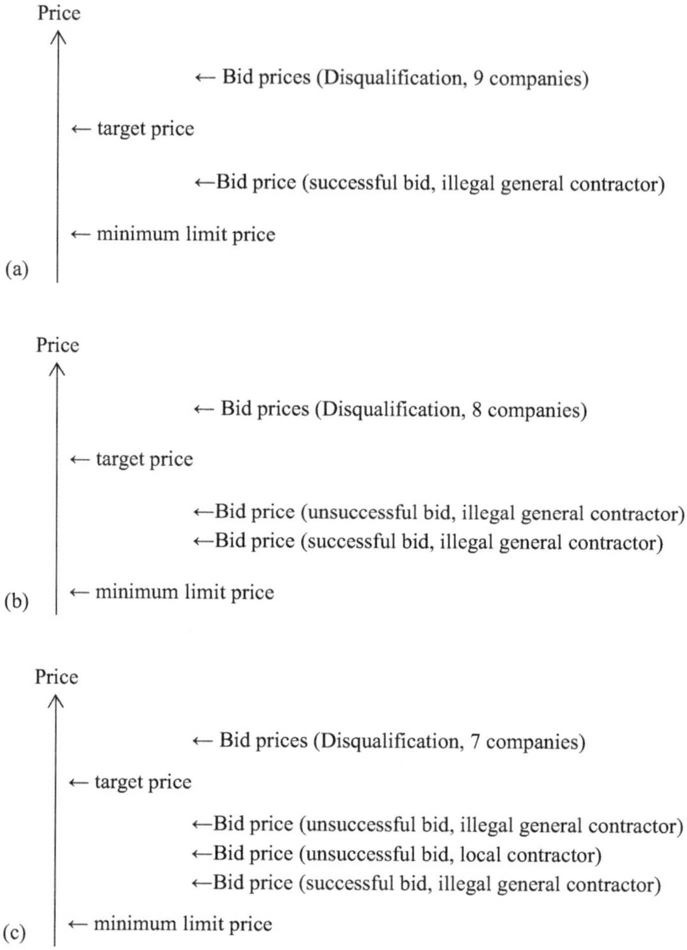

Figure 8.3 (a) Observed bidding status: Type I. (b) Observed bidding status: Type II. (c) Observed bidding status: Type III

In Type III, multiple general and local contractors enter between the target price and the successful bid price. Similar to Type II, competitiveness was judged per whether the successful bid price of the illegal general contractor was close to the target price or the minimum limit price.[6]

6 On the assumption that there was no agreement between the general and local contractors, the local contractors behaved independently. Thus, they appear to have competed. When there is an agreement between the general contractors and the local contractors, it is possible to cooperate, and the successful bid price approaches the target price. Therefore, the successful bid rate reaches unity.

8.2.2.3 The number of applications by the illegal general contractors, the number of successful bids of the illegal general contractor, and the timing of successful bids by illegal general contractor

During the execution period, many violating general contractors won the bid for the property. Five violating general contractors won the bids for two or more properties. Considering the location of the construction site and the timing of the bidding, there was a tendency for continuity of place and time. No contractor received the order for construction works in a completely different location at the same time. Regarding the number of bid applications submitted for the 72 properties, there were eight violating general contractors who applied more than ten during the three-year execution period, but successful bidding was only one for the eight violating general contractors. Thus, there were many opportunities for general contractors to apply for a bid at the request of a prospective bidder.

8.2.3 Making the perfect forecasting target price model: An attempt to explain the data

As an economic model of bid-rigging, it is necessary to consider collusion between general contractors, the strength of cooperation between the local contractors, and the relationship between local and general contractors. In the following, the study sets up a model to determine a successful bid price, identifying competitiveness or cooperativeness. It then tests the realistic validity of the model using the statistical data created in the previous section.

Using the successful bid rate as an indicator, the study presents a perfect forecasting target price model for the bidding behavior of two kinds of contractors (general contractor X_1 and local contractor X_2). It identifies the successful bid price from competition or cooperation per the model. The study sets up the following assumptions about the perfect forecasting target price model regarding a property:

Assumption 1: The general and local contractors accurately predict the target price made by the Public Corporation.

Assumption 2: There are two types of bidding properties: (1) a general contractor wants to make a successful bid for the property, and (2) no general contractor wants to bid on a property.

Assumption 3: When the general contractor wants to make a successful bid, it makes every effort to win the bid.

Assumption 4: The local contractors act after the intention of the general contractors becomes clear.

Assumption 5: There may (not) be a cooperative relationship between the local and the general contractors. There may also (not) be cooperation between the local contractors.

Assumption 6: the local contractors would feed back the results of cooperation or competition among local contractors to the general contractors only

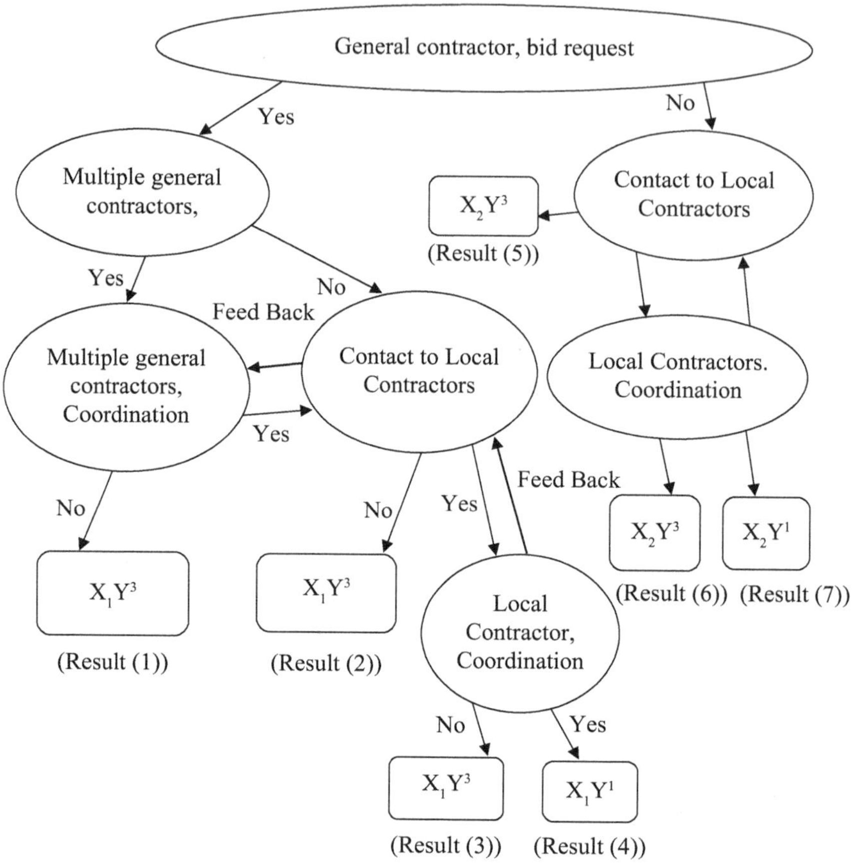

Figure 8.4 Perfect forecasting target price model

(Note 1) Y^1 and Y^3 are the intervals of 97.5% and 100% and that of 80% and 82.5%, respectively. From the figure, Y^1 and Y^3 also indicate the successful bid prices as the price near the target price and that near the minimum limit price, respectively. (Note 2) This flowchart is not a game tree in game theory because feedback is included in the game tree. In such a case, it is not feasible to use the technique of backward induction, which is used to solve expansion-type games.

when the general contractors inform the local contractors of establishing collusion among the general contractors.

Assumption 7: The nominated contractors participate in the bidding regardless of whether they are general or local contractors.

Assumption 8 There are two levels of successful bid prices: the value near the target price by cooperation and the value near the minimum limit price by competition.

With Assumptions 1 through 8, Figure 8.4 indicates the seven decisions in a flow chart. In the figure, there are several branching conditions for decision-making: (1) whether a general contractor wishes to successfully bid on a certain property; (2) whether the basic agreement is accepted among general contractors; (3) whether the basic agreement by the general contractors is communicated to the local contractors; and (4) whether a cooperative relationship can be established between the local contractors for the successful bid.

Now, check the final result with a flow chart that runs from the top to the bottom. When a property is publicized, the general contractors decide whether to bid on the property. When multiple general contractors decide to bid on the property and do not reach an agreement, competition over price inevitably occurs among the multiple contractors regardless of the presence of the local contractors. Here, based on Assumptions 3 and 8, Y^3 is selected for the general contractor to win the bid with certainty. It can be written as (X_1, Y^3). In this case, there was a price competition between the general contractors (Indicated Result (1) in the figure).[7]

Next, consider the case where one general contractor wishes to win the bid, and the basic agreement is reached through collusion between the general contractors. If this agreement is not informed to the local contractor, the decision of the general contractor would be (X_1, Y^3) based on Assumption 3, as indicated in the second result (Result (2) in the figure). Although the agreement was reached between general contractors, there may be competition with the local contractors. Therefore, the successful bid price is Y^3 for the general contractor to win the bid reliably.

If a general contractor wishes to win the bid, the agreement is reached among the general contractors, and the information is sent to the local contractors, what happens to the successful bid price? Results (3) or (4) happen. If the local constructors receive information on the agreement among the general contractors, and they feed information of no cooperation among them back to the general contractors, where this situation also stems from Assumption 3, the general contractor sets the bid to secure the successful bid of Y^3 (Result (3)). When the local contractors receive the agreement between the general contractors and they agree with it and feed back that fact to the general contractor, it surely sets Y^1 as the bid price and wins the bid at Y^1. The result is (X_1, Y^1) (Result (4)).

Next, consider the case where the general contractor does not want the property. Thus, the nominated general contractors to participate in the bid are disqualified by bidding at a bid price higher than the target price or lower than the minimum limit price. The successful bidder becomes a local contractor X_2 from Results (5) to (7). If the general contractor does not inform the local contractor that they do not want to bid on the property, the local contractor will get a bid. The successful bid price is determined by competition as the lowest bid price among the local contractors, which becomes (X_2, Y^3) (Result (5)). Next, consider the case where the local contractors receive a message from the general contractors that they do not wish to bid on the property. Meanwhile, the branch point regards whether cooperation among the local contractors can

7 As explained in the note of Figure 8.4, Y^1 and Y^3 indicate the successful bid prices as the price near the target price and that near the minimum limit price, respectively.

Table 8.2 Successful bidders and contract prices derived from the perfect forecasting target price model and the distinction between competitive and non-competitive by economics definition

General contractor X_1				
Result	(1)	(2)	(3)	(4)
successful bid price	Y^3	Y^3	Y^3	Y^1
	Competition	Competition	Competition	Non-competition
Local trader X_2				
Result	(5)	(6)		(7)
successful bid price	Y^3	Y^3		Y^1
	Competition	Competition		Non-competition

be achieved. If there is no cooperation, the local contractor wins the bid at the minimum limit price as (X_2, Y^3) (Result (6) in the figure). However, if they can cooperate, the successful bid price of Y^1 can be written as (X_2, Y^1) (Result (7)).

Now, consider the question of whether competition occurred. In this case, whether a property is subject to competition can be divided into three kinds of competition: competition among the general contractors, that between general and local contractors, and that among local contractors. Furthermore, one can distinguish between formal and substantive competition. Formal competition is bid-rigging, and the outcome is known before bidding. Substantial competition is assumed in economics. The basis of competition in economics is price competition. The successful bidder offers the lowest bid price.
Table 8.2 shows the distinction between competition and non-competition per the definition in economics. In Results (1), (2), and (3), at least the general contractors are the competitors or the local contractors become competitors against the general contractors. Result (4) has no competitors. Results (5) through (7) are competitions unrelated to collusion between general contractors. Result (5) is potential competition with general contractors. Result (6) is competition among the local contractors. Result (7) has no competitors.

8.3 Evaluation and limitations of the perfect forecasting target price model from observed facts: Does theory contradict facts?[8]

There are eight assumptions in the perfect forecasting target price model. The validity of these assumptions can be confirmed by corroborative evidence. The bidding behavior of Assumption 8 is a bidding method in which unlimited bidding is possible. This process lacks reality. In the actual bidding, only two additional bids are allowed after the first bid fails. However, the observed value in this

8 The basic principle of empirical sciences asks the question, "Does theory contradict facts?" not "Does facts contradict theory?"

Table 8.3 Bid rate frequency table for the general contractors X_1 and the local contractors X_2

	Y^3 (80.0–82.5%)	Y^2 (82.5–97.5%)	Y^1 (97.5–100%)	Total
General contractors X_1				
Total	7 (17.5%)	3 (7.5%)	30 (75.0%)	40
Results	(1),(2),(3)	—	(4)	
Local contractors X_2	8 (25.0%)	5 (15.6%)	19 (59.3%)	32
Results	(5),(6)	—	(7)	
Total	15 (20.8%)	8 (11.1%)	49 (68.0%)	72

bid-rigging approached the target price and the minimum limit price by a small number of bids. In this case, Assumption 8 surprisingly applies to the observed facts. Therefore, the study bases these observations on the theoretical model and considers whether cooperation, as defined by economics, is consistent with the illegality of the contractors involved in the unreasonable restrictions on trade stipulated in the AMA, as indicated in the ruling. From Figure 8.4, Table 8.2 summarizes the successful bid prices and the degree of competitiveness.

According to Table 8.3, the successful bid prices become Y^3 and Y^1 from the perfect forecasting target price model. From the data indicated in Table 8.1, out of the 72 properties, 15 properties are included in the interval of Y^3, eight properties are included in the interval of Y^2, and 49 are included in the interval of Y^1. In the present model, there are no intervals of Y^2, including the theoretical value. The rate of including Y^2 in the observation is 11.1% out of the total observation.

Considering the results divided into general contractors X_1 and local contractors X_2, the present model shows that only the intervals of Y^3 and Y^1 appear. However, according to Table 8.1, there are three observations for the interval of Y^2, with 7.5% of the general contractors, and five observations for the interval of Y^2, with 15.6% of local contractors.

8.4 Comprehensive consideration

Table 8.3 is a summary based on Tables 8.1 and 8.2 and Figure 8.4. Assumption 8 of the model, if there is competition among contractors regarding bid price, the successful bid price would be close to the minimum limit price. However, if there is cooperation, the successful bid price would be close to the target price. Under AMA, competition is not an offense, but cooperation is. Thus, is cooperative behavior in economics the same as unfair restraint of trade, which

Table 8.4 Bid rate frequency table for properties by general contractor X_1

	Low	*← successful bid rate →*		*high*
	Υ^3	Υ^2	Υ^1	*Total*
General contractor X_1 Illegal general contractor property	1 (A)	2 (F)	28 (E)	31
Not illegal General contractor properties	6 (B)	1 (C)	2 (D)	9
Total	7	3	30	40

is a violation of the AMA? To address this economist question, the study considers the conclusions by the judgments.

Section 8.4.1 examines the difference between the conclusions obtained from the economic model and the judgment. Section 8.4.2 examines the results of the action if the parties to the basic agreement are all general contractors but not the 34 general contractors classified in the present case.

8.4.1 Judgment on whether there is competition: Differences in judging competition between jurisprudence and economics in this case

The presence (absence) of competition based on economics can be tested by the perfect forecasting target price model. Moreover, judging whether there is a surcharge based on the judgment, it is possible to judge whether there is competition based on jurisprudence. It is interesting to examine how much the economics- and jurisprudence-based conclusions agree with each other. Table 8.4 shows only the portion of general contractors from Table 8.1.

Table 8.4 is categorized into (A), (B), (C), (D), (E), and (F). From the conclusion of economics, there is competition in the categories of (A) and (B), and there is no competition (cooperation) in the categories of (C), (D), (E), and (F). However, in the judgment, given the relationship between the surcharge payments and competition, (B), (C), and (D) were found to compete (i.e., there was no unfair trade restriction), and (A), (E), and (F) were non-competition (there were unfair trade restrictions). To summarize,

Competition: Economics	A	B			
Judgment		B	C	D	
No Competition: Economics			C	D	E F
Judgment	A				E F

Table 8.5 Details of the ten underlined properties in Table 8.3

Property no.	Category	Successful bid rate	Surcharge payment	Competition
1	B	80.00	None (O)	O
4	B	80.09	None (O)	O
8	B	80.00	None (O)	O
9	B	80.08	None (O)	O
10	A	80.00	Yes (×)	O not matching
25	B	80.08	None (O)	O
46	D	99.60	None (O)	× not matching
57	D	98.56	None (O)	× not matching
61	C	92.61	None (O)	× not matching
66	B	80.00	None (O)	O

(Note) See Table 8.4 for categories A, B, C, D, E, and F. The (O) in the surcharge column corresponds to the O in the competition column, indicating that the court judged that there was competition (no surcharge).

Economics agrees with judgments in B (six properties), E (28 properties), and F (two properties) and does not agree with A (one property), C (one property), and D (two properties). Thus, the study selected A (one property), B (six properties), C (one property), and D (two properties) and examined the characteristics of these ten properties. Table 8.5 indicates details of the ten underlined properties in Table 8.3

Category B has a relationship between no surcharge payment and competition based on Assumption 8, commonly corresponding to the successful bid rate of 80%. However, Categories A, C, and D lead to different conclusions between the judgments and the economic model.

In Table 8.5, category A (one property) won the bid by the illegal general contractor with a successful bid rate of 80%. To the successful bidder, two other illegal general contractors participated in the bidding. The successful bidders obtained the cooperation of the illegal general contractors, and their bid prices were higher than the target prices. Further, the bid prices of the two local contractors were close to the target price (100%). Therefore, the court ruled that there was no competition with the local contractors because of the disparity between the winning bidder's price and the bids of other bidders.

In category C (one property), the successful bidder won property no. 61 with a successful bid rate of 92.61%. The court ruled that although the general contractors participated in the bids for the property, they were not violating general contractors in the bidders. Therefore, they were not the party to the basic agreement and would not be subject to the surcharge payment.

Category D (two properties) is property nos. 46 and 57. The successful bid rates for these properties are 99.60% and 98.56%, respectively, but escaped paying the surcharge. Though a general contractor participated in the bid for property no. 46, the contractor was a collaborator rather than a violating general contractor and was not a party to the basic agreement. Regarding property no.

57, although two violating general contractors participated in the bidding for the property, the court ruled that they were not regarded as violating general contractors because they were subcontractors of the JV and that there were no parties to the basic agreement. Therefore, it was not subject to the surcharge.

8.4.2 Critical comments

In the trial, the judge recognized the existence of the basic agreement and developed its logic after limiting its scope to the 33 violating general contractors. From the law academics, there was strong criticism against dividing general contractors (80 companies) into violating general contractors (33 companies) and collaborators (47 companies), as in this case. However, it was challenging to identify the violating general contractors among the 80 contractors in practice based solely on the evidence. Moreover, it would not be profitable to extend the investigation to include all the general contractors. Some of the general contractors did not have sales. Therefore, the surcharge payment is nothing, as the surcharge can only be imposed on the properties during the execution period of this case. Even if the parties to the basic agreement are expanded to 80 companies, the result regarding the surcharge would not change. That is, the fine is zero for anyone other than the illegal general contractor.

However, combining the legal requirement of communicating intentions with the economic concept of competition can induce other rational decisions about categories A, C, and D. The following view assumes that the parties to the basic agreement are 80 general contractors and that the agreement is a practice that everyone recognizes among the general contractors and is shared knowledge. Probing the actual successful bids reveals that for one property, violating general contractor A is the successful bidder, and violating general contractor B assists. For another property, violating general contractor B is the winning bidder, and violating general contractor A is the assist. This is called the logic of lending and borrowing between two contractors.

The prospective general contractor surely asks for their assistance to get the bid from among the 80 general contractors. Thus, the structure of mutual aid (lean back) between general contractors was maintained. If the parties to the basic agreement were expanded to 80 general contractors and the economic model was applied, there would be the following four changes.

Property no.	*Original category*	*After change*	*Surcharge*
10	A →	B	No
46	D →	E	Yes
57	D →	E	Yes
61	C →	E	Yes

From this new perspective, property nos. 46 (successful bid rate 99.60%), 57 (successful bid rate 98.56%), and 61 (successful bid rate 92.61%) are subject to the surcharge. Property no. 10 (successful bid rate 80.00%) is not subject to the surcharge. Such a decision would eliminate the unfairness related to the successful bid rate for those subject to the surcharge.

8.5 Conclusion

Economics emphasizes concepts such as market, competition, and price. The AMA has the concepts of market, competition, and price. However, there are subtle differences in economics and law. These issues were examined using cases of bid-rigging. The market in economics is replaced as a particular field of trade in the AMA and is a common concept in the domestic market. However, with competition, there are certain differences. Competition in economics is competition regarding price. In the AMA, the focus is on the status of the market. Regarding price, when economics addresses competitive price, it means equilibrium price in a perfectly competitive market. It is, nonetheless, different from competitive price in jurisprudence.

Hence, economics and jurisprudence sometimes have slightly different concepts and definitions regarding technical terms in economics. It is, indeed, one of the factors hindering mutual understanding between economics and law. Education for mutual understanding would be beneficial for the design of future legal systems.

9 Tama district bid-rigging case

Compensation of damages by local residents

9.1 Introduction

Freedom of personality, *freedom of ownership*, *freedom of contract*, and the *principle of liability for negligence* are the major premises of property law in jurisprudence. The principle of liability for negligence is that a person is liable for damages to another person only when there is intent or negligence. Of the four premises, economics does not include the principle of liability for negligence. Its removal from the premises of economics has certainly contributed to the development of economics. If economics includes it as one of the premises, the economic model would be much more complicated, as shown in Chapter 2. The standard economic model based on microeconomics would not easily solve the competitive equilibrium model of the Walrasian system. However, removing the principle of liability for negligence causes various problems when analyzing the actual economy.[1] The economic model is remarkably not aligned with its relevance to the real world. In other words, when economic troubles occur in the actual economic society, many situations cannot be resolved with the current economic model. Specific problems include, of course, consumer damage caused by illegal price-fixing and bid-rigging presented in this book. Moreover, there is the issue of damages to consumers caused by the destruction of the environment, which has frequently occurred in recent years, and compensation for damages related to large-scale disasters.

From that perspective, introducing the premise of the principle of liability for negligence in the analysis is an important theoretical advance while being based on existing economics. This chapter examines two types of legal proceedings,

1 There are some problems with the explicit incorporation of the principle of liability for negligence into the economic model. One problem is that a legal system must be introduced as a standard for confirming illegality in the model. As mentioned in Chapter 2, legal systems differ among countries, making it challenging to ensure the universality of the model. A second problem is that the model needs a block that considers illegality cases. From a model-solving perspective, the introduction of this block requires a feedback loop. Solving the feedback model requires enormous computational power. By the way, the existing model is an open-loop model. The new model itself will not be a Walrasian equilibrium model based on selfishness but would be a Nash equilibrium model based on selfishness that considers reactions to others.

DOI: 10.4324/9781003370444-9

class action lawsuits and civil lawsuits for the cases of consumer damage claims. A class action lawsuit was used in the case of consumers' damage claim related to the price-fixing case of petroleum products in Chapter 3. A class action lawsuit is a civil lawsuit filed by multiple people who share a common interest in the same incident. In class action lawsuits, Article 709 of the Civil Code is the basic provision for claims for damages. However, in a civil lawsuit, there is a case where local residents are the plaintiffs. This lawsuit arose when the plaintiffs recognized that the local government was not properly managing its financial administration. There, the plaintiffs argue for the optimization of the local financial administration as the representative of the interests of all residents (public interest). This lawsuit is based on the resident audit request of the citizen litigation system set forth in Article 242-2 of the Local Autonomy Act.

Continuing from the previous chapter, this chapter examines the case of claiming damages from local residents related to the Tama district bid-rigging cases in Section 9.2. Section 9.3 makes a comprehensive evaluation.

9.2 Tama district bid-rigging Case: Claim for Damages

9.2.1 Overview of the incident

When the general contractors committed illegal acts of collusion and were subject to criminal or administrative matters, they were detained, fined, and surcharged. Meanwhile, in recent years, the general contractors have been sued for damages by local residents (consumers) or local governments. The residents of Hachioji City, Machida City, Hino City, and Tachikawa City, the satellite cities in Greater Tokyo, requested the mayors of their respective cities to exercise their right to claim damages against the general contractors involved in the collusion. However, the Resident Audit Committee of each city rejected the resident audit request. The main reason was that the city was not in a position to independently determine whether collusion existed at the time the JFTC trial was in court. In May 2002, the residents of each city filed lawsuits claiming compensation for damages. In Hachioji City, the 12 general contractors were defendants. In Hino City, there were two general contractors as the defendants, and in Machida City, there were ten general contractors as the defendants. In Tachikawa City, there were three general contractors as the defendants.

The issues in each city were similar. Therefore, the study introduced the points of contention in Hachioji City. There are five points at issue in the claim for damages:

(1) The existence or non-existence of the basic agreement on bid-rigging.
(2) Whether bid-rigging has occurred for individual rigging.
(3) Occurrence of damage in Hachioji City.
(4) The amount of damage.
(5) The failure of the city to claim damages from the defendants under the fact of neglect (illegal omission) referred to in Article 242-2 of the Local Autonomy Act.

Regarding issue (1), the court held that there was a *de facto* practice among the general contractors operating in the Tama district. However, there was not enough evidence to prove that the practice was clearly agreed upon by the 80 contractors or that the basic agreement was specifically established. Moreover, no evidence revealed how binding the practice was. Further, no evidence clarified the circumstances such as what kind of sanctions would be taken if the order for construction was contrary to customary practice. Therefore, the plaintiffs' allegations regarding issue (1) could not be fully adopted. However, issue (2) was examined on the premise that the practice exists individually.

Regarding issue (2), the court ruled that, for the bid-rigging by the illegal general contractors, they should be held liable for tort under Article 715 of the Civil Code. Regarding issue (3), the court acknowledged that the successful bid prices for these biddings were unfairly inflated given collusion by the illegal general contractors. In other words, if there was no bid-rigging and fair competition was ensured, the amount would have been lower. Therefore, the court determined that individual bid-rigging by the illegal general contractors caused damage to Hachioji City.

Regarding issue (4), the court acknowledged that Hachioji City had suffered damages but determined that it would be extremely challenging to prove the amount. Therefore, the court awarded a reasonable amount of damages under Article 248 of the Code of Civil Procedure. The basis for this was the successful bid rate. During the period from October 1997 to September 2000, when bid-rigging occurred, the average successful bid rate for the 72 properties ordered by the Public Corporation was 94.54%. The average successful bid rate for the 139 properties from October 2000 to November 2005 was 89.85%. Therefore, the damage suffered by Hachioji City from collusion was at least equivalent to 5% (i.e., the difference between 94.54% and 89.85%) of each contract amount in these properties.

Regarding issue (5), the court admitted that the Mayor of Hachioji City did not claim damages even though the collusion of the illegal general contractors constituted an unlawful act under the Civil Code. The court ruled that the non-exercise of the Mayor was illegal and that the plaintiffs' claims for damages in this lawsuit had good grounds. The District Court decisions were issued in November 2006 for Hachioji City, July 2007 for Hino City and Machida City, and October 2007 for Tachikawa City. All claims of the plaintiff (residents) were accepted.

The defendants appealed. The High Court's judgments were divided in each city. The ruling of the case of Machida City was dismissing all of these appeals. There was no change in the District Court ruling. In the cases of Hachioji City and Tachikawa City, the claim for damages in the lawsuit by the residents was accepted, but the High Court judges changed the amount of damages. In the Hachioji City ruling, damages were awarded to 11 properties and 11 general contractors recognized by the District Court, but the Tokyo High Court dismissed claims for damages for five of the 11 properties. Thus, damages were awarded for six properties. The amount of damages was determined by the 3%

(not the difference of the successful bid price by 5%) of the contract price. The Tokyo High Court ruling of Tachikawa City accepted the judgment of the District Court regarding the claim for damages, but the amount of damage was significantly reduced. Finally, in the case of Hino City, the High Court ruling was reversed, and the plaintiffs' claim for damages was dismissed.

Dissatisfied with the High Court decision, the appellants in Machida City and the appellees in other cities appealed to the Supreme Court. However, all appeals were dismissed.

9.2.2 Evaluation from the legal perspective

The legal syllogism puts applicable laws as major premises and facts as minor premises and draws a conclusion therefrom. For example,

Major premise (applicable law): Those who intentionally or negligently violate the rights or legally protected interests of others (A) shall be liable for the damages caused thereby (B). (Article 709 of the Civil Code)

Minor premise (relevant facts): The fact that the plaintiffs were paid a price higher than the fair price (C) and that given the bid-rigging of the defendants, the successful bid price was determined to be higher than that of no bid-rigging (A).

The legal syllogism is that (A) is (B) and (C) is (A); therefore, (C) is (B). This syllogism leads to the following conclusion.

Conclusion: As the plaintiffs were paid a higher than fair price (C), the defendants should pay the plaintiffs' damages (B).

For damages to be recognized under Article 709 of the Civil Code, all of the following five requirements must be substantiated: (1) the offending act is intentional or negligent, (2) the perpetrator is responsible, (3) the offending act is illegal, (4) damage has occurred, and (5) there is a causal relationship between the offending act and the damage.

Based on these basic requirements, consider the present case. Taxpayers (residents) claimed damages resulting from collusion between the general contractors involved in public works. The Tama district bid-rigging case was relatively large in scale, with 30 illegal general contractors and 31 illegal properties being the targets of the case. Much of the information is made public through trials and judgments. The direct victims of the Tama district bid-rigging cases were the residents of Hachioji City, Hino City, Machida City, and Tachikawa City. They filed claims for damages against the general contractors, and the cases were decided by the District Courts in Tokyo and the Tokyo High Court. Eight judgments were handed down in the two courts.

The cases that led to the claim for damages were the bid-rigging involving the general contractors. During the trials, the existence of the basic agreement, a requirement for establishing unfair trade restrictions under the AMA, was examined. These materials are also used in cases of claiming damages in the form of written statements. A comparison of these judgments shows that each judgment has a wide range.

Based on these circumstances, Table 9.1 summarizes the changes in the damage of claim amounts of the Tokyo District Court decisions, the Tokyo High Court decisions, and the surcharge payment decisions by the JFTC as the administrative penalty. It shows a list of construction works conducted in Hachioji City, Hino City, Machida City, and Tachikawa City, and the decisions of the District Courts, the High Court, and the surcharge payment by the JFTC.

From the plaintiff's perspective, this study compares the content of the judgment in terms of the degree of acceptability of the claim. In the case of claiming compensation for damages involving Machida City, the plaintiff's claim was broadly accepted. However, in the case involving Hino City, the plaintiff's compensation for damages was not accepted. On the degree of acceptability of claims, the cases of Hachioji City and Tachikawa City were included between Machida City and Hino City.

9.2.3 Comprehensive comments

In the case of claiming damages, proof that the general contractors performed the action of coordinating the order when receiving the order for the property is required. If there were fair competition without order adjustments, evidence would be required that the successful bid price would be lower than the current successful bid price. Elements common to the cases of the Tama district collusion and the case of the Tama district damage compensation include (1) communication of intentions between the general contractors, (2) predictability of the general contractors regarding the target prices, (3) relationship with the local contractors, and (4) the reliability of the testimony record of the JFTC. As there is no direct evidence in the form of documents of the basic agreement, the reliability of the statement of the JFTC strongly affected the judgment of the presence of the elements (1), (2), and (3). Regarding (1), the JFTC and the courts admitted the existence of communication of intentions between the general contractors. Regarding (2), the evidence is that the successful bid rates were close to the target prices of the properties. Now, focus on (3), the relationship with local contractors.

In the case involving Machida City, the order coordinator made a statement about the relationship with local contractors. In principle, prospective general contractors are bound by the long-standing practice (or the basic agreement), but local contractors are not bound by the practice. However, the prospective general contractor and the local contractor discussed the bidding property. In general, on the condition that local contractors will become a subcontractor of the property, they will cooperate with the prospective general contractors. As a characteristic example showing this, a prospective general contractor for a property in Machida City made a mistake during the bidding, and another general contractor won the bid. The prospective general contractor planned to use a specific local contractor as a subcontractor. Therefore, this contractor asked the winning bid general contractor to use the specific local contractor as a subcontractor. The winning bid general contractor entrusted the work to the specific local contractor, except for the on-site management engineers and a few people, according to the request of the prospective general contractor.

Table 9.1 Construction works in Hachioji City, Hino City, Machida City, and Tachikawa City and the corresponding court and surcharge payment decisions

(1) Hachioji City

No.	*Property no.*	*District Court (10,000 yen)*	*High Court (10,000 yen)*		*Surcharge Payment*
1	2	1,283	×	(0.00)	○
2	9	1,475	885	(0.60)	○
3	29	1,921	×	(0.00)	○
4	31	1,207	724	(0.60)	○
5	39	1,246	748	(0.60)	○
6	40	2,483	1,489	(0.60)	○
7	44	1,638	982	(0.60)	○
8	46	1,081	×	(0.00)	×
9	51	×	×	(–)	○
10	56	1,811	×	(0.00)	○
11	59	×	×	(–)	○
12	65	1,512	×	(0.00)	○
13	71	4,147	2,488	(0.60)	○

(2) Hino City

No.	*Property no.*	*District Court (10,000 yen)*	*High Court (10,000 yen)*		*Surcharge Payment*
1	64	1019	×	(0.00)	○

(3) Machida City

No.	*Property no.*	*District Court (10,000 yen)*	*High Court (10,000 yen)*	*Surcharge Payment*
1	7	1,716	Same (1.00)	○
		1,716	Same (1.00)	×
2	6	1,622	Same (1.00)	○
3	13	5,958	Same (1.00)	○
		5,958	Same (1.00)	×
		5,958	Same (1.00)	×
4	22	1,748	Same (1.00)	○
		1,748	Same (1.00)	×
5	27	2,572	Same (1.00)	○
		2,572	Same (1.00)	×
6	38	5,666	Same (1.00)	○

(*Continued*)

7	42	1,538	Same (1.00)	O
		1,538	Same (1.00)	×
		1,538	Same (1.00)	×
8	50	236	Same (1.00)	O
		236	Same (1.00)	×
9	58	1,349	Same (1.00)	O
		1,349	Same (1.00)	×
		1,349	Same (1.00)	×

(4) Tachikawa City

No.	*Property no.*	*District Court (10,000 yen)*	*High Court (10,000 yen)*		*Surcharge Payment*
1	24	409	198	(0.48)	O
2	26	2,719	1,310	(0.48)	O
3	30	2,730	316	(0.12)	O
4	34	8,463	4,874	(0.58)	O
5	52	1,081	125	(0.12)	O
6	57	2,268	306	(0.13)	×

(Note) The Supreme Court has decided not to accept the final appeal. Amounts less than 10,000 yen are rounded down. Regarding the trial decision (whether there is a surcharge), O means yes, and × means no.
(Note) The Supreme Court has decided not to accept the final appeal. Amounts less than 10,000 yen are rounded down.
(Note) The Supreme Court has decided not to accept the final appeal. Amounts less than 10,000 yen are rounded down.

Thus, it is necessary to consider vertical ties in the form of subcontractors between general contractors and local contractors. If the court believes that competitiveness would be maintained when local contractors participate in bidding, it is insufficient as a grasp of the actual situation.

9.2.4 Evaluation from an economic perspective

In the extreme condition that there is no collusion, there is no information on the behavior of the competitors, and the bidding continues infinitely; the bidders act independently to win the bid. The winning bid price would then be the same as the model indicated: the perfect forecasting target price model in the previous chapter. As explained in the model, the successful bid price reaches the minimum limit price.[2] However, considering the distribution of successful bid rates between 80% and 81% during the bid-rigging period, only 15 out of the 72 properties (20.8%) were successfully bided. In the period after the bid-rigging, the successful bid rates between 80% and 81% indicated only 50 out of the 139

2 The assertion of the attorney of the plaintiffs in the court is that if there had been no collusion, the minimum limit price would have been the successful bid price.

properties (35.9%). It is challenging to imagine that the successful bid price in reality becomes the minimum limit price even in the period after the bid-rigging.

In reality, there are uncooperative scrutiny and ulterior motives among contractors. The bidders collect information on the successful bid rates obtained from past successful bids and serial connections between bidding participants. Moreover, contractors consider the topography of the property and the degree of difficulty of construction. Such additional information does not necessarily result in the winning bid price being the minimum limit price. Moreover, the most important factor is that the bidding continues finitely, not infinitely. Therefore, an index based on determining the amount of compensation for damages is a meaningful value by utilizing the difference between the average value of successful bid rates of the bid-rigging period (94.54%) and the average value of the successful bid rates after the period of excluding bid-rigging (89.85%).

9.3 Conclusion

Regarding claims for damages related to the bid-rigging in the Tama district, there was a great deal of variations in the judgments of the District Courts and the High Court on the amount of compensation for damages between Hachioji City, Hino City, Machida City, and Tachikawa City. In the bid-rigging case, the trial decision of the JFTC was the starting point, and the surcharge was imposed on the 30 illegal general contractors by the surcharge payment order. However, a request for cancellation of the trial decision was filed by the general contractors, and five separate trials were held in the Tokyo High Court. In one of the cases, a request for cancellation of the trial decision was accepted, but the decision was overturned by the Supreme Court in one case. The validity and legal stability of the trial decision were secured.

The statements from the JFTC were the basic and common materials in the cases of claiming compensation for damages in resident lawsuits based on the Local Autonomy Act. The Tokyo District Courts ruled that the statements were accepted, but the Tokyo High Court overturned the District Court ruling on Hino City. The High Court ruling reduced the amount of compensation in Hachioji City and Tachikawa City. Clearly, there were variations in judgments stemming from factors such as the reliability of testimonials, which raises issues from the perspective of legal stability.

In the past, lawsuits by residents were a peculiar category, and the reason may be that the Resident Audit Committee of the local governments and various stages of the public check systems functioned sufficiently. One of the foundations of the Constitution is the sovereignty of the people, and it is necessary to consider lawsuits by citizens. Ultimately, it is important to strive for information disclosure, and for the local governments to be more conscious of the fairness and transparency of bidding for public works than ever before.

As shown this time, the scattered judgments of each court must converge in the future. Hence, nurturing legal professionals who are strong in economics or mathematics will also be indispensable in resolving the increasing economic disputes in today's economic society.

10 Sewerage facility bid-rigging case in Tokyo

Changes in the behavior brought about introducing the announcement in advance for target prices

10.1 Introduction

This study has analyzed several bid-rigging cases. The simplest bidding method is that the ordering party sets only the target price for a property. The target price is the maximum price of the successful bid price, and the winning bidder is the lowest bidder among the bidders. Bidders who bid above the target price are disqualified. As a bidding method that complicates the simplest one, a minimum limit price is set. In the case of the Tama district public works bid-rigging in Chapters 8 and 9, the ordering party set the minimum limit price. The minimum limit price is 80% of the target price. In the bidding method, bidders who bid above (below) the target (minimum) price are disqualified.

This chapter examines the case of the bid-rigging for the construction of sewage pump facilities in Tokyo. It probes the relationship between the presence of bid-rigging and the successful bid rates. In the present case, new elements are introduced in addition to the minimum limit price. These include the announcement of the target price in advance and the submission of materials showing the basis for the bid price by the contractors. The additional requirements are different from the cases of the bid-rigging so far. To detect the presence of rigging from the data, the study analyzes the effect of advance announcement of the target price.

Section 10.2 describes the overview, progress, results, and characteristics of the present bid-rigging case. Section 10.3 conducts an econometric analysis of the relationship between collusion and the successful bid rate using econometric techniques. Finally, Section 10.4 concludes the chapter.

10.2 Case of the Tokyo sewerage pump facility bid-rigging

The subject of this case is the facility works for the pumps installed in the sewerage facilities. The contents include installation works for sewage pumps, rainwater pumps, discharge pumps, sludge pumps, and sludge feed pumps. The sewage pump facility works are classified into new and existing constructions. The existing constructions include expansion and improvement works. Improvement works are divided into reconstruction and replacement works.

DOI: 10.4324/9781003370444-10

The basic agreement for the 14 manufacturers aimed to prevent a decline in the order prices for new constructions, expansion works, reconstruction works, and replacement works regarding the main pump ordered by the Bureau of Sewerage of the TMG after April 1999. The basic agreement had three notable points:

(1) For existing construction works, the manufacturer that received the previous order would be the prospective contractor. If the existing manufacturer cannot participate in the bidding, the prospective bidder would be determined through negotiation among the bidders.
(2) For new construction, the prospective bidder will be decided through negotiation among the bidders. Candidates include consultants who undertook the design and manufacturers who made technical proposals to the TMG.
(3) The order price would be determined by the prospective contractor. Other contractors would cooperate such that the prospective contractor can receive the order at the price determined by itself.

There were three bidding methods for ordering the construction works, depending on the target price of the property: designated competitive bidding by request from the manufacturers, designated competitive bidding by public offering, and general competitive bidding. The first was applied to properties with the lowest price range among the three bidding methods. The ordering party appointed ten bidders from the registered bidders and participated in the bid. The second was applied to bidding properties in the middle price range. The ordering party solicited bidders from the registered manufacturers. All bidders who meet certain requirements participate in the bid. The third was applied to the highest price range bidding property. Registered manufacturers who meet certain conditions became bidders.

In this case, a different bidding method from the other cases of bid-rigging was partially adopted in addition to the above three bidding methods. The target prices calculated by the ordering party were announced in advance during a part of the bidding period. The execution period for the case was from April 1, 1999, to July 29, 2003. From July 1998 to July 1999 (Phase I), some of the properties with a target price of 900 million or more were announced in advance. During the period from August 1999 to October 2000 (Phase II), all of the bidding properties with a target price of 900 million yen or more were announced in advance. From November 2000 to March 2002 (Phase III), all of the bidding properties with a target price of more than 700 million yen were announced in advance. From April 2002 onwards (Phase IV), all bidding properties were subject to the prior announcement of the target prices. Table 10.1 summarizes the changes in the announcement method of the target prices and the range of amounts for the designated competitive bidding by request from the manufacturers, the designated competitive bidding by public offering, and the general competitive bidding.

Table 10.1 Prior announcement of the target price and the range of amounts in the bidding methods

(1) Phase I (From July 1998 to July 1999)
April 1, 1999 (the starting date of the execution period of the bid-rigging)
Target price advance announcement: some properties with 900 million or more
Bid method: designated competitive bidding by request (2.5 million to 2.5 billion)
designated competitive bidding by public offering (2.5 billion to five billion)
general competitive bidding (5 billion or more)

(2) Phase II (From August 1999 to October 2000)
Target price advance announcement: all properties with 900 million or more
Bid method: designated competitive bidding by request (2.5 million to 2.5 billion)
designated competitive bidding by public offering (2.5 billion to five billion)
general competitive bidding (five billion or more)

(3) Phase III (From November 2000 to March 2002)
Target price advance announcement: all properties with 700 million or more
Bid method: designated competitive bidding by request (2.5 million to nine million)
designated competitive bidding by public offering (nine million to 2.5 billion)
general competitive bidding (2.5 billion or more)

(4) Phase IV (After April 2002)
Target price advance announcement: All
Bid method: designated competitive bidding by request (2.5 million to 900 million)
general competitive bidding (more than 900 million)

July 29, 2003 (the final date of the execution period of this collusion)

The incident began in July 2003, when the JFTC conducted on-site inspections of 14 manufacturers. In March 2004, recommendations from the JFTC were issued to ten manufacturers. As one manufacturer agreed with the recommendation, nine manufacturers were involved in the trial. The trial decision was issued against them in April 2008. There were 47 bids for sewage pump facility construction related to the case. One of the defendants filed an appeal to the Tokyo High Court to revoke the trial decision. The judgment was issued in December 2008, resulting in the plaintiff's claim being dismissed. An appeal was filed against this ruling but was dismissed by the Supreme Court in October 2009, resulting in a decision of non-acceptance.

In August 2008, the surcharge payment orders were issued to six manufacturers. Of the 29 properties won by the six manufacturers, 22 properties were subject to the surcharges. The following is a summary of the characteristics of this case. There were 47 bidding properties during the period of execution of the violation. Six manufacturers were subject to the surcharge payment, and the number of successful bids from them was 29 properties, of which 22 were subject to the surcharge payment. Regarding the 47 properties, the minimum target price was approximately 21 million yen for property no. 37, and the maximum target price was approximately two billion yen for property no. 16. The average value of all properties was 536 million yen, and the standard deviation was 502 million yen.

Consider the number of properties for which the target price was announced in advance. In the period from August 1999 to October 2000 (Phases I and II), three out of 19 properties priced at 900 million yen or more were announced in advance. In the period from November 2000 to March 2002 (Phase III), four out of 11 properties priced at 700 million yen or more were announced in advance. In the bidding period from April 2002 to July 2003 (Phase IV), all 17 properties were subject to prior announcement of the target price. Therefore, the bidders knew the target price of the 24 properties out of the 47 properties in advance. Of the 24 properties, 16 properties were successful bids by the six illegal manufacturers.

The study examines the effect of the announcement of the target price in advance. The guideline compiled by the Ministry of Land, Infrastructure, Transport, and Tourism discusses the advantages and disadvantages of such an announcement. For the advantage, it is possible to prevent fraudulent acts by the manufacturers such as asking governmental staff for the target price. For the disadvantage, the target price becomes a guideline for the successful bid price, resulting in the successful bid price remaining at a high level and competition being restricted. Moreover, collusion may be conducted more easily. Even manufacturers with inadequate cost estimation capability may receive orders based on the target price in advance.

When the target price is unknown at the time of bidding, the prospective bidder does not have a 100% chance of winning the bid even if the prospective bidder is determined in advance by collusion. If the prospective bidder makes a mistake in predicting the successful bid price, there is room for another bidder to win the bid. Looking at the trends in successful bid prices thus far, prospective successful bidders tend to bid closer to the target price than bid at a lower price far from the target price. This propensity of the successful bidder in the high successful bid rate triggered the JFTC to detect the possibility of collusion, and the JFTC conducted an on-site inspection.

However, when the target price becomes a known figure, there is no possibility that other bidders would bid at a lower bid price than the prospective successful bidders. Therefore, they can erase the evidence of collusion while increasing the confidence that they would be successful bidders, relative to the case where the target price was not disclosed. The bid-rigging bidders can decide the winning bid price with some amount of leeway.[1]

Regarding the advantages and disadvantages of the announcement of the target price in advance, consider the relationship between the presence of collusion and the successful bid rates. Here, the sample is limited to the six manufacturers that were fined. Among the properties they won, the study compares the successful bid rates between properties for which the target price was announced in advance (16 properties) and properties for which the target price was not announced (13 properties), as shown in Table 10.2.[2]

From this table, the successful bid rate on average decreased by two percentage points from 96.86% to 94.98% after the target price was announced in advance. Announcement in advance tends to lower the successful bid rates. Moreover, the tendency of the successful bid rate of the 22 properties subject to the surcharge reveals an interesting observation that contradicts conventional wisdom. In the case of no advance announcement, the average successful bid rate subject to the surcharge was 97.96%, while that not subject to the surcharge was 93.21%; thus, the average successful bid rate subject to the surcharge is 4.7 percentage points higher. This result accords with the effect of collusion. However, the case of the advance announcement was different. The average successful bid rate subject to the surcharge was 94.51%, while that not subject to the surcharge was 96.65%. The properties subject to the surcharge are 2.1 percentage points lower, inconsistent with past results. According to the ruling, the prospective bidder usually bids at a price equivalent to approximately 95% of the target price. However, as an employee at a company was arrested for bid-rigging on a different incident, the company devised a way to avoid the discovery of the order adjustment for the present incident. It adjusted the winning bid rate at a price of approximately 92% of the target price, not 95%.[3]

1 The guidelines also stipulate that the pre-announcement of target prices should be handled so as not to cause any harm. If any harm occurs, appropriate measures would be taken promptly, including cancellation of the advance announcement, the direction of promoting post facto announcement of the target prices in the future, and the introduction of a comprehensive evaluation.

2 Regarding the 22 properties imposed by the surcharge payment out of the 29 properties, the study estimated the properties by utilizing the surcharge payment orders and the trial decisions.

3 The successful bid rates for the three successful bids of this company are 92.66%, 91.62%, and 91.69%.

Table 10.2 Difference between the successful bid rate for no announcement and the announcement of the target price in advance

(1) Successful bid rate for the no announcement of target price in advance

Property no.	*Successful bid price (10 thousand yen)*	*Successful bid rate (%)*	*Surcharge payment*
18	8,000	96.28	○
23	7,000	97.53	○
11	66,200	95.92	
17	11,500	99.15	○
8	9,500	93.15	
6	58,500	97.80	○
19	49,000	97.36	○
30	48,000	99.32	○
24	47,400	99.19	○
27	43,000	94.99	○
29	32,000	98.20	○
12	25,000	90.57	
1	93,000	99.84	○

Average successful bid rate for 13 properties: 96.86%.
Average successful bid rate for ten properties: 97.96%.
Average successful bid rate for three properties: 93.21%.
(Note) The ten properties are those subject to surcharge payment indicated by ○. The three properties are those subject to no surcharge payment.

(2) Successful bid rate for the announcement of target price in advance

Property no.	*Successful bid price (10 thousand yen)*	*Successful bid rate (%)*	*Surcharge payment*
33	3,100	94.66	○
44	48,500	95.35	○
41	14,500	94.93	○
31	75,500	95.60	○
43	24,000	94.79	○
16	195,400	97.51	
26	156,900	96.98	○
45	131,000	92.66	○
46	129,000	91.62	○
7	90,950	96.89	
47	2,880	91.69	○
20	105,400	95.93	
39	103,900	94.85	○
40	80,900	96.09	○
38	44,400	95.28	
37	18,800	94.85	○

Average successful bid rate for 16 properties: 94.98%.
Average successful bid rate for 12 properties: 94.51%.
Average successful bid rate for four properties: 96.65%.
(Note) The 12 properties are those subject to surcharge payment indicated by ○. The four properties are those subject to no surcharge payment.

10.3 Econometric Analysis: Relationship between bid-rigging and high bidding rates

Three cases of bid-rigging in this book provide detailed information, such as the successful bid rate for each property: the case of stoker furnace bid-rigging (Chapter 7), the Tama district public works bid-rigging case (Chapters 8 and 9), and the Tokyo sewage pump facility construction bid-rigging case (this chapter). In chronological order, the execution period of the stoker furnace bid-rigging case began (ended) in April (September) 1994 (1998), followed by the execution of the Tama district public construction bid-rigging case. The period began (ended) in October (September) 1997 (2000), and the implementation period of the Tokyo sewerage pump equipment construction collusion case began (ended) in April (July) 1999 (2003).

A controversial point in these bid-rigging cases is the relationship between bid-rigging and high successful bid rates. This section explains the economic variables used in the empirical analysis conducted in the next section. The economic variables regarding price are the target price, successful bid price, and fair price. Preconditions related to the target price are classified into two categories: pre-announcement and post-announcement. Moreover, the precondition related to the successful bid price is the presence or absence of collusion. This section explains why the successful bid rate is used in economic analysis. Section 10.3.1 discusses the successful bid price and the fair price related to collusion. Section 10.3.2 discusses the target price related to advance and post facto announcements. Section 10.3.3 describes the econometric merits of using successful bid rates but not successful bid prices.

10.3.1 Successful bid price related to collusion and fair price (competitive price)

The successful bid price given bid-rigging (the bid-rigging price) is certainly higher than that without bid-rigging (the fair price). The purpose of bid-rigging is to maintain the winning bid prices as high as possible and increase profits for the companies and the industry.[4] Therefore, the question is how a fair price without collusion can be provided as a reasonable numerical value based on economic theory. A fair price is absolutely necessary in the case of damage claims. In the current situation, although the theory guarantees that the successful bid price given bid-rigging is higher than the price without bid-rigging, it is challenging to give a concrete answer as to the difference between the bid-rigging price and the fair price. In other words, even if the fair price is smaller than the bid-rigging price, it is not possible to define the value of the difference.[5]

4 The excuse of the bidders for the high successful bid price is that the successful bid price happened to be close to the target price but because of collusion.

5 Therefore, Article 248 of the Code of Civil Procedure is necessary. If a causal relationship, which is one of the constituent elements, can be proven by the plaintiffs, the amount of compensation for damages can be determined by the court.

The two emergent problems are the problem of the fair price and the target price. To estimate the fair prices numerically, it is necessary to create an econometric model and conduct empirical analysis using actual data. For example, Chapter 3 of this book quantitatively analyzed the case of the AMA violations through the cartel price agreement among oil wholesalers during the first Oil Crisis. It constructed an econometric model under the assumption that there was no cartel price-fixing and obtained reasonable estimates of the price that would be realized in the absence of the cartel price-fixing. However, in Japan, there are few examples of estimating fair prices using economic models. The importance of empirical analysis on fair prices is a future issue.

10.3.2 Target price

The target price is determined by the ordering party, and the bidders must predict it. With several bid-rigging cases so far, the target price set by the ordering party is predicted by the bidders with high accuracy. The bidders investigate past successful bid prices and explore the method of calculating the target price by the ordering party. Moreover, even if potential bidders do not become bidders for the property, they gather and review information on the target price and winning bid price for the property.[6]

The prospective bidder can predict the target price with a high degree of accuracy. That is, the variance of the probability distribution of the target price is extremely small. However, since the target price is a random variable unless announced in advance, it is a stochastic value for the bidders. Further, if the target price is announced in advance, it becomes the non-stochastic price. Thus, the prospective bidder for the bid-rigging controls the successful bid price with certainty, and the others would not make excuses for misreading the target price. This is the merit of the prospective bidder.

10.3.3 Successful bid rate and its role as an analytical concept

If there is collusion, the bid-rigging price will be higher than the fair price. Therefore, bid-rigging will increase the winning bid price and its rate. When there is a successful bid rate of 99% or more, there is the possibility of collusion. However, as several bid-rigging cases for the successful bid rate are over 99% thus far, it is not always the right decision for the JFTC or the court to recognize bid-rigging. Consider a specific bidding property. If there

6 The Accounting Act stipulates for the central government biddings, and the Local Autonomy Act stipulates for the local government biddings. The target price is the upper limit of the successful bid price calculated by the ordering party. When the target price is not announced before bidding, it is unknown to the bidders, and they must anticipate the target price before bidding. When a bidder offers a bid higher than the target price, the bidding is disqualified. However, when a bid is made at a price significantly lower than the target price, the profit would be reduced even if the bidder won the bid.

is bid-rigging for the property, the successful bid rate would be higher than that of no bid-rigging. This is a reasonable result of the role of collusion. For a particular property (suffixed i), the following inequality exists:

$$\text{Winning bid price without rigging}_i < \text{Winning bid price with rigging}_i$$

Dividing both sides by the target price yields the following inequality,

$$\text{Successful bid rate without rigging}_i < \text{Successful bid rate with rigging}_i.$$

The successful bid rate for a property with bid-rigging is higher than that without bid-rigging for a particular property. Similarly, for another property j,

$$\text{Successful bid rate without rigging}_j < \text{Successful bid rate with rigging}_j$$

which is correct. When property i is recognized as having bid-rigging and property j is recognized as not having bid-rigging, does the following inequality

$$\text{Bidding rate without bid-rigging}_j < \text{Bidding rate with bid-rigging}_i$$

exist? This is not valid, showing a counterexample where the successful bid rate for i property with rigging is 95% and that for j property without rigging is 96%. Regarding the successful bid rate, three points of tendency were found in the trial decisions and the judgments. First, bid-rigging does not exist for properties with a low successful bid rate. Second, properties judged to have collusion have a high successful bid rate. In extreme cases, the successful bid rate is concentrated between 99% and 100%. Third, when there are outsiders, the successful bid rate is close to 80% (in the Tama district bid-rigging case), sticking to the minimum limit price.

In some cases, the presence of collusion is identified by the high successful bid rate according to current bidding methods. An example is the case of bid-rigging for public works in the Tama district. In this case, two price constraints—the target price and the minimum limit price (80% of the target price)—were imposed, and it was possible to clearly distinguish between collusion and non-collusion. Given the distribution of successful bid rates in the case, it was possible to identify that the possibility of collusion was the property near the rate of 95% but not one near that of 80%.

If there is collusion, the winning bid price will be higher than the fair price without collusion. Though there is a target price and a successful bid price for each bidding property, fair prices do not exist. With current knowledge of economics, it is almost impossible to calculate the fair price for each property. Therefore, the study employs information on the average value of the successful bid rate for identifying the existence of bid-rigging and calculating damages.

Suppose illegal and non-illegal properties are determined from direct evidence. As the construction scale of each property is different, it is meaningless to take the average value of the successful bid prices of the illegal and non-illegal properties. As one means of standardization, the study employed the successful bid rate and removed the effect of scale. Then, the difference between the average successful bid rates of illegal and non-illegal properties becomes a key figure when calculating the amount of compensation for damages. By multiplying this constant by the successful bid price of the illegal property, it is possible to calculate the amount of damages.

10.4 Three cases to be considered and their basic data

This section examines the relationship between the successful bid rates and the collision imposed in the surcharge payment. In the bid-rigging cases conducted thus far, three cases disclosed the successful bid rate for each property in the judgments.

The number of properties involved in each case is 84 in the stoker furnace bid-rigging case (out of 86 properties, two properties do not show the successful bid rate), 72 in the Tama district public works bid-rigging case, and 47 in the case of bid-rigging for sewage pump facilities in Tokyo. For econometric analysis, the sample size of the three cases is sufficient. The study reproduced the distribution of successful bid rates and verified them through empirical analysis of how successful bid rates affect the decisions of the trials and court judgments.

Consider the distribution of successful bid rates and the relationship between successful bid rates and the surcharge payments. Figure 10.1 is a scatter diagram of successful bid rates in the stoker furnace bid-rigging case. The highest frequency is in the 95%–100% interval, and the frequency is 64, accounting for 76.1% of the total. The next highest frequency is in the 90%–95% interval, and the frequency is 8. Further, 72 of the bids (85.7%) exist in the 90%–100% interval. The successful bid rates in the 40%–80% intervals are scattered thinly. The bottoms are widely scattered because there is no constraint on the lower limit of bids. In the other two cases, there are upper and lower restrictions regarding the range of the bid price. The target price is the upper limit, and 80% of it is the minimum limit price, which constrains the lower limit of bids.

A characteristic point from this figure is that, regardless of whether they engage in collusion, the manufacturers can predict the target price with considerable accuracy. Now, superimpose the decision on the surcharge payment order on the distribution of the successful bid rates.

In Figure 10.2, the horizontal axis shows the successful bid rates, and the vertical axis shows the property that imposed the surcharge (vertical axis = 1) and the property that imposed no surcharge (vertical axis = 0). The properties that imposed the surcharge payment given collusion were scattered with a successful bid rate of over 90%. However, some properties imposed no surcharge even if it is 90% or more. When it is lower than 90%, no surcharge payment is imposed without any exception.

Next, consider the frequency distribution table for the successful bid rate of the bid-rigging case of Tama district public works, as in Figure 10.3, where the winning bids were characterized by two modes. One is in the range of

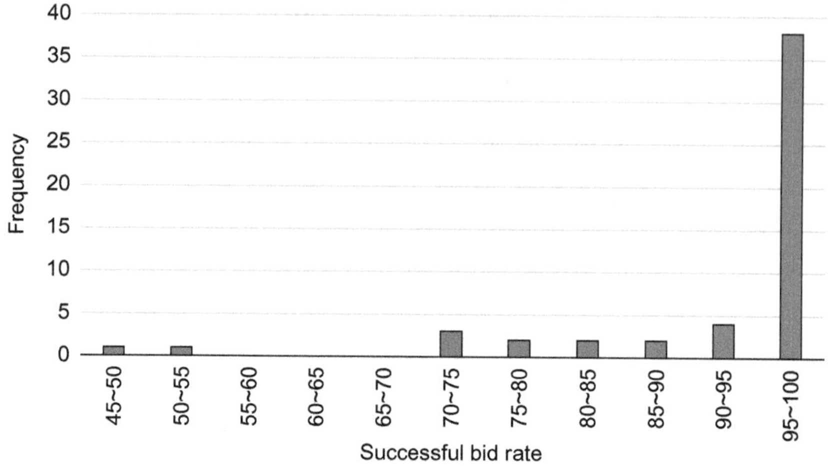

Figure 10.1 Histogram regarding the successful bid rates in the stoker furnace case

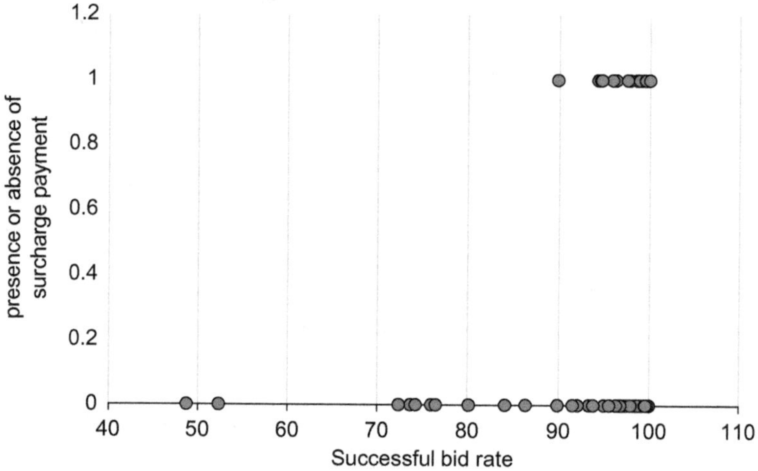

Figure 10.2 Relationship between the successful bid rate and the surcharge payment: the stoker furnace case

the successful bid rates from 97.5% to 100%, and its frequency is 49 (68.0%). The other is in the 80%–82.5% interval, and the frequency of the successful bid rates included in the range is 15 (20.8%). Combining the frequencies of these two intervals, they account for 88.8% of the total. As described above, the minimum limit price is imposed on the bidding properties. Thus, the successful bid price fell given competition among contractors.

Figure 10.4 shows a scatter diagram of the successful bid rates on the horizontal axis and the presence of the surcharge payment for the properties on the vertical axis. In this figure, there is a mixture of properties whether the

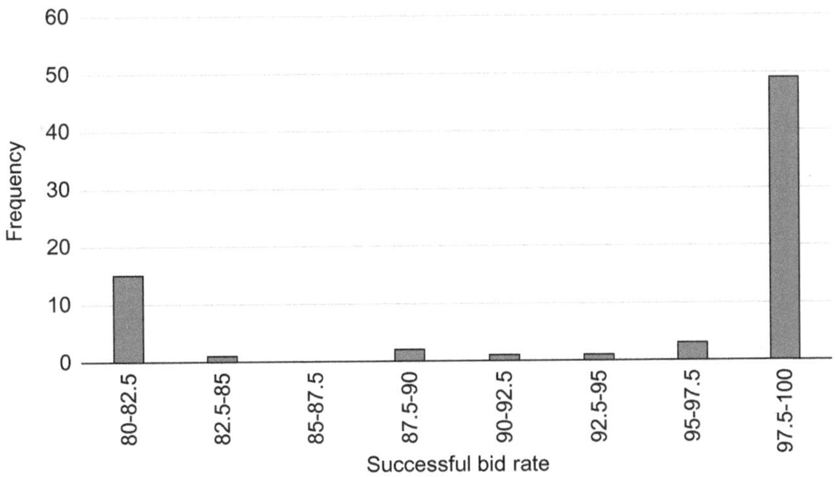

Figure 10.3 Histogram regarding the successful bid rates in the Tama district public works bid-rigging case

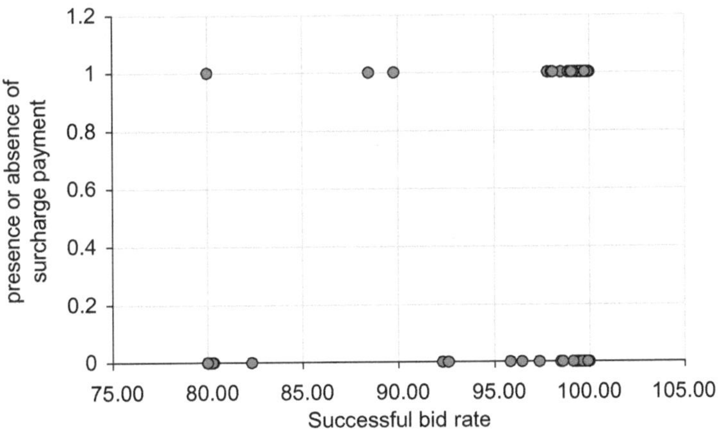

Figure 10.4 Relationship between the successful bid rate and the surcharge payment: the Tama district public works bid-rigging case

surcharge has been imposed in the interval of the high successful bid rate of more than 90%. Meanwhile, there is only one property with a low successful bid rate and the surcharge was imposed.

The final case is the bid-rigging case for the construction of sewage pump facilities in Tokyo (see the histogram in Figure 10.5). In this case, the upper limit is the target price, and the lower limit is 80% of the target price. Unlike the Tama district public works bid-rigging case, the highest frequency was not in the top interval between 97.5% and 100% but in the 95%–97.5% interval. The successful bid rates for all properties were over 90%, except for one property.

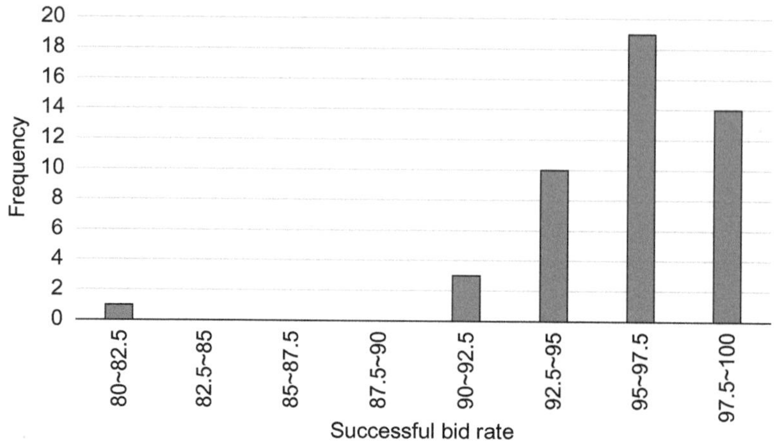

Figure 10.5 Histogram regarding the successful bid rates in the construction of sewage pump facilities in Tokyo bid-rigging case

A scatter of the successful bid rates and the presence (absence) of the surcharge payment for the properties is depicted in Figure 10.6. When the successful bid rate is low, no surcharge payment is imposed. However, when it is at a level of 90% or more, there is a mixture of properties for which surcharges have been imposed or no surcharges have been imposed.

Regarding these three incidents, the study examines the relationship between collusion and the high successful bid rates. As the first step, an econometric model is used to test whether the successful bid rate is related to the presence of the surcharge payment. As a second step, the study will examine whether the successful bid rate imposed by surcharge payments would be higher than for the properties not imposed surcharge payments. [7]

As an econometric model, the study introduced a qualitative response model and tested the relationship between the successful bid rate and the presence of administrative sanctions. At first, it examined the general causal relationship in collusion cases. From the legal perspective, the cause is the basic agreement, and the effect is the bid-rigging. Another way of expressing this causality is that the cause is the basic agreement and the effect is a higher winning bid. Considering the condition that the bidders accurately estimate the target price, a high winning bid price is synonymous with a high winning

7 In principle, after admitting a property as the result of collision by the court, the successful bid price with bid-rigging is compared with the successful bid price without bid-rigging using an econometric model. The amount of compensation for damages is calculated as the difference between the observed successful bid price and the fair price derived from the model. In the current situation, this procedure is not possible in cases of collision. Therefore, the method of comparing the bid rates but not the bid price between the illegal and legal biddings is used for the judgment of collision and the calculation of the compensation for damages.

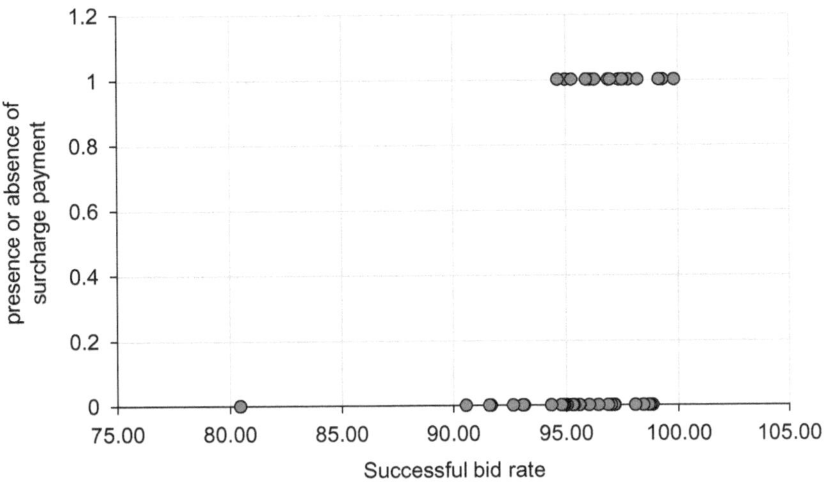

Figure 10.6 Relationship between the successful bid rate and the surcharge payment: the construction of sewage pump facilities in Tokyo bid-rigging case

bid rate. The basic agreement includes the legal element of unfair trade restrictions and the economic element of a high winning bid rate. Thus, the relationship between the existence of bid-rigging and a high bidding rate is not causal but a correlation derived from the basic agreement.

If a basic agreement is reached, bid-rigging will take place and the winning bid rate will be high. If no basic agreement is reached, bidders will compete and the successful bid rates will vary. Thus, the study verifies the correlation between the existence of bid-rigging and the high bidding rate. Figure 10.7 shows the causal relationship and correlation between the bid-rigging and successful bid rates.

Table 10.3 summarizes the characteristics of the three cases before conducting the econometric analysis.

10.5 Econometric analysis of the three cases: Logit and probit models

This section examines the relationship between the successful bid rates and surcharge payment orders using a qualitative variable model (see Maki, 2011). In the qualitative response model, the probability distribution is specified in the model.

Qualitative response models introduce the latent variables in the model. For the latent variable y_i^*, the study specifies the following linear relation:

$$y_i^* = \beta_0 + \beta_1 x_i + \varepsilon_i \ (i = 1, 2, \ldots, n)$$

where ε_i is a random variable. The relationship between observed values y_i and y_i^* is as follows:

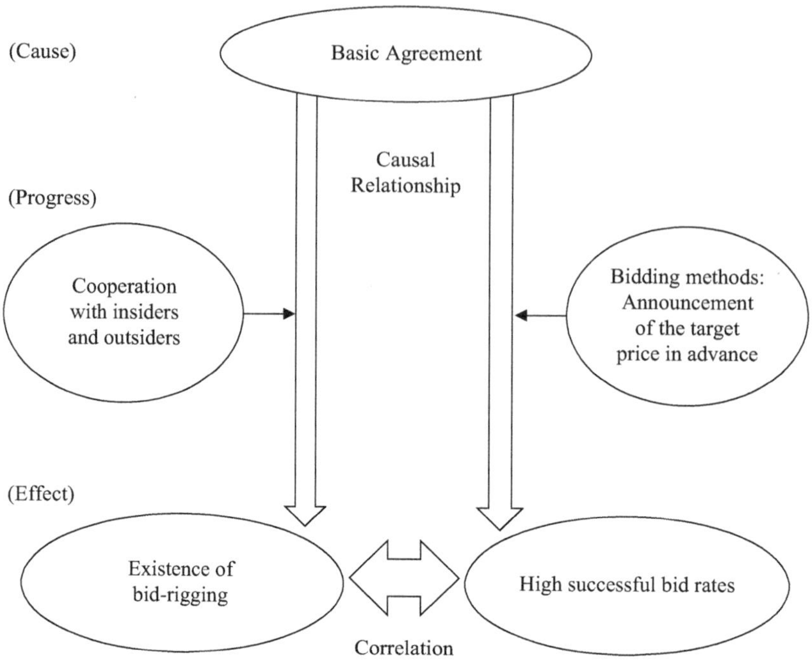

Figure 10.7 Causal relationship and correlation in the bid-rigging case

$$y_i = 1, \text{ if } y_i^* > 0$$

$$y_i = 0, \text{ if } y_i^* \leq 0$$

Here, a model is called a logit model in which the following distribution functions are specified as the distribution functions of random variable z:

$$F(z) = \exp(z) /(1 + \exp(z).$$

However, a probit model assumes the probability density function representing the normal distribution as the distribution function:

$$F(z) = \int_{-\infty}^{z} f(t)dt$$

where f(t) is the probability density function of the standard normal distribution with mean 0 and variance 1.

These two distribution functions have an S-shaped curve; at both ends (the region of the horizontal axis where the vertical axis is close to 0 or 1), there is little difference between the two distribution functions. However, there is almost no difference regarding the S-shape in the other regions.[8] In the econo-

8 See Maki (2011) for details on the qualitative response model.

Table 10.3 Characteristics of the three cases

	Stoker furnace	*Tama district*	*Tokyo sewerage system*
Number of properties	84	72	47
Number of properties Imposed the surcharge	31	31	22
Start of implementation	1994	1997	1999
Minimum	3.34 billion yen	40.35 million yen	21.65 million yen
Maximum	40.13 billion yen	1.14 billion yen	2.0 billion yen
Average	15.04 billion yen	290 million yen	530 million yen
Standard deviation	10.18 billion yen	190 million yen	500 million yen
Participating companies	Five major companies	General contractors	Manufacturing companies
	Outsiders	Local contractors	
Property subject to a surcharge			
Average successful bid rate	98.25	98.04	96.15
Standard deviation	2.12	4.24	2.33
Property not subject to a surcharge			
Average successful bid rate	92.90	91.89	95.43
Standard deviation	11.43	9.10	3.69
Difference in average successful bid rate	3.35	6.15	0.72

metric analysis using the qualitative response models, Table 10.4 presents the estimated values for the logit and probit models.

Consider the estimation results. In the logit and probit models, the successful bid rate coefficient is positive and significant in the stoker furnace and Tama district cases, indicating that the t-value is significant at the level of 5% (P-value is less than 0.05). As the estimation results for the stoker furnace and Tama district cases, the successful bid rate is related to the determination of the surcharge payment. However, in the sewage pump facilities bid-rigging case, the result is different from these two cases. Although the coefficient of the successful bid rate is positive, the t-value is not significant at the 5% level (P-value is greater than 0.05), and the null hypothesis of H_0: $\beta_1 = 0$ cannot be rejected at the 5% level. Clearly, the reason lies in the advance announcement of the target price. The present econometric analysis shows that the correlation that existed in the past collapsed given the announcement of target prices in advance.

Now, examine from a different perspective that bid-rigging increases the successful bid rate. The study employs the significance test regarding the difference in the statistical method. It conducts a hypothesis test with the mean and standard deviation of the successful bid rates of the surcharged and uncharged samples. Accordingly, there is no difference in the population averages between the two groups, and the alternative hypothesis is that the successful bid rate of properties subject to a surcharge is higher than that of other properties.

Table 10.4 Logit and probit model estimates

	Stoker furnace	*Tama district*	*Sewage pump*
Logit model			
Intercept (β_0)	-22.67	-12.61	-5.20
	(2.22)	(2.86)	(0.53)
	[0.026]	[0.004]	[0.59]
Coefficient of successful			
Bid rate (β_1)	0.2273	0.1289	0.052
	(2.18)	(2.84)	(0.52)
	[0.029]	[0.004]	[0.60]
Probit model			
Intercept (β_0)	-13.49	-7.502	-3.345
	(2.23)	(3.17)	(0.54)
	[0.025]	[0.002]	[0.586]
Coefficient of successful			
Bid rate (β_1)	0.1351	0.07675	0.0345
	(2.19)	(3.13)	(0.53)
	[0.028]	[0.002]	[0.594]

(Note) Round brackets are t-values and square brackets are P-values.

$$H_0: \mu_1 = \mu_2$$

$$H_A: \mu_1 > \mu_2$$

If the H_0 is true, then the following statistics

$$z = (x_1 - x_2 - (\mu_1 - \mu_2)) \cdot \sqrt{(n_1 \cdot n_2 \cdot (n_1 + n_2 - 2)/(n_1 + n_2))} / \sqrt{((n_1 - 1)s_1^2 + (n_2 - 1)s_2^2)}$$

follows a t-distribution with $n_1 + n_2 - 2$ degrees of freedom. Table 10.5 shows the results of the significance test of the difference.

From the table, H_0 is rejected at the 1% significance level in the cases of the stoker furnace and the Tama district public works bid-rigging. On the successful bid rate, bid-rigged properties and other properties showed a statistical difference, and the successful bid rate is higher for the bid-rigged properties. However, in the sewage pump facilities bid-rigging case, H_0 was not rejected at the 1% significance level. That is, statistically speaking, there

Table 10.5 Significance test result of the difference between the two averages

	Stoker furnace	*Tama district*	*Sewage pump*
Value of z	2.56	3.48	0.78
$n_1 + n_2 - 2$	82	70	45
Significance level of 1%	2.37	2.39	2.41

is no difference in the successful bid rates between bid-rigging and no bid-rigging. Thus, direct evidence plays an important role as the reason for the difference in character between the surcharged population and the non-surcharged population.

10.6 Conclusion

This chapter employs the qualitative response models to verify whether there is a relationship between successful bid rates and bid-rigging. The data used for verification are the legal data in the three cases of the stoker furnace, Tama district, and the sewage facilities. No minimum limit price was set for the stoker furnace, and the other two had a minimum limit price. In the case where the minimum limit price was set, the results showed that when there is competition with outsiders, the successful bid prices would stick to it.

Further, a part of the target prices was announced in advance for the case of sewage facilities, but the other two cases did not announce the target price in advance. Conventionally, the courts used the information on the high successful bid rates as evidence of collision. It would be challenging to judge the impact of bid-rigging based only on the high successful bid rates in the case of sewage facilities. To identify the existence of bid-rigging, the data on the successful bid rates and other evidence such as direct evidence is necessary.

Econometric analysis is never the definitive and unique piece of evidence in trials and judgments. Econometric analysis results do not replace conventional direct evidence but merely comprise one piece of evidence. Even so, if econometrics can provide new insights into matters that could not be proven in the conventional legal world, that would be the role of economic analysis in the legal world.

11 Policy theory based on empirical analysis of law and economics

11.1 Introduction

Legal backing is necessary for economic policies to be implemented in a country ruled by law. The Diet enacts and amends laws, and the government run by the politicians and bureaucrats carries out policies based on the law entrusted with administration by the people.

Government failure is a new topic in recent years. It regards the situation where bureaucrats prioritize the interests of the bureaucracy over national interests and prioritize the private interests of some politicians and specific industries over the people. It impairs market efficiency given competition inhibition restrictions to the market. An example of the competition inhibition restriction was found in the bid-rigging case. Ultimately this situation wastes taxes.[1]

The conclusion of policy theory based on normative economics is relatively simple. It is based on the fundamental theorems of welfare economics, and the conclusion should be to create a competitive market that maximizes economic welfare. The policies for this purpose are *deregulation* and *privatization*. However, as mentioned in Chapter 2, deregulation and privatization have taken place, and marketization that pursues efficiency and fairness are not necessarily synonymous.

The policy theory based on empirical analysis of law and economics does not simply propose the realization of a competitive market. In the actual world, various economic disputes occur, and there are many cases in which these disputes

1 As the scale of the Japanese economy measured by GDP has grown, the budget of the government also expanded. Moreover, it is gradually challenging for people to judge the appropriateness of government spending. Symbolically, a household's decision-making in units of 10,000 yen is equivalent to the government's decision-making in units of ten billion yen. For example, a household expenditure of 100,000 yen is equivalent to a government expenditure of 100 billion yen. Under these circumstances, if 1% was wasted in the above example, the household would have wasted one thousand yen, but the government would have wasted one billion yen. Moreover, bureaucrats and politicians feel no monetary hurt even if 1% of the money is wasted given, for example, bid-rigging. Under this sense of money, bureaucrats and politicians make decisions in large expenditures.

DOI: 10.4324/9781003370444-11

have been settled in the form of court proceedings. In the actual economic society, a standard of *rule of law* exists. In making policy recommendations for the actual economic society, it is insufficient to evaluate them only from the perspective of economics. A policy theory that sets the evaluation of *efficiency and fairness* and incorporates jurisprudence based on justice is necessary.

This chapter examines policy theory based on empirical analysis of law and economics. Judicial precedents are used as data, so legal justice is the standard of justice. It identified unjust acts that violate the law and the factors that produce injustice through actual incidents. The factors that created the injustice are removed through legal reforms. In this way, justice is realized in the real world. To create a fair market, a policy theory based on empirical analysis of law and economics clarifies the deficiencies in the operation of laws and the laws themselves.

Section 11.2 examines the gap between the results of empirical economic analysis and the desirable policies based on normative economics. It examines the gap between the empirical and normative analysis of economics, including its relationship with law. Section 11.3 continues the discussion on Weber's claims regarding social science and its policy. He argued that analysis (science) and policy (politics) are not a continuum. He distinguished that analysis is the job of academics and policy is that of politicians. Myrdal also proposed value premises of respect for life and egalitarian principle as values underlying economic analysis.

Section 11.4 offers a proposal of how to use the knowledge of empirical analysis and theoretical analysis of law and economics. Section 11.4.1 presents specific examples of the use of estimation results by econometric models. In the case of cartel price-fixing, it estimated the retail price in the absence of cartel price-fixing. Further, it estimated the target price of the manufacturing plant installation by scale. Moreover, it estimated the relationship between the successful bid rates and collision using the qualitative response model. Section 11.4.2 considers a case of loss guarantee and loss compensation in the financial market. Section 11.5 examines the basic laws related to the six cases of bid-rigging analyzed in this book. Section 11.6 examines various problems related to the government's fiscal deficit, which has become entrenched in the Japanese economy, as a continuation of the wasteful use of government spending through bid-rigging and other means. This study employs macroeconomics rather than microeconomics. It shows that there is a discrepancy between the fiscal deficit policy Keynes thought of and the fiscal policy implemented in Japan. Section 11.7 examines economic disparities and the logic of the strong, which are problems that cannot be solved by economic theory alone.[2]

2 Today's economic issues include environmental pollution regarding global warming, new infectious diseases, alternative energy issues other than fossil fuels and nuclear power, human rights issues, and inter- and cross-state issues. A wide range of economic issues involves politics, but this section will be limited to economic disparities.

11.2 Policy gap between empirical results and normative analysis

The fundamental theorems of welfare economics conclude that the competitive market maximizes economic welfare. Therefore, the best economic policy is to make a competitive market through deregulation and privatization in the real world. However, the results of the empirical analysis showed that implemented deregulation and privatization policies did not necessarily match the intent of the promotion of competition policy.[3] With deregulation, in reality, the strong won, and the uncompetitive weak withdrew from the market. Contrary to the intent of the legislation, there was a tendency to reduce competitiveness in the actual market. Below is a reconsideration of the policy effects of deregulation in the empirical analysis discussed in Chapter 2.

11.2.1 Domestic and foreign price differences and deregulation policies that have been implemented

The final report of the Japan-US Structural Talks was released in 1990, and Japan's market structure with high retail prices was viewed as a problem. The inefficiency of the distribution industry became one of the focal points. From the results of the empirical analysis described in Chapter 2, the retail prices in the Japanese market were higher than those in the United States, the United Kingdom, France, and Germany. There was a revision of the law as a means of deregulation.

Now, examine the series of legal reforms. The law that existed at the time of the Japan-US Structural Talks was the Large-Scale Retail Stores Law.[4] However, it was abolished in June 2000, and the Act of Large-Scale Store Location was enacted for deregulation. By arranging the Department Store Law, the Large-Scale Retail Stores Law, and the Act of Large-Scale Store Location in chronological order, the direction of policy becomes clear by looking at the purpose of each law. The Department Store Law is aimed at the sound development of the national economy. The Large-Scale Retail Stores Law aimed at the normal development of the retail industry. The Act of Large-Scale Store Location aimed to maintain the living environment. Thus, the purpose of the law shifted from human-oriented to environmental-oriented.

3 Conditions for a competitive market include several small-scale participants, homogeneity of goods, complete information, and free entry (exit) to (from) the market. The merit of creating a competitive market is to maximize the economic welfare of society. Thus, it is necessary to create a fair market (a market regulated by fair rules) in which individual demanders and suppliers participating in the market maintain equal competitiveness.

4 The Large-Scale Retail Stores Law was enacted in 1973, following the abolishment of the Department Store Law. The old Department Store Law was abolished because department stores and large-scale mass retailers expanded into regional cities. Given the diversification of the management scale and product lineup of large-scale mass retailers, sales competition in local cities has intensified with local shopping districts. To protect small- and medium-sized rural shops, the new law was needed to accommodate department stores and large retailers.

The study examines the changes in Japanese society given policy changes accompanying the revision of laws. The advantage was that consumers could complete shopping within the mall. One of the reasons for this was the increase in the holding rate of automobiles in Japanese households. Consumers benefited from suburban malls and large-scale retail stores, and the large-scale retailers also benefited. These measures made progress in improving the efficiency of the distribution industry, called *Price Destruction*. In particular, the retail prices of clothing and electric appliances dropped given the emergence of mass retailers.

However, it is undeniable that the three Acts of Community Building including the Act of Large-Scale Store Location did consider local small retailers in provincial cities and the elderly who did not have a means of transportation. Currently, the regional revitalization policy is among the important policy issues. In those days, small-scaled individual retailers in provincial cities no longer had hopes for the future. The so-called *Shattered Streets* were left in the center of the provincial city. The large-scale retailers drove out small retailers; thus, the retail industry has become less competitive. Given the normative analysis, it is appropriate to promote deregulation and privatization based on the fundamental theorems of welfare economics. However, based on the empirical analysis, it would be necessary to reexamine whether the legal revision for deregulation was appropriate as an economic policy for the people.[5]

11.2.2 Changes in living standards by income group and economic disparities given deregulation

New Zealand was heavily regulated among developed countries before the 1980s, and it implemented large-scale deregulation in the 1980s. Given the empirical economic analysis introduced in Chapter 2, the high-income group benefited the most from the deregulation. The next beneficiaries were the low-income group, not the middle-income group. This inevitably means the downfall of the middle-income classes. That is, society would become polarized. It suggests that economic disparities would widen across society, increasing the probability of a civil society collapse.

In Japan, income disparity among workers has also become a problem. It is the income disparity between regular and non-regular workers. The regular workers are directly employed by the company in which they work, and they work full-time until retirement age. The merits are that they have a stable life by being paid bonuses and retirement allowances. Disadvantages include time constraints and heavy work responsibilities. The non-regular workers are workers other than the regular workers. They include part-time workers, dispatched workers, contract workers, and temporary workers. The benefits are not tied to the company, and they have freedom of time. However, the disadvantage is the low stability of life because of the wage difference to the regular workers.

5 The study will consider the point again in detail in Section 11.3 of this chapter.

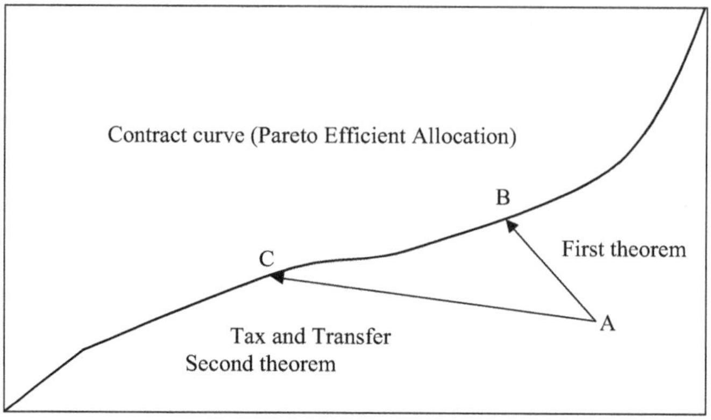

Figure 11.1 Fundamental theorems of welfare economics: first and second theorem

Currently, the ratio of regular and non-regular workers is approximately 60% and 40%, respectively. Regarding income, the average hourly wage is 1.5 times higher for regular workers than for non-regular workers and 1.8 times higher on an annual income basis.

Thus, there is a large disparity in the treatment of regular and non-regular workers. In Japanese society, the economic disparity has become a major social issue. Legislation on non-regular workers aimed to allow them to work freely without time constraints. In reality, however, legislation creates a different situation where economic inequality widens. There is a gap between ideals and reality. Moreover, from the concept of equal work and equal pay, Japanese society is in a situation where it is necessary to consider how future labor laws should be.[6]

Given such empirical results, it is not meaningless to reconsider the policy treatment of the fundamental theorems of welfare economics. If deregulation and privatization were implemented as actual policies to create a competitive market, it would be necessary to verify whether such policies would yield satisfactory results for the people in the real world. This chapter examines the contents of the fundamental theorems of welfare economics, as explained using Edgeworth's box diagram (see Figure 11.1).

According to the first theorem, regardless of the initial point of the combination of goods, the individuals move to the equilibrium point on the contract curve that maximizes economic welfare through competitive markets (from point A to B). The second theorem states that through a competitive market, the individuals move to a particular equilibrium point C on the contract curve, utilizing taxes and subsidies (from point A to C). However, microeconomics does not refer to who determines point C and how, nor does it say how long it takes to get from point A to B or C.

6 Laws directly related to regular and non-regular workers include the Labor Standards Law, Labor Contract Law, Part-Time Labor Law, and Worker Dispatch Law.

According to Arrow's Impossibility Theorem, it is impossible to aggregate individual ordinal utilities to form social preference in a society where general democratic rules exist. Regarding the distribution problem of wealth among the people, nothing can be solved from the fundamental theorems of welfare economics. Economics advocates deregulation and privatization through the first theorem, but it has no solution where the best is on the contract curve. Indeed, this is a question of politics that goes beyond the role of economics. In economics, even if several simulations are possible for the correction of disparities, the final decision of which one to adopt rests with the people.

11.3 Weber's claims on social science and social policy and Myrdal's value premises

Weber's argument on the separation of analysis and policy and Myrdal's value premise have important implications for considering *analysis* and *policy* in economics. Weber argued that analysis and policy should be distinguished. As introduced in Chapter 2, economic analysis is the field of economics, and economic policy is that of politics to draw consensus from people's diverse values. Weber's argument can be stated in two ways. (1) The philosophy and methodology of social science should not be regarded as the same as those of natural science represented by classical mechanics. Therefore, those of natural science should not be uncritically incorporated into social science; and (2) The model (*idealtypus*) used for economic analysis is nothing more than one aspect of human activities. A model is not an exact representation of reality. Model-based policies may not be fully satisfactory to the public.

In empirical analysis, data are collected per the purpose of the analysis. As an example of observational data in natural science, consider planetary motion data. Consider the motion of celestial bodies from the framework of classical mechanics that Newton completed. In the middle of the 16th century, precise observation data existed by Tycho Brahe. Using this data, Kepler discovered Kepler's three laws of planetary orbits in the early 17th century. Newton showed that all of Kepler's laws can be derived from the laws of motion and universal gravitation.

When one reconstructs Newton's works from the perspective of analysis and policy, the model used in the analysis is the laws of motion and universal gravitation. From there, Kepler's laws were derived and tested via Brahe's observational data to verify that the theory accords with the facts. Following the analysis, policy responded to the expansion of the applicability of the Newtonian theory. For example, the theory could predict the motion of the planets. The Law of universal gravitation holds not only between the sun and the planet but also between the earth and every object such as a ball, as illustrated in Figure 11.2. In classical mechanics, analysis and policy are positioned

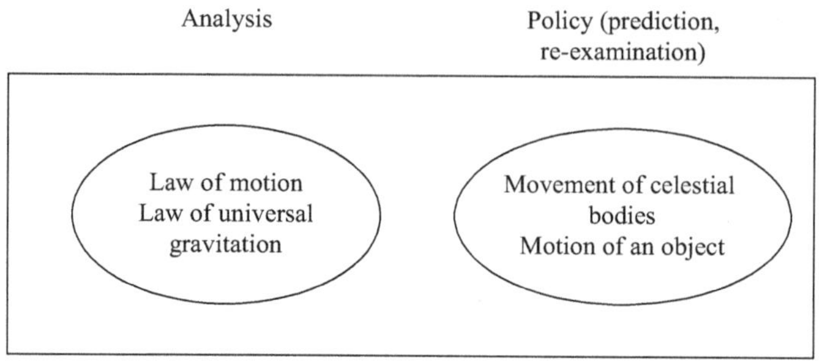

Figure 11.2 Relationship between analysis and policy in natural science (classical mechanics)

(Note) In natural science, analysis and policy correspond perfectly to classical mechanics (policy as an extension of analysis) in the closed world.

in an equivalent relationship within one closed system. It is the big difference from the social science.[7]

In social science, though the results of human behaviors are collected as data, the nature of human beings is diverse. Human beings in the real world do not act solely for economic motives but are influenced by their personality such as their ethics, religious views, and aesthetic sense. Moreover, the society to which individuals belong has a great influence on their behavior. Based on these circumstances, the study examines the concept of economic rationality in empirical analysis. In the ideal type (economic model), a fictitious individual called *homo economicus* is assumed to act to maximize utility. However, considering actual economic behavior, each consumer does not always keep the condition of equal marginal utility when shopping. The utility maximization principle is the *analysis principle* when analyzing observation data but not the truth of individual economic behavior. When one analyzes the observation data from the economic rationality perspective and obtains reasonable results, one can only confirm that the model is consistent with the observation data but does not represent real individual behavior.

Further, modern society is a civil society, where the individuals making up society are respected. Moreover, individual values are diverse. Wealth is an important factor for individuals but is not everything for them. Citizens are

7 There are several reasons why the model of classical mechanics is consistent with the observed data. The properties of an object's motion are determined by a relatively small number of factors: distance, mass, and time. Moreover, the motion of real celestial bodies and objects is an environment that holds as the first-order approximation of the first law of motion (law of inertia). Despite many objects in reality, the multi-body motion can be sufficiently approximated by the two-body motion, namely the relationship between two objects. Motion that considers resistance (e.g., friction) requires conditioning with additional information about the object being analyzed. To obtain the solution of multi-body instead of two-body motion, even today, a huge amount of calculation is required.

not necessarily concerned only with economic aspects. Considering societies throughout recorded history before the emergence of civil society, power was concentrated in the privileged classes. As a privileged class, there were royal aristocrats and big merchants. The privileged classes restricted the behavior of non-privileged people to secure their power and interests. They used rules to their advantage in the form of oracles and edicts as a means of restraint. However, the civil revolution shifted power to the citizens. Citizens have diverse values and unlimited desires. Too much respect for the liberties advocated during the civil revolution violates the rights and interests of individuals supposed to be equal. When new powers are created in certain groups of citizens, democracy becomes threatened. In a civil society, rules called laws are necessary to protect individual rights. It is the duty of the Diet representing citizens to make laws to coordinate the interests of all citizens. The government elected by the Diet implements policies for the people.

Human society is not a world of pre-established harmony that automatically leads to ideals. It needs rules to prevent repeated violations of other individuals' rights given personal desires. Meanwhile, laws necessary for the ideals of how society should be shaped in the future are needed. That is the reason for the development of the legal system in civil society. The purpose of a law is to achieve justice in the society. The laws of motion and universal gravitation of classical mechanics hold true in Japan and the United States. However, the shape of the indifference map derived from the utility function is not common across countries because of the differences in the culture and history of each country and the available amounts of resources. Accordingly, empirical analysis in social science has inherent complexity beyond the empirical analysis of natural science, as shown in Figure 11.3.

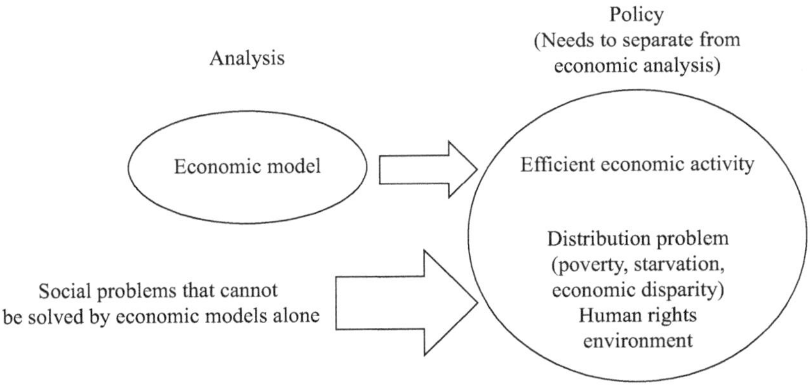

Figure 11.3 The relationship between analysis and policy in social science (the world is a society where humans exist)

(Note) The scope of social science is not necessarily the same regarding analysis and policy. The analysis only corresponds to a part of the policy that the society needs.

In Weber's own words, Figure 11.3 can be described as follows.[8]

(I) Practical social science first establishes a "principle" and scientifically confirms it as valid. It then employs the principle to solve practical individual problems. The opinion that a norm for solving problems should be deduced unambiguously is still held by some experts, but this is originally just a naive belief (Page 26).

(II) It is necessary to make a sharp distinction between relating reality to an ideal type in a logical sense while logically comparing it with evaluating reality from the ideal and making value judgments. Again, the "ideal type" in this sense has nothing to do with evaluative judgments and is nothing but purely logical "completeness" (Page 128).

(III) For astronomy, celestial bodies are of interest and considered exclusively in their quantitative, measurable relationships, whereas, in social science, the qualitative nature of the phenomenon is what matters. Moreover, in social science, the collaboration of mental phenomena is a problem, and, of course, "understanding" this phenomenon while reliving it can be solved by the formula of precise nature recognition. The peculiar nature being different from the subject of study is also a problem (Page 69).

Regarding Weber, Myrdal (1969) proposes *Respect for life* and the *egalitarian principle* as value premises. They are challenging to incorporate into an economic analysis but are fundamental conditions for formulating policy.

11.4 How to use the results of empirical analysis of law and economics

11.4.1 Use of estimation results from econometric models

11.4.1.1 Method of estimating retail prices in the absence of cartel pricing

Regarding damages for the price-fixing denoted in Chapter 3, the plaintiffs' claim for damages was ultimately dismissed by the Supreme Court. It was necessary for the victims to prove the causal relationship between wholesale and retail prices and estimate the amount of damages. The court found the plaintiffs' evidence insufficient. Based on the Supreme Court judgment and the condition in which there are significant changes in retail prices in the economy, the main points of evidence to be verified by the plaintiffs are as follows:

(A): There is a causal relationship between the increase in the wholesale price and the increase in the retail price.

(B): If the price-fixing had not been implemented, the hypothetical retail price would be lower than the actual retail price.

8 See Weber (1904).

Table 11.1 Compensation amount per 18 liters for residents who purchased from Tsuruoka Co-op and residents who purchased from retail stores other than Tsuruoka Co-op

	Purchase from Tsuruoka Co-op	*Purchase from retail stores other than Tsuruoka Co-op*
March 1973	–	–14 yen
April	–	37 yen
May	–	46 yen
June	–	44 yen
July	2 yen	41 yen
August	–1 yen	44 yen
September	6 yen	41 yen
October	9 yen	43 yen
November	1 yen	69 yen
December	–2 yen	88 yen
January 1974	5 yen	84 yen
February	1 yen	70 yen
March	–14 yen	58 yen
April	–	35 yen

(C): The hypothetical retail price formed when the price-fixing had not been implemented is estimated numerically given the calculation of the compensation for damages.

To prove items A, B, and C ruled by the court, the only way is to create an econometric model to estimate the parameters included in the model using actual data, estimate the hypothetical retail price, and calculate compensation for damages as the difference between the actual and hypothetical retail price. Therefore, the study built a model assuming a competitive market without price-fixing and calculated the hypothetical retail price in Chapter 3. Table 11.1 shows the damage claim period for consumers who purchased from Tsuruoka Co-op and consumers who purchased from retail stores other than Tsuruoka Co-op.

The difference in the purchase price between Tsuruoka Co-op and that from retailers other than Tsuruoka Co-op is the reason Tsuruoka Co-op purchased a large amount of kerosene from wholesalers, who shipped kerosene to Tsuruoka Co-op at discounted prices. By using empirical analysis of law and economics, the study showed all the conditions the Supreme Court demanded for the plaintiffs. Had this analysis been known before the Supreme Court's decision, the Supreme Court's decision might have been different.

11.4.1.2 Gap between actual target price and estimated target price by scale

In a bid-rigging case related to the stoker furnace plant construction, the study compared the successful bid prices for the construction works with the same scale as the stoker furnace and the target prices set by the ordering party. They were significantly different despite the unified scale. The target price calculated by the ordering party is the rational cost, including the profit for contractors. Regarding plant construction works, the accumulation of empirical economic analyses shows that when the scale is the same, the cost (target price in the present case) per unit scale would be almost the same. As the scale increases, the cost per unit scale would decrease given economies of scale. In the empirical analysis in Chapter 6, it decreases as the scale increases.

Using the standard error of the equation, the 95% confidence interval of the unit price was calculated. Two properties exceeded the upper confidence interval, indicating that there may be a problem with the target price calculation by the ordering party. This result, using knowledge of economics, is interesting. If the local governments set the target prices higher than the market price, the difference between the two corresponds to tax wastage.

11.4.1.3 Relationship between the successful bid rates and the pre-announcement of the target prices in the case of bid-rigging

The target price was not announced before the bidding. However, in the bid-rigging case for the sewage pumps in Tokyo, a different bidding method was used. When it was announced in advance, there was a change in the bid-rigging behavior among the manufacturers. According to the ruling, an agreement was reached among the bidders to keep the successful bid price at approximately 95% of the target price. This was a big change from the conventional bidding rate of approximately 99% in the bid-rigging case. The relationship between the successful bid rate and surcharge payment orders was examined using a qualitative response model. Table 11.2 shows some of the results from Chapter 10.

The coefficient of the successful bid rate is not significant in the bid-rigging case of the sewerage pumps in Tokyo when the target price is announced in advance for some of the biddings. In this case, the information on the high successful bid rate cannot be used as one of the influential indexes appearing in conventional bid-rigging. This analysis, using the knowledge of econometrics, yielded an interesting result. Moreover, the pre-announcement of the target price is not suitable to point to the bid-rigging as evidence.

Table 11.2 Estimates obtained by the Probit model

	Stoker furnace	*Tama district*	*Sewage pump*
Coefficient of the successful bid rate	0.1351 (2.19) [0.028]	0.07675 (3.13) [0.002]	0.0345 (0.53) [0.594]

(Note) Round brackets are the t-values and square brackets are the P-values.

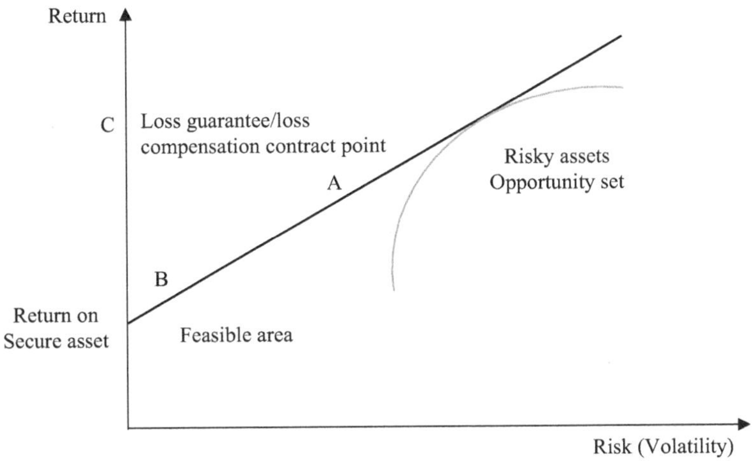

Figure 11.4 Relationship between risk and return, and loss guarantee and loss compensation

11.4.2 Use of conclusions drawn directly from economic theory[9]

After the bubble burst in 1990 in Japan, there were cases of loss compensation given the fall in stock prices. Stocks and bonds are financial instruments in which investors should take risks. A loss guarantee is a contractual act in which a brokerage company guarantees compensation for the loss. Although the practice is illegal, it was not recognized as a strict offense among the stock market practitioners in Japan in the 1980s.

In financial economics, the financial instruments with *zero risk and high returns* do not exist theoretically in the fair market. The relationship between risk and return, *high risk and high returns* and *low risk and low returns*, are well-known, as in Figure 11.4. Comparing points A and B on the investment opportunity line, the point of *high risk and high returns* (point A) and that of *low risk and low returns* (point B) are feasible. However, the loss compensation contracts realized the point of *zero risk and high returns* (realization of point C in Figure 11.4). If there is a financial instrument of *zero risk and high returns*, everyone wants to buy it. By common sense in economics, a *zero risk and high returns* contract is insane and unfair. The problem here is the relationship between the principle of freedom of contract and the market.

The Civil Code stipulates the principle of freedom of contract and states that contracts between individuals must be protected no matter what. However, even if it exists for contracts between individuals, there are certain rules for market transactions. The existence of the market imposes certain restrictions on

9 See Rokusha and Maki (2012) for details of the loss guarantee and compensation case.

the principle of freedom of contract.[10] Now, examine the consistency between the Japanese financial system and international financial markets. Considering financial cases from the United States antitrust casebook, there are descriptions of market manipulation, insider trading, and corporate misstatements. However, there are no cases or provisions regarding loss guarantees or loss compensation (see Gavil, Kovacic, Baker, and Wright, 2017). The New York Stock Exchange is said to date back to the end of the 18th century. When the rules made by the members were violated, the penalty of expulsion was established. The regulations on loss guarantees and loss compensation were created naturally (see Macmillan, 2002). Thus, the United States and European countries do not have legal provisions on loss guarantees and compensation in financial markets. This does not mean that loss compensation is legal; rather, it is insane even if it is not regulated by law.

11.5 Basic laws related to the six bid-rigging cases

Some bid-rigging cases have accompanying damage claims from residents. Now, divide the process from the public notice by the ordering party to the residents' claim for damages into five stages and consider the issues that arise in each of the following five stages: (1) determination of bid property by the ordering party and determination of bidding method. The method of designated competitive bidding was usually used in the bid-rigging case; (2) determination of the target price by the ordering party and selection of bidders for designated competitive bidding. Regarding the former, there were problems regarding its calculation method; (3) determination of the successful bidder and contracts; (4) examination of the settlement of accounts, trial decisions, and judgments of the courts and resident audits, as collision is acknowledged by the courts; and (5) claim for damages from local residents.

Regarding (1), (2), and (3), the basic laws concerning bidding are the Public Accounting Act and the Local Autonomy Act. There are Enforcement Orders under these laws. The Public Accounting Act rules the bidding by the central government. The bidding method is stipulated in Chapter 4 of the contract in the Public Accounting Act. The specific contents are stipulated in Chapter 7 of Cabinet Order on Budgets, the Settlement of Accounts, and Accounting. The Local Autonomy Act stipulates bidding for the local governments. Moreover, penalties for bidding are stipulated in the AMA, the Criminal Code, and the Government-Manufactured Bid-Rigging Prevention Law. Regarding (4), the national accounting is audited by the Board of Audit in accordance with the

10 In economics, the market is a place for trading and exchanging information. Regarding the incident, the market is the place of trading where stocks and bonds are bought and sold. Moreover, it is a place for exchanging information about prices and quantities traded in the past, present, and future. The market has strict rules. Price is the only signal. Market participants are treated homogeneously and equally. Even a large-scale demander or supplier cannot intervene in the market price according to his or her wishes at the market.

law. Local residents have the right to request an audit according to Article 242 of the Local Autonomy Act and file a resident lawsuit according to Article 242-2 of the Local Autonomy Act.

For these clauses to function, active disclosure of information is required to scrutinize the settlement of accounts by the local council and local residents. It is natural to eliminate the wasteful use of public funds by enhancing the auditing functions of the central and local governments. Regarding (5), the underlying laws regarding compensation for damages are the Civil Code and the AMA. These basic provisions are Article 709 of the Civil Code and Article 25 of the AMA.

11.6 Legal basis of macroeconomic policy

Shifting the perspective from microeconomic policy theory to macroeconomic policy theory. Section 11.5 examined several bid-rigging cases. When the government procured at a relatively high price for the bidding properties, efficient allocation would not be realized, and the budget might become deficit with limited government revenues. As mentioned in McMillan (2002), public works cost 15% to 30% higher, and taxpayers were wasting their money. As an extension of the bid-rigging cases, Section 11.6.1 examines the current state of deficit finance in the Japanese economy. Section 11.6.2 introduces the legal basis for fiscal policy in macroeconomics. Section 11.6.3 examines the essence of deficit finance as advocated by Keynes, and Section 11.6.4 considers the legal system regarding deficit finances in the United States and European countries.

11.6.1 Current state of the fiscal deficit in Japan

Considering the current state of Japan's finances in the report, *Fiscal Situation in Japan* (December 2019), compiled by the Ministry of Finance, the government's debt exceeds 1.125 trillion yen, which is almost double the GDP. It is the worst financial situation relative to other developed countries. From the international comparison of debt outstanding as a percentage of GDP, Italy (134%) and the United States (108%) exceed the 100% level, while France (99%), the United Kingdom (85%), Canada (85%), and Germany (55%) were less than 100%. Among developed countries, Japan stands out at 239%. However, fiscal reconstruction has not become a major concern in Japan.

From a common sense economics view, when a household continues to live in debt with more expenses than income, the situation will eat up its assets and induce bankruptcy. Moreover, when a company has more expenses than sales, its profit will become negative; eventually, it will go bankrupt. The deficit in the government continues every year, and the total accumulated debt exceeds 1,000 trillion yen. However, the government would not go bankrupt. Despite discussions about fiscal reconstruction and fiscal discipline, the government and the people have not reached the stage of serious consideration. Perhaps, the Japanese people believe that it is not necessary to actively deal with government debt or reduce government debt through modern macroeconomic theory.

11.6.2 Legal basis for fiscal policy

Fiscal policies and monetary policies are cited as policy theories in macroeconomics, but their implementation is supported by laws such as the Public Finance Act and the Bank of Japan Act. Now, consider the legal basis for the two pillars of macroeconomic policy: fiscal and monetary policy. From macroeconomics, fiscal and monetary policies are shown by shifting the IS and LM curves. The former is shifted by increasing government spending, mainly by increasing tax revenue or the issuance of government bonds. Starting with the legal basis for fiscal policy, the basic law is the Public Finance Act, especially Articles 4 and 5.

Article 4 of the Public Finance Act prohibits the issuance of government bonds. However, by the proviso, the issuance of construction bonds is permitted when the Diet approves it, while the issuance of deficit-covering government bonds is prohibited. However, the issuance of deficit-covering government bonds became possible under the Special Debt Law enacted in 1975. The law was effective only in 1975, but similar laws were enacted every year in Japan, resulting in the regular issuance of deficit-covering government bonds. Article 5 of the Public Finance Act stipulates the prohibition of debt financing. Thus, the fiscal policy explained by macroeconomics is based on legal rules and procedures. [11]

Modern macroeconomics neither emphasizes fiscal deficit nor concerns about accumulated government debt. It is optimistic about government debt and has an inherent expectation that the current fiscal deficit and government debt will be eliminated through GDP growth in the future. However, the schools of thought based on public choice theory, such as Buchanan Wagner (1977), sounded a strong warning against deficit finance. This theory pointed out the harmful effects of deficit finance and proposed a balanced budget, lying in the propensity of politicians and bureaucrats, which is commonly referred to as *government failure.*

Keynes considered that economic policy is in the hands of wise men. When sages are in charge of policy, they think about society as a whole. When aggregate demand is insufficient, the government increases aggregate demand by increasing public works and tax cuts. Such policies result in a budget deficit. When aggregate demand is sufficient, the government decreases aggregate demand by decreasing public works, and the tax increases. The tax increase results in a budget surplus. The repetition of budget deficit and surplus does not cause a monotonous increase in the government debt. Therefore, deficit and surplus finance intersect in chronological order.

11 Regarding monetary policy, the purpose of the Bank of Japan is to stabilize prices. The Bank of Japan is a competent agency, including discount rate operations, financial market adjustments, and reserve adjustments as policy measures. The policy committee of the Bank of Japan decides how to combine these policy measures. The main articles are Articles 2 (Philosophy), 14 (Establishment), and 15 (Authority) of the Bank of Japan Act.

Economists who adhere to modern Keynesian theory and Ricardo's equivalence theorem also have a common understanding that the current deficit is compensated by the taxation of future generations. Thus, the disposable income of future generations will become smaller, resulting in a lower standard of living.

11.6.3 The essence of deficit finance advocated by Keynes

Since Keynes passed away in 1946, it is unclear how he thought about the long-term vision of deficit finance and economic growth written in modern macroeconomics textbooks. Though there were few debates among economists on the concept of long-term deficit finance considered by Keynes, it would be possible to infer from Harrod (1951).

Harrod (1951) notes that "he also gave his support to the idea of a double budget, one for current expenditure and the other for capital expenditure, which should be manipulated in accordance with the trade cycle." The capital expenditure is linked to the Sinking Fund. When the economy is good, it is increased from tax revenues, and when the economy is bad, a part of it is allocated to the budget for fiscal policy. This is not a strictly balanced budget every year but sets the limits of public spending as the amounts of the Sinking Fund. The source is the accumulation of past fiscal surpluses. Moreover, fiscal policies fall within that range. Following this way of thinking, there will be no burden on future generations.

Keynes would not have imagined the execution of deficit budgets conducted in various countries today. If Keynes looks at today's finances, he might consider that policy is not based on his theory. Keynes envisioned that deficit finance was limited to times when national survival was at stake, such as the Great Depression of 1929 or World War I and II. However, in modern Japan, a deficit budget is constantly set every year, and the government debt continues to increase in the form of government bond issuance.

11.6.4 Basic attitudes and laws of the United States and European countries toward deficits and government debt

In Japan, it is possible to issue deficit-covering government bonds with the approval of the Diet according to Article 4 of the Public Finance Act and Article 1 of the Special Debt Law. With government debt exceeding 1,000 trillion yen, economists who adhered to Keynesian theory pay limited attention to this problem. As a realistic policy, Japan's fiscal situation is unique internationally.

This section reviews the laws relating to the issuance of deficit-covering government bonds in the United States and European countries. In the United States, Congress introduced legislations to stem the rise in federal budget deficits since the 1980s. These include the Gramm-Rudman-Hollings Act of 1985 during the Republican Reagan administration and the Comprehensive Fiscal Adjustment Acts of 1990 and 1993. These laws mandated a fiscal balance.

The Comprehensive Fiscal Adjustment Act of 1993 was introduced under the Clinton administration after the Reagan administration. In 1995, he proposed a constitutional amendment requiring the federal government to maintain a balanced budget. It was passed by a majority in the House of Representatives but was defeated by one vote in the Senate. Further, regarding the State Governments, there is a balance clause in the State Constitution, except for the State of Vermont.

In European countries, the Maaslicht Treaty sets deficit and outstanding government debt limits. Thus, in the United States and European countries, return to balanced budgets or caps are imposed as constraints by State Constitutional balance clauses or Treaties. Behind the addition of such legal measures, there seems to be general support among the public for a balanced budget given the awareness that future generations should not be left behind. In the United States, the public's awareness of balanced finance is widespread as embodied in the law. The State Constitutions impose restrictions on balanced finances, and US people understand that maintaining balanced finances within the legal system is a matter of course. Based on the balanced budget, they recognize the room for deficit finance as a part of federal economic policy. However, for the US people, it is unacceptable that the deficit budget would continue and the government debt would increase. Clearly, in the United States, the balanced budget is the primary objective and the deficit budget is the secondary one. In Japan, it is the reverse. A clause (Article 4) in the Public Finance Act seeks to balance between revenue and expenditure. However, while creating loopholes by overinterpreting the exemptions, modern macroeconomics plays a major role in the legitimacy of those loopholes.

11.7 Economic disparities and the logic of the strong: Policies considering empathy and tolerance

Many people distrust economics for the following reasons: (1) Economics oversimplifies society. Economics concludes with competitive markets and privatization but lacks consideration of the harmful effects of marketization and privatization that exist. Moreover, economics rarely talks about justice. Therefore, there is little interest in contemporary issues such as human rights in the economic society. (2) Economics treats human beings as homogeneous objects and does not see human diversity. It lacks consideration for the weak and leans too much toward the logic of the strong.

Consider the simplification of the economic model. Economics emphasizes results. Models are constructed based on the assumptions of economic theory to derive economically meaningful results. Based on this line of analysis, economics simplifies things. A simplified model solves the problem of efficiency (the first theorem of welfare economics). Strictly, however, a unique answer cannot be obtained for the distribution problem (see the second theorem of welfare economics). Even so, jurisprudence examines legal texts according to the course of a case; thus, it is necessary to assume various possibilities. This situation naturally complicates the logic.

Jurisprudence emphasizes intention, and economics emphasizes conclusions. Hence, law and economics approach social problems from different starting points. Given the differences in methodology, economics (jurisprudence) tends to be simplified (complicated). By approaching social problems from this different angle, reaching valid conclusions that seek efficiency and justice is likely. Consider justice. Although the content of justice varies, legal justice becomes the concept in empirical analyses using judgment data. Regarding justice, consider inequality or economic disparity regarding policy. Inequality is a challenging problem with no solution in economic theory. Ordinal utility theory does not solve the inequality argument because it is not possible to compare the utility between different individuals. However, economic disparity exists as a real problem. Weber's claim of *wertfrei* (value free) is an argument that provides an answer to this problem. He argued for the separation of analysis and policy. Analytical judgments should not be equated with policy judgments.

Now, consider the logic of the strong and compassion for the weak. Economics cannot compare the utility between different individuals. Thus, although it is possible to optimize the average value of society, there is a lack of an analysis method that optimizes the variance among individuals. To shift from the real economic system to a competitive market where economic welfare is maximized, the government's role in implementing policies is important. Hence, it is necessary to develop a policy mix that does not disadvantage the socially vulnerable. From the second fundamental theorem of welfare economics, the transition to a desirable economic system involves redistribution by taxes and subsidies through a competitive market. Therefore, after the people have agreed, the government must implement the agreed items appropriately. To bring the real world closer to the ideal world, it is necessary to improve the system. History and lessons learned from incidents help establish a safety net during the transition period. Law-based policies also lead to the realization of distributive justice. The answer to economic inequality cannot be solved by the second theorem of welfare economics alone. The answer to this problem is to recognize that it is not an economic problem but a social problem regarding a collection of individual citizens.

12 Conclusion of the book

This study explores the methodological differences between natural science (i.e., classical mechanics) and social science (i.e., economics) from an empirical science perspective. The models of classical mechanics, as developed by Newton, explain and predict object motion with high accuracy. One of Newton's famous quotes is *Hypotheses no fingo.*[1] However, in economics, creating a model that explains existing data does not necessarily mean high predictive power. When drastic economic phenomena occur, predictions are often incorrect because, although economic models maintain logical consistency, they lack the necessary elements to explain actual economic society. When comparing classical mechanics with the empirical analysis of the economy, as depicted in Figure 11.3 in Chapter 11, it becomes evident that economic models do not encompass the full spectrum of economic and social issues. Figure 12.1 summarizes the differences between the methodologies of natural science and social science, examining three elements: target of analysis, observation, and analysis.

The target of analysis in economics is the economic society (i.e., a collective of human beings). Observers and researchers are also human beings and have the discretion to select the scope of observation and viewpoint of analysis based on their intentions. In other words, they can choose to ignore undesirable events.

Economics presupposes a civil society. Societies that contradict this notion are dominated by privileged classes such as feudal lords, absolute monarchs, and guild members (c.f. Smith, 1776). *The Wealth of Nations* is a work that challenges conventional society and justifies civil society. In it, Smith (1776) researched the merits of an exchange economic system through markets in civil society. The general equilibrium theory provided by modern economics assumes a competitive market; however, gaps remain between the actual economic society and the model. Specifically, there is (1) a deviation between the actual market and the mathematical model of a competitive market (e.g.,

1 To paraphrase Newton, a hypothesis is not a mathematical figment but should be backed by experiments (reality).

DOI: 10.4324/9781003370444-12

	Natural science (classical mechanics)	Social science (economics)
Target of analysis	Objects	Human society
Observation	Human beings	Human beings
Analysis	Human beings	Human beings

Figure 12.1 Differences between methodologies of natural science and social science

market failure), (2) a lack of solutions for wealth distribution among society members (per the second fundamental theorem of welfare economics, there is no standard to determine the best, as an *egalitarian principle* is lacking), (3) disregard for the economically weak (ignorance of *respect for life*), and (4) ignorance of the existence of fraud and other wrongdoing in real economic activities (a need for empirical law and economics). Based on the four noted gaps, we will consider the scope for further research to build on the results of this study. Point (4) directly addresses the issue under investigation in this study.

Indeed, to elucidate the reality of point (4), economic actions require a standard of justice (fairness) in addition to efficiency based on competition. This study is an empirical analysis of how fraudulent activities induce market distortions. It focuses on case law on price-fixing and bid-rigging and conducts several econometric analyses related to the incidents. It also focuses on the principle of liability for negligence, which is not covered in orthodox economics textbooks. Hence, this study examines cases in which citizens requested compensation for damages related to price-fixing and bid-rigging. Economic incidents that fall outside the scope of this study include financial or securities incidents and those related to consumer protection. These cases will be the focus of future research in the field of law and economics.

Regarding points (1) through (3), the areas of market failure in the contemporary market system are extensive. The confirmation of the existence and stability of general equilibrium solutions under various factors of market failure is a direction in theoretical economics. Distributional issues related to the second fundamental theorem of welfare economics are tied to economic policy. The type of distribution that society desires is a policy issue that extends beyond the realm of economics and is linked to both economics and politics. The issue of economically disadvantaged individuals is also a matter to be resolved by societal consensus, much like the issue of distribution. However, to comprehend the reality of the economic society, empirical economic analysis is essential. Based on the results of empirical analysis and the consensus of the citizens comprising the society, the adjustment of interests will be debated in the Diet, and the conclusions will be legislated. Subsequently, the government will implement it as a policy.

This study also examines the separation of analysis and policy. Policy regards changing the future resource allocation (economic environment).

Therefore, individuals today must decide on the future of society even if they are not economists, bureaucrats, or politicians (*government failure*). Once the future allocation of resources has been agreed upon among the people, the job of economics is to ascertain how to distribute those resources efficiently. An Ancient Roman poet Decimus Junius Juvenalis warned against political apathy among Roman citizens with the phrase "*panem et circenses*" (bread and games). The crisis of a healthy democracy is largely due to citizens' political apathy. The academic contributions of empirical law and economics will help develop a healthy civil society.

References

Legal materials

(Remarks)

(1) Legal material includes Case name, Court name (JFTC indicates decision at the JFTC court), Case number [(Year.(Code).Number)], Date of the judgment (Year. Month.Day)
(2) Minshu (abbreviation of Supreme Court reports: Civil precedents) Vol.No.Start page,
(3) Keishu (abbreviation of Supreme Court reports: Criminal precedents) Vol.No.Start page.

Chapter 3 Petroleum Product Price Agreement Criminal Case and Consumer Damage Claim Case

Case of violation of law concerning the prohibition of private monopoly and ensuring fair trade [Oil cartel (Production adjustment) case], Tokyo High Court, 1974.(No).1, 1980.09.26.

Case of violation of law concerning the prohibition of private monopoly and ensuring fair trade [Oil cartel (price agreement) case], Tokyo High Court, 1974.(No).2, 1980.09.26.

Case of violation of law concerning the prohibition of private monopoly and ensuring fair trade, Supreme Court, 1980.(A).2153, 1984.02.24, Keishu Vol. 38, No. 4, 1287.

Case of Claims for Damages, Supreme Court, 1981 (Gyo-Tsu).187, 1987.07.02, Minshu Vol. 41, No. 5, 785.

Case of Claims for Damages, Supreme Court, 1985.(O).933, 1989.12.08., Minshu Vol. 43, No. 11, 1259.

Chapter 4 Case of bearing bid-rigging

Case of price cartel by bearing manufacturers (Fujikoshi), Tokyo District Court, 2012 (Toku-Wa). 956, 2012.12.28.

Case of price cartel by bearing manufacturers (NSK), Tokyo District Court, 2012 (Toku-Wa). 956, 2013.02.25.

Case of price cartel by bearing manufacturers (NTN), Tokyo District Court, 2012 (Toku-Wa). 956, 2015.02.04.

Case of pricing cartel by bearing manufacturer (NTN), Tokyo High Court, 2015 (U). 551, 2016.03.22.
Case of price cartel by bearing manufacturer (NTN), Supreme Court, 2016 (A). 650, 2017.12.05.
Case for bearing manufacturers, JFTC, 2013 (So). 6, 2013.03.29.
Case for Bearing Manufacturers", JFTC, 2013 (Nou). 9, 2013.03.29.
Case for NSK, JFTC, 2013 (Han). 23, 2017.03.29.
Case for NTN, JFTC, 2013 (Han). 22, 2019.11.26.

Chapter 5 Case of water meter bid-rigging

The first incident
Case of Kinmon Seisakusho Co., Ltd. and 23 others, JFTC, 1992 (Kan). 33, 1993.01.29.
Case of Toko Seiki Co., Ltd. and 10 others, JFTC, 1992 (Kan). 35, 1993.01.29.
Case of Kinmon Seisakusho Co., Ltd. and 19 others, JFTC, 1992 (Kan). 34, 1993.01.29.
Case of Kinmon Seisakusho Co., Ltd. and 23 others, JFTC, 1994 (Nou).1 to 1994 (Nou). 23, 1994.0310
Case of Toko Seiki Co., Ltd. and 10 others, JFTC. 1994 (Nou). 33 to1994 (Nou). 40, 1994.03.10.
Case of Kinmon Seisakusho Co., Ltd. and 19 others, JFTC. 1994 (Nou). 24 to 1994 (Nou). 32, 1994.03.10.
The second incident
Case of Kinmon Seisakusho Co., Ltd. and 24 others. 1997 (Kan).3, 1997.04.18
Case of Kinmon Seisakusho Co., Ltd. and 24 others, JFTC. 1997 (Nou).149 to1997 (Nou). 172, 1997.12.18.
Case of Violating the Law Concerning Prohibition of Private Monopoly and Ensuring Fair Trade. 1997(No).1, Tokyo High Court, 1997.12.24.
Case of Violating the Law Concerning Prohibition of Private Monopoly and Ensuring Fair Trade. 1998 (A).148, Supreme Court, 2000.09.25.
District Court:
Case of request for cancellation of disposition of non-disclosure of official documents. 1997 (Gyo-U). 24, Yokohama District Court, 1998.10.26.
Case of Damage Compensation Residents Litigation. 1998 (Gyo-U). 9, Tsu District Court, 1999.09.09.
Case of Appeals for Residents' Litigation for Damages. 1999 (Gyo-Ko). 27, Nagoya High Court, 2001.08.21.
The third incident
Case of Aichi Tokei Denki Co., Ltd. and 17 other companies. 2003 (Kan).20, 2003.08.07.
Case of Kinmon Seisakusho Co., Ltd. 2003 (Han).38, JFTC, 2004.02.05.
Case of violation of law concerning prohibition of private monopoly and ensuring fair trade. 2003 (No).1. Tokyo High Court, 2004.03.26.
Case of bidders of water meters ordered by Tokyo, JFTC, 2005 (Nou).24 to 2005 (Nou). 36, 2005.02.07.

Chapter 6 Case of Government bid-rigging

Case of Violation of Law Concerning Prohibition of Private Monopoly and Ensuring Fair Trade. 2004 (A). 1478, Supreme Court, 2005.11.21, Keishu Vol. 59, No. 9, 1597.
Case of Breach of trust, ex post facto bribery, aggravated bribery. 2005 (A).246, Supreme Court, 2009.03.16, Keishu Vol. 63, No. 3, 81.
Case of accused bribery, consignment bribery, violation of the law concerning witness's oath and testimony in the House of Representatives, and violation of the Political Funds Control Act. 2008(A).738. Supreme Court, 2010.09.09, Keishu Vol. 64, No. 6, 865.

Chapter 7 Stoker Furnace Bid-rigging Case

Case of Hitachi Zosen Corporation and 4 others. 1999.(Han). 4. JFTC, 2006.06.27.
Case of Hitachi Zosen Corporation and 4 others. 2007.(Han). 6. JFTC, 10, 2010.11.10.
Case of Appeal for Subrogation of Damages. 2006(Gyo-Ko).223, Tokyo High Court, 2007.11.28.
Case of Request for Cancellation of Trial Decision. 2006(Gyo-Ke).11. to 2006(Gyo-Ke).13, Tokyo High Court, 2008.09.26.
Case of claim for damages. 2007(Wa).4520, Nagoya District Court, 2009.08.07.
Case of Request for Cancellation of Trial Decision. 2009(Gyo-Tsu).8 to 2009(Gyo-Tsu).10, Supreme Court, 2009.10.06.
Case of Appeal for Subrogation of Damages. 2009(Gyo-Tsu).101. Supreme Court, 2009.11.12.

Chapter 8 Tama District Bid-Rigging Case (Part 1)

Case of Taisei Corporation and 33 others. 2002 (Han).1 to 34. JFTC, 2008.07.24.
Case of Request for Cancellation of Trial Decision. 2008.(Gyo-Ke).16, 2008.(Gyo-Ke).22, 2008.(Gyo-Ke).28, 2008.(Gyo-Ke).34, Tokyo High Court, May 29, 2009.05.29.
Case of Request for Cancellation of Trial Decision. 2008.(Gyo-Ke).17, 2008.(Gyo-Ke).23, 2008.(Gyo-Ke).29, 2008.(Gyo-Ke).31, Tokyo High Court, 2009.10.23.
Case of Request for Cancellation of Trial Decision. 2008.(Gyo-Ke).18, 2008.(Gyo-Ke).24, 2008.(Gyo-Ke).30, 2008.(Gyo-Ke).37, Tokyo High Court, Dec. 18, 2009.12.18.
Case of Request for Cancellation of Trial Decision. 2008.(Gyo-Ke). 21, 2008.(Gyo-Ke).27, 2008.(Gyo-Ke).33, 2008.(Gyo-Ke).39, Tokyo High Court, 2010.01.29.
Case of Request for Cancellation of Trial Decision. 2008.(Gyo-Ke). 25, 2008.(Gyo-Ke).26, 2008.(Gyo-Ke).32, 2008.(Gyo-Ke).38, Tokyo High Court, 2010.03.19.
"Case of Request for Cancellation of Trial Decision", 2010 (Gyo-Hi). 278, Supreme Court, February 20, 2012.02.20, Minshu Vol. 66, No. 2, 796.

Case of Kinmon Seisakusho Co., Ltd. and 24 others. 1997 (Kan).3, JFTC, April 18, 1997.04.18.
Case of Violation of Law Concerning Prohibition of Private Monopoly and Ensuring Fair Trade. 1998 (A) .148, Supreme Court, 2000.09.25, Keishu Vol. 54, No. 7, 689.

Chapter 9 Tama District Bid-rigging Case (Part 2): Damage Compensation Claim Case

Case of Claims for Damages. 2002 (Gyo-U).228, Tokyo District Court, 2007.07.26.
Case of claim for damages. 2002 (Gyo-U).231, Tokyo District Court, 2007.07.26.
Case of Appeal for Damages. 2007 (Gyo-Ko). 287, Tokyo High Court, 2009.05.21.
Case of claim for damages.2002 (Gyo-U).229, Tokyo District Court, 2007.10.26.
Case of Appeal for Damages. 2007(Gyo-Ko).388, Tokyo High Court, 2009.05.28.
Case of claim for damages. 2002 (Gyo-U).230, Tokyo District Court, 2006.11.24.
Case of Appeal for Damages. 2008 (Gyo-Ko).342, Tokyo High Court, 2008.07.02.

Chapter 10 Tokyo Sewage Works Bid-Rigging Case

Case of Ebara Corporation and 8 others. 2004 (Han).4, JFTC, 2008.04.16.
Case of Request for Cancellation of Trial Decision. 2008 (Gyo-Ke).9, Tokyo High Court, 2008.12.05.
Case of Request for Cancellation of Trial Decision by Shin-Maywa Industry Co., Ltd. 2009 (Gyo-Tsu). 76, 2009 (Gyo-Hi).89, Supreme Court, 2009.10.22.

References: (Books and Papers)

Allen, R. G. D. and A. L. Bowley (1935), *Family Expenditure: A Study of the Variation*, London: PS King & Son.
Ando, A. and F. Modigliani (1963), "The life cycle hypothesis of saving: The aggregate implications and tests," *American Economic Review*, vol. 53, 55–84.
Bacon, F. (1620), *Novum Organum* (Translated into Japanese by J. Katsura, 1978, Iwanami Bunko).
Buchanan, J. M. and R. E. Wagner (1977), *Political Economy of Deficit Finance*, New York: Academic Press.
Descartes, R. (1637), *Discourse on the Method of Rightly Conducting One's Reason and of Seeking Truth in the Sciences* (Translated into Japanese by T. Ochiai, 1953, Iwanami Bunko).
Douglas, P. (1934), *The Theory of Wages*, New York: Macmillan.
Duesenberry, J. S. (1949), *Income, Saving, and the Theory of Consumer Behavior*, Cambridge: Harvard University Press.
Engel, E. (1895), *Belgian Workers' Family Living Expenses* (Translated into Japanese by T. Morito, 1968, Kurita).
Friedman, M. (1957), *A Theory of Consumption Function*, Princeton: Princeton University Press.
Gavil, A., W. E. Kovacic, J. B. Baker and J. D. Wright (2017), *Antitrust Law in Perspective: Cases, Concepts and Problems in Competition Policy*, 3rd ed., St Paul: Minn.

Greene, W. H. (2012), *Econometric Analysis*, 7th ed., Essex: Pearson.
Harrod, R. M. (1951), *The Life of John Maynard Keynes*, London: Macmillan.
Hicks, J.R. (1939), *Value and Capital: An Inquiry into Some Fundamental Principles of Economic Theory*, Oxford: Clarendon Press.
Hüschelrath, K., K. Müller and T. Veith (2016), "Estimating damages from price-fixing: The value of transaction data," *European Journal of Law and Economics*, vol. 41, 509–535.
Ito, M. (1990), "Claim on compensation of damages due to the violation of AMA; I and II," *Jurist*, no. 963, 54–61 and no. 965, 53–61.
Johnson, C. (1982), *MITI and the Japanese Miracle*, Stanford: Stanford University Press.
Kaneko, A. (1990), "On the Supreme Court decision for the Tsuruoka kerosene compensation for damage case," *Kose Torihiki*, no. 473, 18–25.
Keynes, J. M. M. (1936), *General Theory of Employment, Interest and Money*, London: Macmillan.
Klein, L. R. (1950), *Economic Fluctuations in the United States 1921–1941*, New York: John Wiley.
Kuznets, S. (1942), Uses of national income in peace and war, Occasional paper no.6 (NY, NBER).
Kuznets, S. (1966), *Modern Economic Growth*, New Haven: Yale University Press.
Komiya, R., M. Okuno, K. Suzumura (1988), *Industrial Policy of Japan*, Tokyo: Academic Press.
Leontief, W. W. (1941), *Structure of American Economy 1919–1929: An Empirical Application of Equilibrium Analysis*, Cambridge: Harvard University Press.
Maki, A. (1998), "How high consumer prices are in Japan," *Japan and the World Economy*, vol. 10, 173–183.
Maki, A. (2002), "Changes in New Zealand consumer living standards during the period of deregulation 1984–1996," *Economic Record*, vol. 78, 443–450.
Maki, A. (2005), "The statistical price index as an approximation of the constant-utility price index: An empirical analysis using Japanese data-sets," *Journal of the Japanese and International Economies*, vol. 19, 37–50.
Maki, A. (2011), *Introduction to Estimating Economic Models*, London: Routledge.
McMillan, J. (1990), "Dango: Japan's price-fixing conspiracies," Research Report 90–03, Graduate School of International Relations and Pacific Studies, University of California, San Diego, 24pp.
McMillan, J. (1992), "Dango: Japan's price-fixing conspiracies," *Economics and Politics*, vol. 3, 201–218.
McMillan, J. (2002), *Reinventing the Bazaar: A Natural History of Markets*, New York: Norton.
Myrdal, G. (1969), *Objectivity in Social Research*, New York: Pantheon Books.
Moore, H. L. (1914), *Economic Cycles: Their Law and Cause*, New York: Macmillan.
Porter, R. H. and J. D. Zona (1999), "Ohio school milk markets: An analysis of bidding," *RAND Journal of Economics*, vol. 30, 263–288.
Prais, S. J. and H. S. Houthakker (1955), *The Analysis of Family Budget*, Cambridge: Cambridge University Press.
Rokusha, A. and A. Maki (2012), "Anticipated loss and compensation: Collaboration between law and economics," *Journal of Law, Politics and Sociology*, vol. 85, 81–124.
Rousseau, J. C. J. (1762), *On the Social Contract; or, Principles of Political Right* (Translated into Japanese by T. Kuwahara and T. Maekawa, 1954, Iwanami Bunko).

Schultz, H. (1938), *The Theory and Measurement of Demand*, Chicago: University of Chicago Press.
Scruton, R. (2002), *A Short History of Modern Philosophy*, London: Routledge.
Shoda, A. (1990), "Kerosene case and the Supreme Court," *Horitsu Jiho*, vol. 62, no. 3, 6–16.
Sims, C. A. (1980), "Macroeconomics and reality," *Econometrica*, vol. 48, 1–48.
Smith, A. (1776), *An Inquiry into the Nature and Causes of the Wealth of Nations* (Translated into Japanese by H. Ouchi and S. Matsukawa, 1969), Iwanami.
Smithies, A. (1945), "Forecasting postwar demand: I," *Econometrica*, vol. 13, 1–14.
Stigler, G. J. (1965), *Essays in the History of Economics*, Chicago: Chicago University Press.
Stone, R. (1954), *The Measurement of Consumers' Expenditure and Behaviour in the United Kingdom 1920–1938*, Cambridge; Cambridge University Press.
Tobin, J. (1951), "Relative income, absolute income and saving," in *Essays in Economics: Consumption and Econometrics*, Vol 2, Amsterdam: North-Holland.
Tsuneki, A. (2015), *Economics for Lawyers*, Iwanami Shoten (in Japanese).
Weber, M. (1904), "The 'objectivity' of knowledge in social science and social policy," in *Collected Methodological Writings* edited by Bruun, Hans Hendrik, and Sam Whimster, London: Taylor & Francis Group, 2012.
Weber, M. (1919), *Science as a Vocation* (Translated into Japanese by K. Odaka, 1936, Iwanami Bunko).
Weber, M. (1919), *Politics as a Vocation* (Translated into Japanese by K. Waki, 1980, Iwanami Bunko).
Wold, H. (1953), *Demand Analysis*, New York: John Wiley.
Yang, Y. (2005), "Can the strengths of AIC and BIC be shared?" *Biometrika*, vol. 92, no. 4, Dec, 937–950.

Index

Kolibri 360 GmbH
Ferdinand-Jühlke-Straße 7
99095 Erfurt, Deutschland
produktsicherheit@kolibri360.de